Famous Battles and How They Shaped the Modern World, 1558 – 1943

Famous Battles and How They Shaped the Modern World, 1558 – 1943

From the Armada to Stalingrad

Beatrice Heuser and
Athena S. Leoussi

Pen & Sword

MILITARY

AN IMPRINT OF PEN & SWORD BOOKS LTD.
YORKSHIRE – PHILADELPHIA

First published in Great Britain in 2018 by
Pen & Sword Military
An imprint of
Pen & Sword Books Ltd
Yorkshire - Philadelphia

ISBN 978 1 52672 741 1

Printed and bound in England
By TJ International Ltd.

Pen & Sword Books Ltd incorporates the Imprints of Pen & Sword Books Archaeology, Atlas, Aviation, Battleground, Discovery, Family History, History, Maritime, Military, Naval, Politics, Railways, Select, Transport, True Crime, Fiction, Frontline Books, Leo Cooper, Praetorian Press, Seaforth Publishing, Wharncliffe and White Owl.

For a complete list of Pen & Sword titles please contact

PEN & SWORD BOOKS LIMITED
47 Church Street, Barnsley, South Yorkshire, S70 2AS, England
E-mail: enquiries@pen-and-sword.co.uk
Website: www.pen-and-sword.co.uk

or

PEN AND SWORD BOOKS
1950 Lawrence Rd, Havertown, PA 19083, USA
E-mail: Uspen-and-sword@casematepublishers.com
Website: www.penandswordbooks.com

Contents

List of Contributors

Andreas Behnke is Associate Professor in International Political Theory at the University of Reading. His research interests include the political theory of international relations, in particular Carl Schmitt, critical security studies, critical geopolitics and the aesthetics of global politics. He is the author of numerous books and articles on international security and terrorism, including *NATO's Security Discourse After the Cold War* (2013) and the editor of *The International Politics of Fashion* (2017).

J. D. Davies won the Samuel Pepys prize for *Pepys's Navy: Ships, Men and Warfare 1649-89*. He is a vice-president of both the Society for Nautical Research and the Navy Records Society, and a Fellow of both the SNR and the Royal Historical Society. He is also the bestselling author of the naval historical fiction series, 'the Journals of Matthew Quinton', set during the Restoration period.

Alan Forrest is Emeritus Professor of History at the University of York. He has published widely on the history of the French Revolution and Empire and the history of war. His publications include *Napoleon's Men: The Soldiers of the Revolution and Empire* (London, 2002), *The Legacy of the French Revolutionary Wars: The Nation-in-Arms in French Republican Memory* (Cambridge, 2009), *Napoleon* (London, 2011), and most recently *Waterloo* (Oxford, 2015), a study of the battle and its place in public memory.

Beatrice Heuser is Professor of International Relations at the University of Glasgow. She is a specialist in Strategic and Military Studies, and has worked as Consultant at NATO. Her books include, *Reading Clausewitz* (2002), *The Evolution of Strategy* (2010), *The Strategy Makers* (2010) containing translations of early texts, and *Strategy Before Clausewitz* (2017). She is keenly interested in myths invoked in foreign policy making, treated in (edited, with Cyril Buffet) *Haunted by History* (1998).

Andrew Lambert is Laughton Professor of Naval History in the Department of War Studies at King's College, London. His books include: *The Crimean War: British Grand Strategy against Russia 1853-1856* (1990), *The Foundations of Naval History: Sir John Laughton, the Royal Navy and the Historical Profession* (1997), *Nelson: Britannia's God of War* (2004), *Franklin: Tragic Hero of Polar Navigation* (2009), and *The Challenge: the Naval War of 1812* (2012), and *Crusoe's Island* (2016).

Athena Leoussi is Associate Professor in European History at the University of Reading. She is a founder of The Association for the Study of Ethnicity and Nationalism, based at LSE, and the journal, *Nations and Nationalism*. She has published extensively on the role of the visual arts in nation-building and the influence of the classical Greek cult of the body in re-defining modern European national identities. She was one of the organisers of the British Museum's exhibition, 'Defining Beauty' (2015). Her publications include, *Nationalism and Classicism* (1998), the *Encyclopaedia of Nationalism* (Transaction, 2001) and *Nationalism and Ethnosymbolism* (edited with Steven Grosby, 2006).

Major General **Mungo Melvin** CB OBE retired from the British Army in 2011. His major published works include *Manstein: Hitler's Greatest General* (2010) and *Sevastopol's Wars: Crimea from Potemkin to Putin* (2017). He also edited the British Army's Battlefield Guide to the Western Front of the First World War (2015). A senior visiting research fellow at King's College London, Mungo Melvin served as President of the British Commission for Military History from 2012 to 2017.

Georg Schild is Professor of North American History at the University of Tübingen. He received his Ph.D. from the University of Maryland. His research interests mainly concern the history of the American constitution and of US foreign and security policies. He is author of *Abraham Lincoln: Eine politische Biographie* (2009) and *1983: Das gefährlichste Jahr des Kalten Krieges* (2013).

Chapter 1

Introduction to the Second Volume

Beatrice Heuser & Athena Leoussi

This is the second of two volumes on famous European battles and the legacy they engendered in the form of a variety of narratives or interpretations. Although each volume stands alone, the two volumes, taken together, offer a historical panorama, from Antiquity to the present, of some of those battles that captured the collective imagination of the Europeans – and frequently peoples beyond Europe – which made them famous and wove them into myths.

As noted in the introduction to Volume 1, we are not concerned here with engaging in the argument on whether certain battles were 'decisive', i.e. whether they changed history, defined frontiers, made or destroyed kingdoms, and achieved what no other event could have done. Much ink has been spilled on this and that is another issue altogether.[1] What we are interested in is fame, not real or supposed decisiveness; battles that were remembered for many generations, that acquired a mythical quality, that were interpreted as expressing something greater than the political configurations that lead to them, as a fight between Good and Evil, a sign of the favour or the anger of gods, as a great sacrifice atoning for the sins of the people, as a legitimation of a regime or dynasty, as the justification of a larger, long-term policy, as a terrible mistake never to be repeated, and so on. They tend to be used by later generations as exhortations to follow the examples of those who fought, suffered and perhaps died in these battles, to take revenge, to keep memories of friend and foe alive, to resist some new enemy – always cast as successor to the old – valiantly and uncompromisingly. Very occasionally, they are evoked to argue for a peaceful settlement of a conflict. More frequently, since 1945, they have been commemorated as an exhortation to break with the past fratricidal wars that have darkened European history for millennia, and which have only been contained and overcome with the process of European integration which has led to the creation of the European Union.[2] As we shall see, many such famous battles would be interpreted in many different ways over time, often serving as instrument for political causes.

In this volume, we look at the political myths that were constructed around two naval battles, the Spanish Armada (1588) and Chatham (1667). Then we move on to the myths engendered by the siege and relief battle of Vienna (1683), and of the battles of Culloden (1746), Waterloo (1815), Gettysburg (1864), the Somme (1916), and finally Stalingrad (1942/43).

Values, Wars, and the Politics of Commemoration

The eighteenth-century philosopher and literary critic, Johann Gottfried Herder (1744-1803) rejected the study of the history of peoples, dominated as it was by wars and battles, favouring instead the study of their literature. For Herder, literary studies would give access to the diverse views of the world, the diverse cultures that human societies had created. It was this knowledge that was important for understanding humanity as it really was – a garden with many flowers:

> Has a nation anything more precious? From a study of native literatures we have learnt to know ages and peoples more deeply than along the sad and frustrating path of political and military history. In the latter we seldom see more than the manner in which a people was ruled, how it let itself be slaughtered; in the former we learn how it thought, what it wished and craved for, how it took its pleasures, how it was led by its teachers or its inclinations...[3]

Herder's exclusion of military history from the study of humanity was unwarranted. For it is precisely through the study of wars and battles that we can often understand what really matters to a people – what a people is prepared to die for. Indeed, it is in military confrontation, when one places one's own life and that of one's own family and community on the line, that we can discover the role of values in human life. Such values are often believed by their carriers to be irreplaceable and worth protecting by the force of arms against destruction by the rule of others holding different values.

Surrender, however, is always a tempting alternative to fighting. Political and military leaders have always had to persuade their men to fight and not to surrender, not to run away from the battlefield in order to save their lives. Indeed, often, military confrontations have been seen and fought out as clashes of civilisations. Values and ideals are at stake

–values constituting the *way* of life of a community as distinct from that of another. We find such admonitions to fight for ideal ends, including the protection of the political culture and institutions of a community, in memorable speeches from Antiquity, such as Pericles' Funeral Oration, that urged defence of the freedoms of Athens, down to Winston Churchill's plea to the British people to fight for their liberties at the cost of their comforts in his 'we shall never surrender' House of Commons speech of 4 June 1940.[4] And it is precisely for this reason that Herder had argued against empire and against war itself – for they destroy the forms of life of the invaded and subjected peoples.

While there have been many battles fought in history, certain battles have achieved special, and lasting, fame. They have become 'places of memory' – of commemoration – in two senses: first, as great military events whose physical sites, the battlefields, may sport a visitor centre or some other physical monument to identify the site, or serve as the setting for grand commemoration ceremonies. Secondly, as manifestations of core cultural and especially political ideas and exempla of behaviour, either to be imitated or avoided, as children are already taught at school. This ideal or cultural dimension that specific battles have assumed may also be evoked in political speeches, novels, poetry and films. Of particular poignancy are battles which have captured the cultural and especially the political imagination not only of those who lived through them, but also of subsequent generations, both locally and globally.

The commemoration of battles has taken different forms. These may coincide with the battle, but may also lie centuries later. Chronologically, usually the first and most immediate commemorative activity is collective. Its primary aim is to channel the grief of the relatives and friends of the fallen and give it some formal outlet, and public recognition. Indeed, as the deaths of the fallen concern many families, the common sorrow is addressed collectively, to provide mutual comfort. In Christian Europe, collective commemoration normally began with a mass said on the day after the battle on the very battlefield, in fact a funerary service for the fallen, who were then buried nearby. In the words of the French author Paul Hay de Chastelet, writing for Louis XIV of France, 'On the subsequent day, on the same battlefield, they will say masses and will serve with funerary pomp in military solemnity, at the end of which all corpses will be thrown into the graves that will have been prepared for this purpose, and which will have been dug as deeply as possible. In the meantime word will have been sent to the enemy to notify them of what one intended to do with the corpses, so that they can come and fetch those corpses which they want to take away.'[5]

A further church service, soon after a battle, would again serve the purpose of the commemoration of the dead, and, on the part of the victorious party, a thanksgiving. Sometimes a further commemorative mass is said after a year or several years, and in the case of truly famous battles, even centuries thereafter – thus in 2015 a memorial service was held at St Paul's Cathedral in London to commemorate the 200th anniversary of the battle of Waterloo. The memorialisation of battles has also been pursued through the creation of a public secular monument, or an ecclesiastical foundation (an abbey, a chapel).

Then the poets and novelists may seize hold of a subject, and later perhaps the film makers, whether with feature films or documentaries. This may be merely for entertainment, but there may also be deliberate political purpose behind this – Soviet morale was to be uplifted in 1938 by the state production of Sergei Eisenstein's film about Aleksander Nevsky who beat the Teutonic Knights at the Battle on Frozen Lake Chudsko; meanwhile, the National Socialist regime in Germany commissioned films about Frederick II 'the Great' of Prussia, one of which, *Fridericus* (dir. Johannes Meyer, 1936) predictably, glorifies the Prussian role in the Seven-Years War. That Britain in 1944 released a film version of Shakespeare's *Henry V*, with its high point being the English triumph at the Battle of Agincourt (with Laurence Olivier both in the main part and as director), is hardly surprising. Interestingly, *The Chorale of Leuthen* (dir. Carl Froehlich), a film about a Prussian victory in battle in the Seven Years' War that was produced before and first screened only days after Hitler came to power (30 January 1933), was already brimming with the sort of nationalism resonating with Nazism. Artistic treatments of a subject are manifestations of the *Zeitgeist*, the spirit of the times, even if no political prescriptions for how to deal with a subject were imposed with sponsorship.

Commemoration often has a political agenda. Fallen heroes and collective sacrifices of the past are evoked by political leaders in order to admonish new generations to make themselves worthy of them by being prepared to make similar sacrifices. Past battles are evoked as the moments that gave birth to the nation, where in blood and sacrifice a community pulled together and (actually, or supposedly, as later claimed) developed a joint consciousness of belonging to one group, fighting against another, or a sense of 'we-ness' against the 'other', as sociologists like to put it. This is how some battles have been turned into foundation myths for tribes as well as modern nations. With the rise of nationalism in the course of the nineteenth century, we see in many countries the state-sponsored emergence and growth of such interpretations of battles as foundries of nations, where individuals meld into a single collective entity. George L. Mosse showed how, from the early 1800s to the 1930s, the 'myth of the war experience' was created, visually evoked by commemorations of wars, by monuments both at the sites of major battles and in the towns and villages from which the fallen soldiers had hailed, and by war cemeteries. These collective commemorations of war made a great contribution to 'the nationalisation of the masses'.[6] This pattern itself existed much earlier in some cultures, as was illustrated by the chapters in volume one: the Battle of Marathon and the Battle of Thermopylae were commemorated as foundational even in Antiquity, as were the Trojan Wars that were commemorated in the great Homeric poetry that nourished the minds of the Athenians well beyond the fifth century BC, and Western civilisation in general until our own times. Elsewhere, battles originally commemorated to celebrate a dynasty of rulers descendent from the victor of the battle were re-invented as birth of nationhood and national consciousness, usually in the nineteenth century.

Different forms of commemoration feed off each other – they cannot be separated neatly from one another. At the same time, the practical implications of commemoration also vary, some turning the original grief of the bereaved and of (possibly mutilated) survivors into furious calls for revenge, and others calling for reconciliation and the rejection of war. This has much to do with how the battle is subsequently narrated, how its origins and unfolding are told, and into what myths it is cast – myths in the sense of words, or stories narrated and transmitted in writing, which imbue events or configurations with explanations and meaning.

Political meaning has been attributed to particular battles, transforming deadly clashes of armed men into great political symbols. Such interpretations have been adopted by many states in the schooling of their young citizens by way of history classes and textbooks. In this way, these political meanings become widely known among the citizenry, engendering, keeping alive and feeding identification with those states through national pride on the one hand and old animosities on the other. With this in mind, we examine the variety of meanings or interpretations that surrounds a large number of 'famous' battles, making them speak in many and sometimes contradictory tongues. These meanings have accrued over time as battles became and remained famous, their particular interpretations periodically revived or recast to suit new fashions, new political configurations, new times.

Varieties of myths

We have identified a great variety of myths – or patterns of interpretation, if you prefer – that have been attached to famous battles of Western civilisation.[7] One way of classifying such narratives is by the agent they glorify. This agent may be metaphysical (some supernatural power acting on behalf of this side or that), monarchical/princely and populist. Starting with the first category, a number of battles – usually modelled on Emperor Constantine I's triumph at the Milvian Bridge – have been interpreted as a God-willed triumph of Christianity over paganism, in a test between the two religions, resulting in the victor or indeed the defeated party accepting baptism. Battles of the second category, in which a crown was contested, were cast mainly as triumph for the victorious side's ruling dynasty, such as the Battles of Ourique (1139), Aljubarrota (1385), Agincourt (1415), Bosworth (1485), or St Quentin (1557), respectively celebrating the Portuguese Burgundian, the Aviz, the Lancastrian, the Tudor and the Spanish Habsburg dynasties. While this type of commemoration had great appeal in the regnalism of the Middle Ages, its appeal has declined with the rise of nationalism, and then that of modern democratic ideals about the power and agency of 'the people'. Our third category of battles belongs to this modern era of national consciousness and liberal democracy one of whose greatest symbols has been Eugène Delacroix's *Liberty leading the people*, of 1830 (Fig. 1.1). Nationalism and liberalism led to the re-interpretation of history as a history of peoples and not of kings and princes. It also led to the re-interpretation of the great battles of the past as nation-building battles and also as battles between nations. The battle of Leipzig of 1813 that became known as 'the battle of the nations' might be seen as emblematic of the nationalisation of war in modern times.

Mythical interpretations of famous battles, like all myths, simplify. They tend to be binary – the good against the bad, one group against another, both depicted as homogeneous, both ideally identified with groups (*ethnies*, nations) that exist today. In collective memory, there is no room for complexity, as our chapters on the Thermopylae, Culloden and the Somme illustrate. This also applies to the Polish commemoration of Grunwald, in which the Lithuanians barely feature, and the battle of Aljubarrota, in which in fact Spaniards fought alongside Frenchmen, and Portuguese alongside Englishmen. And Britons like to think of Waterloo as a British-French tryst, and of the Somme as an exclusively British-German encounter.[8]

INTRODUCTION TO THE SECOND VOLUME

Some battles achieve mythical fame not only on the side of the victors. There is also the myth of moral victory in death and defeat, inspired by Christ's triumph over evil in his own death.[9] Thus battles lost or won in which a heroic commander died, or even a battle lost at great human cost to one's own side, have been turned into great myths – in Antiquity, the Battle of Thermopylae is an outstanding example which would inspire many future generations. Medieval examples in this category are those of the defeats of the Christian (Silesian) forces of Duke Henry II of Silesia and the death of the duke at the battle of Legnickie Pole against the Mongols in 1241, and of the Christian (Serb) host and the death of its leader, Prince Lazar, at the Battle of Kosovo Polje against an Ottoman army in 1389. Both battles were commemorated over centuries: the former along with a battle in Hungary as the turning point of Mongol expansion (due not to a Christian victory but to the death of the Mongol Great Khan, Ögedei), and the latter as the symbol of Christian suffering under Muslim rule. The memory of Kosovo Polje battle would still fuel the wars that broke out six centuries later following the collapse of former Yugoslavia in the closing decade of the twentieth century.

Civilian victims of war – especially in sieges – are only rarely commemorated in any epic fashion: there seems to be something more admirable about the fallen soldier. He could take many to the grave with him, giving as good as he got, as told in the battle epics of European culture since the Iliad. Or else, especially when wearing a smart coloured uniform well before photography could record the full horror of battle, he could be imagined almost as a painted tin soldier being knocked out of the game, only to be resurrected for a later one. Civilians by contrast are rarely cast in a heroic role: even the Stalinist USSR's commemoration of the sieges of Leningrad or Stalingrad preferred to dwell on the fallen soldiers rather than on the starved civilians.[10] There are exceptions to this pattern: the siege and fall of Masada in the spring of 74 CE, during the Great Jewish Rebellion against Rome that began in 66 CE, when a thousand Jewish men, women and children burnt down the fortress of Masada and killed each other, preferring death to being servants of Rome, remains a great symbol of national self-sacrifice, involving both armed men and unarmed civilians. Masada is believed to have inspired the civilian uprising of the Warsaw Ghetto.[11] Modern Greek historians and writers have celebrated the mass suicide of women and children from Souli in 1803, during the Greek War of Independence from the Ottoman Empire. The women, trapped in an enclave, preferred to die rather than surrender to the Ottoman army. By contrast, it is with horror and bafflement that Westerners at least look upon the tragic mass-suicides of the inhabitants of Okinawa at the end of Second World War.

Turning to further ways of categorising the politically-motivated commemoration of battles, some few have been turned into anti-militarist myths: one, discussed in this volume, is the Battle of Culloden of 1746. As even most Communist-governed states embraced the notion that the use of force and the entertainment of a large military is the legitimate right of any sovereign state, such anti-militarist narrations of battles have enjoyed little support from authoritarian states which in turn determine school curricula, public holidays, and, to a good extent, media coverage of commemorations. By contrast, the number of battles commemorated as reminders of the need for reconciliation and international co-operation has seen a great upturn since the beginning of European integration in the 1950s: reconciliation over the graves and the joint commemoration of the dead constitute the spirit of the great anniversary celebrations of, for example, the Spanish Armada in 1988, Trafalgar in 2005, and the Somme in 2016. This is also how key battlefields of the First and Second World Wars are commemorated at or near battle sites or large cemeteries such as the Mémorial and ossuary outside Verdun (Fig. 1.2) and Centre Mondial de la Paix in the city itself, or the museums-cum-visitor centres in France – the the Historial de la Grande Guerre in Péronne for the First and the Mémorial de Caen for the Second World War. [12] All are classic destinations for school visits, and especially the latter two provide extensive facilities, special tours and didactic activities.

While Trafalgar Day is marked only by the Royal Navy, national holidays commemorate especially the First and Second World Wars. The armistice after the First World War is marked particularly in Britain by rituals on 11 November – the day it came into force in 1918 – and by a special mass on the Sunday nearest this date. Americans tend to commemorate D-Day – the landing in Normandy in 1944 – on 6 June, if only through the annual tribute of the widely printed Peanuts cartoons of Charles M. Schulz. Throughout Europe the end of the Second World War in 1945 is commemorated with 'VE' or 'Victory in Europe Day' – on 8 May in most of Europe, and on 9 May with great military parades in Russia, which was already on the other side of the time line when the armistice entered into force. Significantly, on the European Continent, VE Day is symbolically followed by the Day of Europe on 9 May, commemorating the proposal, in 1950, for a European Coal and Steel Community, an early step on the way to the European Union. The two hang together as Good Friday does with Easter Sunday, death with resurrection. The Day of Europe is a holiday which, equally significantly, Britain never espoused, not having been party to the Coal and Steel Community scheme. Indeed, in the minds of the general British public, the link between the rejection of war as an instrument of politics and European integration as an alternative way to settle conflicts and to replace rivalry with co-operation has never been firmly established, as the British 'Brexit' referendum of 23 June 2016 – against the background of centennial commemorations of the Battle of the Somme – demonstrated. And in a spirit of mourning, Japan and much of the Western world annually remember the nuclear bombing of Hiroshima and Nagasaki on 6 and 9 August with newspaper articles and other mentions in the media. Especially in recent times, these ways of commemorating battles and wars are not marred by *revanchisme*, militarism, or other bellicose intentions, but are dominated by grief, and increasingly, one has reason to hope, a spirit of reconciliation.

Thanatourism or pilgrimage? The future of memory

Narratives or myths sustaining mere mourning or diverse political agendas are not alone in keeping memorials and visitor centres well frequented. Commercial dimensions are not absent. There is certainly, on the part of regional councils, the motive of creating and sustaining tourism for the benefit of that region. Such tourism is at times called, with disapproval, 'thanatourism' (tourism of death) – with the implication that some visitors derive ghoulish pleasure from visiting sites of mass death.[13] Undeniably, the tourist industry benefits from physical centres of commemoration of famous battles, from Culloden in Scotland and Aughrim in Ireland to Aljubarrota in Portugal in Europe's Western extremities, to the memorial parks and visitor centres of Grunwald in Poland (Fig. 1.3), Mohács in Hungary, and Thermopylae (Lamia) in Greece in Europe's South-East.

But this is not necessarily evidence of less than respectable motives on the part of those who visit them. Already Alexander the Great wanted to walk in the footsteps of his hero, Achilles. 'Once arrived in Asia, [Alexander] went up to Troy', Plutarch wrote,

> sacrificed to Athena and poured libations to the heroes of the Greek army. He anointed with oil the column which marks the grave of Achilles, ran a race by it naked with his companions, as the custom is, and then crowned it with a wreath.[14]

Indeed, famously the Athenians, but also Megarans, Tanagrans and Thespians erected monuments to their dead soldiers; while some of these were (in the case of Athens and Thespiae) erected in the city itself, others were constructed on the very battlefield, suggesting that somebody went there to see them and to engage in some form of commemoration.[15] The Romans by contrast seem rarely to have commemorated their war dead, except for the occasional monument erected in Rome for a fallen general. While soldiers and officers might receive their individual monument in places where they were stationed, these were not erected to commemorate particular battles. One sole exception seems to be the altar listing the names of fallen soldiers erected at what today is Adamklissi in Romania, which complements a victory monument dated to the reign of Trajan. Again, the construction of such monuments suggests that somebody visited them for commemorative purposes.[16]

Inspired by such models of Antiquity, a form of worshipful pilgrimage to the places where great men had fought and fallen in the past was revived in modern times. When the great French strategist of the Enlightenment, Guibert, travelled through the German lands in 1773, he made a detour to visit the battlefield of Lützen, where Gustavus Adolphus of Sweden had been slain in 1632. Indeed, he had a little sketch made of himself at the very place where the great Swede had succumbed, and wrote in his diary:

> Three miles before Leipzig, the plain of Lützen. One crosses the village; the battle took place on the other side. As the theatre of great events, and especially great events that took place under great men, immediately affect one's imagination, the army, the reputation of Gustavus, seemed to fill this vast plain. Suddenly my postilion who had not told me anything, whom I had not asked anything, got off his horse, and indicated a large broken rock at the side of the way, resembling more a milestone than a monument. 'It is at this stone, there', he said, 'that the king was killed, the great king.' He did not add of which country ...: 'there, there exactly, he was killed.' That epithet of 'great king' which, as by convention, escaped this simple mouth, was elevated by my imagination to be the voice of Posterity. ... I approached the stone. ... I imagined laurel bushes and cypresses shedding their shade on it. And [the Swedish king] Charles XII, vanquisher of Saxony, like me, has seen this battlefield! He has seen this

stone, he, successor of Gustavus, descendant of Gustavus: is it surprising that he sought glory just like *him*?[17]

Half a century later, on 27 June 1830, as he noted in his journal, Sir Walter Scott as a child paid a visit to the battlefield of Prestonpans, site of the last uncontested victory of the Jacobites in 1745; this and Culloden later inspired him to write his *Waverley* novels. As Alan Forrest shows in this volume, the battle of Waterloo was itself almost something of a spectator sport, and visits to the battlefield began immediately after the battle.[18] But the true surge in visits to nearby battlefield came after the American Civil War,[19] and in Europe after First World War, especially with relatives now able to use railways to travel to the places where their loved ones had been killed and buried.[20]

In the spirit of pure mourning and commemoration of the victims of war – whether they were fallen soldiers, or whether they were unarmed civilians – and as a reminder of the advantages of settling conflicts by means other than war, we say: would but more tourists visited the battle sites of *other* countries, to understand their past traumas, to complement the teaching of national history! This does not happen enough, as we discovered in two polls that we conducted, one among school children and another among historians (see Appendices).

Either way, battles continue to occupy a central place in the collective consciousness. Their memory may divide or unite as circumstances change. Most benignly, a spirit of reconciliation, alongside that of the mourning of the dead, even the dead of times long past, is found in the commemoration of the battles of the American Civil War: already US President Abraham Lincoln at the end of the war itself aimed to heal wounds and mark a new departure for a united country. Also in Europe, since the First World War and even more so since the Second, contacts between war widows' associations and later war graves commissions initiated at grass-root level reconciliation across the graves, especially in Franco-German relations.[21] There are also battles which have marked the collective consciousness of people way beyond those of the sides directly involved – most notably we can mention here the Battle of Stalingrad, which came top of our poll (together with Waterloo) even though very few of our respondents were Russian or German. It is undeniable that some battles have either decided history on a larger scale than that concerning only the polities directly involved, or have marked turning points in history on a larger scale. But all battles deserve to be remembered on account of the suffering they caused.

FAMOUS BATTLES

The ultimate aim of this project, of these two volumes on famous battles and their myths, has been to stimulate among our readers a critical approach to historical narrative and especially to narratives about war. By presenting our readers with a rich gamut of stories about battles, we have shown how history can be oversimplified and popular opinion manipulated. Public commemorations of battles and wars, in all their forms (visual and verbal), are major determinants of public feeling and collective behaviour. As sites of memory and mourning they can promote not only national unity and solidarity, but also reconciliation with former enemies. By contrast, they may also nurture hatred and aggression, boisterous nationalism, and perpetuate collective animosities. We hope that the following chapters will help the former, not the latter, through a more complex understanding of battles and their myths.

Chapter 2

The Defeat of the Spanish Armada 1588: 'Prose epic of the modern English nation'

Andrew Lambert

The events of July and August 1588 have long exercised a powerful hold on the English imagination. They combine all the elements necessary to create an enduring myth. On one side overwhelming power, vaulting ambition, and despotic rule, on the other men made brave by their faith and their freedom, relying on superior skill and daring to save their country from invasion and tyranny. It would not be too much to say that the Armada is a core foundation myth of the English, later British, state. It remained the nation's 'Finest Hour' until 1940, when Churchill shifted the focus to the equally mythic, and far less significant 'Battle of Britain'. The quatercentenary in 1988 prompted a rash of new books, a nationwide chain of signal fires, exhibitions, and television. It returned the subject to the core of the national identity, and reminded everyone in the English speaking world just how much they owed to the heroes of 1588. However, we should not assume that this status merely reflects the importance of the subject, much of it was consciously created as propaganda.

When nations adopt specific battles as defining moments in their history, the ultimate expressions of their identity, almost all choose events on land. Sea battles have been routinely disregarded since antiquity, the sea being an alien environment, the domain of cultural outliers and foreign ideas, too fluid for heroics. While Greece was saved by a naval victory over the Persians at Salamis, the Athenian elite preferred to celebrate the earlier hoplite victory at Marathon, while the Spartans positively delighted in the heroic sacrifice of their king and his elite troops at Thermopylae. These noble combats involved elite citizens, fighting in a socially cohesive formation, within a spear push of the enemy, not the skilled manoeuvres of common sailors serving for pay.[1]

By adopting the Armada as their iconic battle the English consciously set themselves apart from other nations, privileging their sea-power identity, and the insularity upon which that identity had been built. While the campaign of 1588 remains one of the great dramatic set-pieces of English history the construction of the narrative was a far more complex process than it might appear. The challenge for history was to reconcile the uncertain, contingent pattern of events with the demand of national propaganda and the ambitions of the leading men. If the final outcomes of the process would be a 'definitive' account and a major piece of public art they were unplanned.

The Armada achieved iconic status as the fulfilment of a long held and very specific dream of English naval glory and sea-empire, already fostered in the 1430s, at the humanist Court of Duke Humphrey, and shaped by contact with the growing maritime power of Burgundy, where a rich iconography of ships and the seas decorated Antwerp and Brussels, the great cities of maritime trade and economic power. Henry VIII had hired Flemish artists to record and paint his fleet, in the iconic *Embarkation for the Field of the Cloth off Gold* of 1539, an image created to hang at the entrance to his audience chamber at Whitehall, as the ultimate symbol of royal power, combining the king, his ships and their great bronze guns.

The Campaign

Desperately short of money the English tried to pre-empt the attack by sending squadrons to the coast of Spain in May 1588, but three times they were driven back by gales, a frequent occurrence in this year. Charles Howard, the Lord High Admiral, was left with a wide discretion and a fully mobilised fleet, although supplies and food were always short. When the Spanish finally managed to leave Lisbon on 28 May they were also hampered by gales, the main English force was well placed at Plymouth.

Warned of the Spanish approach the English fleet hastened to sea, and took station astern of the vast crescent formation that the Spanish Commander, the seventh Duke of Medina Sidonia, used to protect and control his transports. Medina Sidonia's mission was not to win a sea battle, or to launch an invasion, but to rendezvous with the Duke of Parma and his invasion army on the coast of modern Belgium. Phillip II of Spain convinced himself the English, whom he knew to be superior in seamanship and gunnery, would have to give battle at close quarters, where they would be overwhelmed by Spanish infantry.

On 20 July the two fleets came into contact, Howard issued a formal challenge, sending in a pinnace to fire a single shot, and then split his force to attack the two wings of the Spanish crescent. Two big Spanish warships were damaged, the *Rosario* by a series of collisions, the *San Salvador* by a powder explosion. Both were left to their fate. In the night Sir Francis Drake slipped away to take the valuable *Rosario*, the fleet picked up the *San Salvador*. After several days of fighting the Spanish were still forging along towards their destination, English gunnery had not stopped the Armada. At a Council of War on the 26th Howard re-organised the fleet into four squadrons, under himself, Sir Francis Drake, Sir John Hawkins and Martin Frobisher, to co-ordinate the attacks. The following day Medina Sidonia tried to anchor in the Solent, but Drake's squadron drove his seaward flank too close to Selsey Bill and the Owers Shoal for comfort, and the attempt failed.

Having won a major strategic victory the English fell back to conserve powder and shot. The Spanish could not anchor in the only other suitable location, the Downs, because these had been heavily fortified by Henry VIII. They had to link up with Parma, on an open coast without a deep-water harbour. Without a force of oared galleys, which had failed to weather the Bay of Biscay, the Spanish could not cross the local shallows, to open the passage for Parma's boats in the face of Dutch and English light warships. On Sunday 27 July Medina Sidonia anchored off Calais, in an open roadstead. Although this was relatively close to Parma, the duke was not ready, had not received any of Medina Sidonia's letters, or any other useful intelligence. The English anchored to windward, and fitted out eight fireships. That night they were sent down on the wind and tide, although none took effect they forced the Spanish to cut their cables and stand out to sea. In the process they lost their cohesion. The next morning Medina Sidonia had only a handful of fighting ships to meet the English. Howard went to finish off a beached galleass, the only warships in the campaign that could stem the wind and tide, while the rest of his fleet attacked at close range, probably about 50 yards. Short of ammunition for the small guns, and unable to reload the big ones, the Spanish were heavily pounded. One ship sank, two more were driven ashore and captured by the Dutch, others were badly damaged, yet Medina Sidonia's iron discipline ensured most of the fleet managed to reform. However, wind and tide were driving the Spanish fleet towards the lethal Zealand Bank, to their certain destruction. Only a timely shift in the wind early the next day allowed Medina Sidonia to set a course north and round the hazard. While Howard continued the pursuit he had run out of ammunition and was only putting on a bold front. The English continued the pursuit up to the Firth of Forth, on the coast of neutral Scotland, before sailing back to the Thames. Howard detailed a few small craft to continue shadowing.

Although English guns and fire ships had stopped the Armada joining up with the Duke of Parma's army, the key move of the campaign, they had not destroyed the Armada as a fleet or a fighting force. That role would be filled by the wind and waves, the coast or Ireland, and the inevitable collapse of Spanish logistics on a prolonged voyage. Driven north, and then north east by the wind, the Spanish struggled to keep together. Medina Sidonia knew he had to get out into the Atlantic to avoid the dangers of the Irish coast, but his battered ships and starving men were caught in the tail end of a south westerly hurricane, and many sought shelter.[2] Some ships, mostly Mediterranean built transports, were simply unequal to the weather, others badly damaged by gunfire, and short of anchors and cables, could not hold the ground. Few escaped the treacherous coast, while their crew found equally unforgiving Irish and English forces ashore. Approximately half of the fleet made it back, a testament to Medina Sidonia's resolute leadership and professionalism.

The big question was how the events of July August and September 1588 would be recorded. History is written by the winners, and here the key battle was about to begin. By modern standards the fighting had been indecisive, but the results were clear. To the contemporary mind it was the outcome that mattered, and the role of the divine in a religious war could not be over-estimated. The English and their Dutch allies, with the active support of other Protestant groups were quick to launch a full scale propaganda offensive, this was so effective that one historian observed: 'It is hard to resist the conclusion that the victory was of the pen rather than of the sword.'[3] When the English lost sight of the Spanish fleet on 2 August it still contained around 100 ships. Drake and Howard thought it might go to Denmark or Norway for masts, anchors and stores, before returning to the Channel. Drake recognised the real danger came from Parma's troops, who he feared far more than Medina Sidonia's fleet, and urged the Belgian coast should be watched closely to prevent a surprise invasion. This was a serious possibility, Parma had embarked 18,000 troops in flat boats by 12 August, and stood ready to sail until the 31st. Clearly Parma was still expecting the fleet, but none came.

On 13 August the English suspended the militia mobilisation for service in the south-east, but left the 17,000 men already assembled by the Earl of Leicester at Tilbury on the Thames. The Queen sailed down to inspect them on the 17th, and launched the propaganda campaign with a famous speech stressing her willingness to die among them, and that she had the heart and stomach of a King of England. Whoever wrote the speech, and it may well have been Elizabeth, was a master of the English language and of the politics of the image. This was grand theatre, beautifully contrived, and delivered with a far wider audience in mind. The Queen made the voyage after the danger of battle had passed and two days later the army began to demobilise. By the end of the month only 1,500 men remained at Tilbury. Fear of invasion was quickly replaced by fiscal probity. The under-nourished and ill-clothed men of the fleet died in droves, saving the state the cost of their pay; £400,000 had been spent on the campaign, of which a mere £180 went as sick and disabled benefits.

Within days the State began to exploit the victory. The trials of suspected Roman Catholic agents began and many were hung. On September 8th captured enemy banners featured in a second service of thanksgiving at St. Paul's Cathedral with some of the naval commanders present. A third, and more magnificent, event on 24 November was attended by the Queen, who arrived in a chariot 'imitating the ancient Romans.' While this was the capstone of the official pageantry, the propaganda offensive was only beginning. Among the many agendas that would be served the most important was to use the success to draw James VI, King of Scotland, into Elizabeth's orbit, and ensure he met her requirements for the succession.

Phillip II was stunned by the disaster, for him it indicated the withdrawal of God's support, and the defeat of God's cause. In his despair the king expressed his feelings on a report of the Gravelines battle 'I hope that God has not permitted so much evil.'[4] This was the avenue of attack for Elizabethan state propaganda, and it was an opportunity that was not spurned. Only in late September did the full extent of the catastrophe come home to the north coast of Spain, borne on crippled galleons full of dying men. Now Phillip was left to hope that his God would send him a miracle, and that his sins had now been sufficiently punished. The entire country, it appears, was devastated by the defeat, and the loss of respect and military reputation that it would occasion. Suddenly it seemed that Phillip's interest were everywhere doomed to failure. His French ally, the Duke of Guise, was murdered in December, soon after Parma's siege of Bergen Op Zoom had failed in October. For such a man, and such a belief system, defeat had a meaning far deeper than it carries today. In this age God still made the decisions. Only in the eighteenth century would men take full credit for their work.

Creating the mythology

Elizabeth watched these developments, well aware that they were adding to her security without draining her purse. English ballads, supposedly including one by the queen, celebrated the triumph in stark terms of good and evil, and religious divides. In September Lord Burghley, the English Chief Minister, commissioned a pamphlet masquerading as a letter from an English Jesuit to the Spanish Ambassador in France. It emphasised the injustice of the Spanish cause, the skill of the English defence, named specific Spanish ships and men lost and observed the safe return of the English. The pamphlet was quickly published in French, Italian, Dutch and German and we can imagine the impact of the concluding sentence, 'So ends this account of the misfortunes of the Spanish Armada which they used to call INVINCIBLE.'[5] The last word was capitalised, it was also the first time this expression had been used to describe the fleet. The irony was not lost on a European audience. The pamphlet had a long and often misleading history, the original intent, and authorship being forgotten until the 20th century, leaving it to stand as curiosity at once supporting anti-Catholic prejudice while appealing for English Catholic loyalty.

The success of the propaganda counter-offensive was fortunate, Drake's counter-armada campaign of 1589 signally failed to destroy the remnants of Phillip's fleet. Drake came ashore, and Phillip decided to carry on the war, building a new fleet to secure his aims. Despite a stunning English victory at Cadiz in 1596, where the Lord Howard and the Earl of Essex took the city and destroyed a large Spanish fleet, fresh Armadas sailed in 1596 and 1597.[6] They were larger and better organised than that of 1588, but both were scattered by storms. English privateers continued to profit, while Elizabeth backed wars in the Low Countries and France that kept Phillip busy.

Spanish pamphlets and other literature published before the event were now translated to show the scale of their power, and the magnitude of their defeat. Religious issues dominated the Anglo-Dutch response to 1588. This unusual wind and weather was immediately seen by the English as a divine message. They had driven the Armada off, and God had then destroyed it. The great medal struck to celebrate the event showed a fleet being dispersed by wind and lightning. The original design and execution of the die, like so much of the Armada iconography was Dutch. The legend around the design 'Jehovah blew and they were scattered' was linked to the image by the thunderbolts issuing from the than name of God. The reverse showed the true church under attack, but remaining unharmed.

The first 'official' account written in Latin by Florentine exile scholar Petruccio Ubaldino appeared in 1590, accompanied by eleven charts, also based on information supplied by Howard. Drawn under the direction of the Lord High Admiral by Robert Adams, Surveyor of the Queen's Buildings, and engraved by the nautical instrument maker Augustine Ryther, it provided a step by step overview of the campaign.[7] Engraved and published in 1590 they remain a major source for the campaign, although their ultimate purpose was to assert the importance of Howard's role, rather than to tell the national story. In the same year a new portrait of the Queen was created by George Gower, placing her between two scenes from the campaign, first the fleets in battle and then the wreck of the Spanish ships on the coast of Ireland. Overhead is the canopy used in the St. Paul's procession, the crown to the right conveys royal power, while the globe under her right hand implies the world circling extent of that power. The picture is reputed to have been commissioned by Drake. Like the ballad attributed to the Queen it conveys the divine power that 'made the winds and waters rise, to scatter all mine enemies.' In the aftermath of the victory Elizabeth had regenerated into a national icon. In 2016 the picture was bought for the nation after a multi-million pound public appeal and now hangs in the National Maritime Museum at Greenwich.

A heroic literature.

Ubaldino's account had been crafted to justify the Lord High Admiral's conduct in October 1588. In response Drake provided Ubaldino with notes, leading to a second narrative of April 1589, to justify his own rather mysterious actions. Here the key audience was the court and especially the Queen, for whom an Italian account would be doubly useful. It lent a stamp of authority to the story that could not be provided by an English account and was easily accessible to critical foreign observers. Drake's version was overtaken by events. The unsuccessful 1589 expedition to Lisbon saw him fall out of favour, and the manuscript of this version was given to Lord Chancellor Sir Christopher Hatton and lost to view for 300 years.[8] In consequence, Ubaldino's first, and rather less full, version translated into English in 1590, printed and circulated by Howard, became the basis for Armada histories for three decades. While Ubaldino's written account had no doubt the victory was divinely inspired, he may, as a Catholic, have had more problem with this interpretation at a personal level. His humanist approach ensured he credited the skill and courage of his patrons, Howard and Drake.

Edmund Howes' edition of John Stow' *Annals*, published in 1615, was the first text to mention the men of the fleet playing bowls at Plymouth, but did not mention the most famous Armada myth; that of Drake refusing to interrupt his game on Plymouth Hoe. A century later Drake was associated with the game of bowls and nineteenth century writers found this heroic sangfroid so appropriate a gesture that they cited it in history and fiction; the very emblem of English superiority.

In 1589 the analyst of English maritime aspiration, geographer, spy, economic advisor and cleric Richard Hakluyt, boasted of 'that victorious exploit not long since achieved in our narrow seas against that monstrous Spanish army'.[9] He provided more detail in a second edition ten years later, using the Armada to demonstrate that England had become a great maritime and imperial power.[10] To sustain the new identity Hakluyt added naval history to the original commercial and exploring voyages, providing a long history of battles by sea from King Arthur to the Armada.[11] Hakluyt's great book, like his friend William Camden's *Britannia* of 1586, was an attempt to recover a useable past as a key instrument in the creation of 'an identity of England defined by its past and independent, at least in part, of its sovereign and court.[12] This was a serious business. Hakluyt carefully crafted the second edition as a coherent compendium of English maritime identity on either side of the Armada.[13] When the first edition of Hakluyt's text appeared in 1589 it was a major contribution to the long running project to create a free-standing English identity that had dominated the years of hopes and dreams before the Armada. The three volume second edition of 1598-1600 was produced in a very different country, rendered confident by the Armada, and certain that the future lay on the oceans. This edition confirmed that the English had an identity on the oceans, something that was based on 1588.

Hakluyt's friend William Camden was appointed to be the queen's regnal historian by a patron they shared, Secretary of State Robert Cecil. Cecil needed a text to pave the way for a Stuart succession. While Camden based his account of the Armada on Ubaldino's text, he added an emphasis on the supporting role of private armed vessels, democratising the victory. He also highlighted the supposed claim that the Armada was invincible, and the incompetence of Medina Sidonia, highly questionable interpretations that persisted until the twentieth century. For Camden the battle provided the basis for a peaceful Protestant succession, and the security of the kingdom. His assessment might not have been especially profound, or overly concerned with fine detail, but it was excellent propaganda that lasted for 300 years.

The art of the myth.

Having won the battle of words with Drake, Lord Howard set out to cement his place in the national political pantheon, annexing the glory to his family. To overmatch Drake's cheap and quick oil he commissioned a tapestry cycle from Hans Sperincx, the Delft master weaver, transforming Urbaldino's text and Robert Adams striking coloured charts into the ultimate art form of the age, something fit for the halls of princes and beyond the threadbare pockets of his cousin the queen. It would convey his version of the Armada to high status visitors. Here the national and the personal combined in a cultural form that melded art, craftsmanship and the public display of wealth. Made rich by the legal revenues of his office, as Lord High Admiral of England Howard took a percentage of the proceeds of all prize cases in a very long war with Spain.[14] Tapestry had been the art of kings for centuries, sumptuous wall hangings that reflected royal power, and helped take the chill off the draughty halls of Northern European princes. Painting in oil was, in comparison, a cheap format, used when speed of execution was paramount.[15] Tapestry was the ultimate art of the age, a vast, costly display of wealth, and status, conveyed through technical ability, artistic prowess and costly materials. To wait the necessary span of years was the mark of a great man, a king, or a mighty Lord. The Armada tapestry set Howard apart from his subordinates, especially Drake, who could not afford to deal in the same symbols.

The ten massive tapestries, each 14 by 28 feet, were designed by pioneer Flemish marine artist Hendrik Cornelis Vroom (1566-1640). Vroom transformed Robert Adams' maps into images with remarkable, innovative skill.[16] The designs were in the tradition of Bayeux, and other great celebratory wall hangings, composed to be seen from below, picking out the key moments of the story, with a full cast of characters set in the broad borders, with a few sea-monsters, charts and other conventional adornments for good measure. The truly novel aspect was that the perspective was taken from a ship, not the land. Howard, who had seen an earlier Flemish cycle commemorating the Spanish Conquest of Tunis in 1554, set a high standard for his team, and was so pleased with them on their delivery in

1596 that he gave Vroom an extra hundred guilders.[17] Vroom created the most commonly repeated images of the Armada, and it is fortunate that he also produced a painting of the fireship attack off Gravelines, again using Adams's charts for the layout of events of the day in question.[18] It is among the first sea-battle pictures, profiting from his extensive experience of sea voyages. It is not the least of the ironies of this deeply Protestant subversion of a Catholic art form that Vroom (meaning pious in Flemish) was almost certainly a Catholic.[19]

Woven with gold, silver and coloured threads, the hangings cost £1,582 a staggering sum by contemporary standards. They were delivered to Howard in 1595 and after hanging in his Chelsea manor they were moved to Arundel House on the Strand in 1602, specifically to be shown to the Queen. Hoping to cash in his asset Howard had hoped the Queen would buy them, but Elizabeth appears to have expected her cousin would hand them over as a gift. In 1612 Howard, by now aged, and impecunious, having spent his fortune maintaining his status, sold the set to King James I for £1,628. House of Lords Researcher Justin Dee recorded:

> James displayed them in the Banqueting Hall to receive the Spanish Ambassador. It has been suggested that in so doing perhaps he could pursue dialogue with Spain without the appearance of weakness.[20]

The Banqueting Hall hang was so overtly triumphalist that the Spanish Ambassador feigned illness – to avoid being confronted by the images, and possibly humiliated by references to them in Royal speeches.[21] The tapestries having served their purpose, James then displayed them in the royal quarters in the Tower of London. Dee went on to observe that, 'By contrast, his son Charles I folded these martial images away for much of his reign.'[22] Cromwell, who understood the importance of the images, had them removed to the House of Lords in 1644, 'as reminders of English naval glory'. They featured in Wenceslaus Hollar's image of the fateful Trial of Archbishop Laud in that year, a key stage in the downfall of Charles I's personal monarchy.[23] The tapestries dominated the debating chamber, whose walls they covered entirely, effectively transforming Lord Howard's self-aggrandising Armada images into a core element of English national identity. The impact of such images on the work of the Lords is unknown, but the message they conveyed would be reflected in their lordships' rhetoric on many occasions.

It must be assumed that Cromwell was consciously administering to their Lordships a lesson in the realities of power, and the needs of the English Commonwealth, just before closing their House. There is an obvious connection with his decision to declare war on Spain in 1652, just after the hanging became permanent. Nine panels covered every inch of the walls, and the door. They provided the debating chamber with the perfect backdrop for debating the growth of English and later British sea-power identity, and the concomitant naval might that secured an empire of trade and power. Clearly the Armada tapestries satisfied Cromwell's taste for art as power; his own accommodation at Hampton Court featured Andrea Mantegna's majestic 'Triumph of Caesar'.[24]

When tension with Spain began to rise once again in the early 1730s, the commercial classes sought a return to the 'good old days' of Elizabethan war. London engraver John Pine produced a fine print edition of the tapestries, describing the Armada as the 'most glorious victory that was ever obtained at sea, and the most important to the British nation'.[25] He also claimed that he had produced the pictures to ensure they were not lost to the nation. Pine's timing was perfect. War with Spain broke out in 1739, the year he published his luxurious portfolio. The issues at stake retained much of imperial, economic focus of the mythic 1588. Here as always, the renewal of interest in these images was driven by current concerns.[26]

Although the Armada tapestries provided the backdrop for eighteenth century high politics only one artist managed to exploit their allegorical riches, and their luminous fabric. In 1781 American born artist John Singleton Copley exhibited his great canvas 'The Death of the Earl of Chatham'. Chatham, architect of Britain's greatest victory, the Seven Year's War, suffered a fatal stroke in the Chamber on 7 April 1778 while declaiming against making concessions to the American rebels, or the old enemy, in this case France. Chatham referenced the Armada as France and Spain were gathering their forces for a fresh attempt.

> Shall this great kingdom, that has survived, whole and entire, the Danish depredations, the Scottish inroads, and the Norman conquest; that has stood the threatened invasion of the Spanish Armada, now fall prostrate before the House of Bourbon? … Let us at least make one effort; and if we must fall, let us fall like men![27]

Copley posed Chatham, the aged hero, surrounded by family, friends and admirers, against the brilliant Armada backdrop to which he had gestured.

The allegorical counterpoint between Chatham's slumped figure, beneath the depiction of England's greatest naval victory, and his imperial vision of an expanding British Empire of commerce secured and sustained by sea-power, was too real to require any sleight of hand. Copley made a fortune exhibiting the picture, backed up by sales of a print marketed by Boydell.[28]

The heightened fear of invasion that Britain endured at various times between 1779 and 1805 prompted a renewal of old Armada ceremonies, notably the laying up of trophies in St. Paul's in late 1797. Whenever the mortal danger of 1588 was revisited interest in the original campaign was raised. The new art of the 'Apocalyptic Sublime', propelled by Edmund Burke's essay and the French Revolution, prompted émigré Alsatian artist and stage designer Philippe Jacques de Loutherbourg to produce a suitably dramatic technicolour canvas. The looming threat of invasion prompted saw James Gillray, caricaturist of Britishness in adversity, commissioned to produce a series of prints in 1798 to 'rouse all the People'. In 'Consequences of a successful French Invasion' the Armada tapestries were slashed and torched by a gleeful horde of marauding French sailors. Clearly he believed that the evocation of such an assault on the 200 year old tapestries retained the power to stiffen the resolve of a nation.[29]

While the Revolutionary War ended with their debating chamber inviolate, their lordships moved to a larger space in 1801, and took the precious tapestries with them. This was no time to give up on the heroic past. Such sentiments endured while Napoleon threatened to invade. 'When it was said that Napoleon wanted to put the Bayeux Tapestries on a pre-invasion tour of France, it was suggested the same be done in Britain for the Armada ones.'[30]

After Trafalgar the need for the Armada waned, as a new heroic iconography was been created around the sainted redeemer Horatio Nelson, just in time for a rapidly changing war in which Spain and Catholicism were allies against the Imperial tyranny of Bonaparte. The 74-gun HMS *Armada* was built, but the heroic imagery of the next generation would be more Carthaginian than Elizabethan.

Then on 16 October 1834, disaster struck. The Old Palace of Westminster was ravaged by fire, the House of Lords Chamber being burnt to the ground and with it the precious tapestries. This loss was widely regarded as a national catastrophe, so deeply engrained was their connection with English identity. The ancient battle, like the old landed houses represented in the Chamber, reflected a record of resilience, stability and success.

The Armada always had a place in the rebuilt Palace of Westminster, a Gothic celebration of English democracy, amidst a wider scheme of national historic decoration, in statues, pictures and stonework. Chaired by Prince Albert, a master of the invention of tradition, the Royal Commission on Fine Arts, settled on a six picture cycle based on the Tapestries.[31] The paintings would fill panels in the Prince's Chamber, leading into the Lords debating chamber. Albert also found space for another iconic naval battle, a majestic fresco of Trafalgar shared space with Waterloo in the Royal Gallery, demoting the Armada to secondary status. Richard Burchett painted the engagement off Fowey, but the death of Albert in December 1861 stalled the great Westminster project. Burchett's picture was put in store, the Armada replaced by Pugin wallpaper.

However, the Armada was not forgotten. In 2007, an American benefactor offered to pay for two more pictures, this resulted in the completion of the five 'missing' panels by artist Anthony Oakshett (Figs. 2.1-3 and 2.4-6). They were hung in 2010, along with Burchett's cleaned panel, to considerable acclaim. With that the Armada came back to the centre of British political life, albeit in a secondary role, no longer the vibrant backdrop of unfolding history, but still a potent presence in the mental self-image of a sea-power state.

Re-working the history.

While Edward Creasey's inclusion of the campaign in his 1851 text *Fifteen Decisive battles of the World; From Marathon to Waterloo* was full of symbolic meaning, his book, one of the most successful publishing phenomena of the century, reflected and shaped contemporary political agendas. A year later James Anthony Froude described Richard Hakluyt's naval material as 'the prose epic of the modern English nation', a judgment that reflected his Imperial ideology.[32] In 1888, England celebrated the Armada at the apogee of imperial grandeur, reflecting on Spain, a decayed relic of her former glory. Tercentenary Armada scholarship included John Laughton's *State Papers Relating to the Defeat of the Spanish Armada* of 1894 and Julian Corbett's *Drake and the Tudor Navy* of 1898, which demonstrated the English had been stronger, the Armada largely composed of transports, not warships.[33] When underwater archaeologists addressed the physical legacy of the Armada they found the Spanish ships less heavily armed than the English, and had not fired much heavy calibre ammunition, although they ran out of antipersonnel projectiles. American diplomatic historian Garrett Mattingley placed the Armada in the context of the Counter-Reformation. The Armada will remain a heroic English legend, but it takes on a more coherent form when viewed in a European perspective.

While popular culture found endless opportunities to address the subject, in fiction and art, the technical difficulties of filming large scale sea battles encouraged directors to avoid placing the actual fighting on centre state. In *Fire Over England* (1937) the action took place at night. While *Elizabeth: the Golden Age* of 2007 made good use of CGI technology it made Sir Walter Raleigh, a figure well known to Americans, the hero of the fight. Raleigh actually spent the campaign ashore. This treatment prompted some well-merited mockery from *The Simpsons*. An episode in the twentieth season saw Homer Simpson playing Raleigh, accidentally setting the only English ship alight, which then burnt the entire Spanish fleet.

Conclusion:

The Armada was placed at the heart of a rapidly evolving English national identity by a highly skilled group of statesmen, publicists, and artists, including some who were neither English nor Protestant. Their words and images defined the English sense of self; a sea-faring, Godly in a peculiarly English way, an outward looking people, free from continental tyranny, temporal and spiritual. That identity would evolve and broaden, notably with the Act of Union in 1707, but 1588 remained the iconic moment of the national story down to 1805, when another naval battle eclipsed the Elizabethan drama, a greater victory, a more dangerous opponent, a new national hero. Trafalgar took the national love affair with sea-power outdoors, clearing a space in central London for a Roman column that celebrated the efflorescence of an oceanic imperial destiny foretold in the heroics of 1588. It helped that Trafalgar was truly British, the heroes included men from all four parts of the kingdom, and a much wider British world. The Armada tercentenary in 1888 found the Empire at its apogee, prompting a major revival, notably around Plymouth, as long forgotten deeds were re-imagined: Drake the Pirate became Drake the Admiral, a proto-Nelson, his name graced great warships, and naval bases. The quatercentennial celebrations, for such they were, must be read as a reflection of rising national confidence, post-Falklands War, when rhetoric about Armadas and invasions had been strikingly common. That the four hundredth anniversary should herald the cusp of a new world order, one in which the global maritime world of Elizabethan enterprise became more resonant than it had been for generations, remains suggestive. British optimism, fuelled by the recent defeat of another Armada, rising prosperity, and growing public interest in the sea and history returned the story to centre stage.

For 500 years the English lived in a world where a united Europe constituted an existential threat to their existence. The fear that a superpower would force them back into a system dominated by distant rulers and distant ideologies, brilliantly brought to life by Thomas More, was exploited by the Tudors to secure their power. The turn to the ocean provided an identity largely free from contemporary peers, one which led to empires in America and Asia, established colonies peopled by Anglophone settlers, who multiplied the Anglosphere, carrying with them an English culture shaped in the sixteenth century.

In the twentieth century Britain engaged in three titanic contests to sustain the European balance of power, and prevent the creation of a hegemonic bloc. In the process it was bankrupted, lost the Empire, and consequently the naval dominance that it had sustained slipped away. In the struggle to find a post-imperial mission in the Cold War era a large part of the political class settled on Europe, an economic community hoping it could aid the recovery of industries wrecked by the loss of imperial markets. After the end of the Cold War the attractions of Europe to a recovering British economy were challenged by the prospect of European political integration. Having deliberately cut themselves off from Europe to avoid falling under an alien hegemony, propelled by different ideologies 500 years before, the negative reaction of many in England was only a surprise to those with no sense of a past in which 1588, 1805 and 1940 remain powerful. Security and sovereignty were the key issues in the 2016 referendum, as they had been when Henry VIII adopted an Imperial Crown and took charge of a national Church. He blocked recourse to extra territorial jurisdictions and built a Navy to ensure those jurisdictions could not be brought to England. In 1588 his daughter used that Navy to defeat the threat that Spain would re-impose the old faith and, more pertinently, the old subservience to the Papacy. Elizabeth's speech at Tilbury reminded her people of Henry's choice.

In 2016, yet another Spanish blockade of Gibraltar emphasised what the English fought for in 1588 and the press enjoyed reminding Spain what had happened on that occasion. Insularity, the ocean and a global vision still mark the English out from other Europeans. This distinction may break up the United Kingdom, but a culture shaped by the defiance of

European aggression will endure for as long as the Armada is remembered, Shakespeare is read, and Nelson stands in Trafalgar Square. The ideas and traditions of 1588 may have been invented, at least in part, but they have been owned by the English for too long for their truth to be in doubt. The Englishness that was shaped by 1588 has long since escaped the bounds history.

Chapter 3

Chatham 1667: A Forgotten Invasion and the Myth of a Moth

J. D. Davies

At about 10 in the morning of Wednesday 12 June 1667, a squadron of Dutch warships, detached from Admiral Michiel de Ruyter's fleet, sailed down Gillingham Reach on the River Medway. Ahead of them lay a great chain, stretched taut across the river blocking their way to the British warships that lay beyond, off the great naval dockyard at Chatham.[1] Most of the British ships were dismasted and virtually unarmed. Lacking the money to send a proper fleet to sea for that summer's campaign (and believing in any case that peace was imminent), King Charles II had ordered the ships to be laid up, trusting that the chain and the forts guarding the Medway would be sufficient to protect the navy against just such a Dutch attack. But most of the forts were still incomplete, and the largest and most important of them, that at Sheerness, had already fallen to the Dutch two days earlier. Still, the great chain appeared to be an insuperable obstacle and so it might have proved but for the audacity of Jan van Brakel, a Rotterdam captain, who volunteered to lead his ship, the *Vrede*, in an attack on the barrier. Under heavy fire, he attacked the guardship which protected the chain and took her without a serious fight.[2] This allowed the fireship *Pro Patria* to sail directly at the chain, which broke on impact (according to the Dutch) or else sank under its own weight (according to the English).[3] Beyond lay the most seaward of Charles II's great ships, the *Royal Charles*: the very ship that had carried the king back to England at the Restoration, and which he had named after himself and his father (Fig. 3.1). Only thirty-two of her hundred guns were still aboard and she had virtually no crew embarked. The men ordered to tow her to safety up river simply turned and fled when they saw that they were too few and too weakly armed to resist the approaching Dutch, thus enabling a small prize crew quickly to take possession of the ship. The Dutch resumed their attack on the following day, albeit under heavy fire. Three more great ships – the *Royal James, Royal Oak* and *Loyal London* - were attacked, and all were set ablaze. Friday 14 June brought further humiliation. Despite the immense navigational difficulties presented by the River Medway, and under fire from British forces ashore, the Dutch managed to get the *Royal Charles* down river to Sheerness, where the Dutch flag still flew over the fort, and thence back to Holland.

***

The semantics of warfare are often overlooked, but they can be at once loaded and highly revealing. Consider, for example, the subtle but important distinctions conveyed by 'the American Revolution' as against 'the American War of Independence', or 'the Dutch Revolt' as against 'the Eighty Years War'. This is certainly true of the events of June 1667, too. In British history, the Dutch attack has always been known as 'the Raid on the Medway', while in the Netherlands, it is the *tocht naar Chatham* – literally, 'the trip to Chatham' – or else the *slag bij Chatham*, the battle at Chatham. While the Dutch terms conjure up visions of a jolly outing (and thus, one without serious opposition) or else a full scale engagement, the British description downplays the seriousness of the whole affair: in the popular imagination, after all, a 'raid' is generally something carried out by the likes of bank robbers or cattle rustlers. The place-names serve the same purposes, with the name of a river making the action more impersonal and remote than the name of a town, which implies the presence of both people and destruction (one cannot, after all, destroy a river). Similarly, in British history the Medway attack is described as an invasion only rarely. While it invariably appears on lists of 'greatest British defeats' (and, naturally, on those of greatest Dutch victories), the status of the events at Chatham in June 1667 is somewhat anomalous – not quite a naval battle, not quite a land battle, perhaps not quite an invasion either.

Even before the Dutch ships sailed out of the Thames estuary, the genesis of a number of myths about the attack was already taking shape. Inevitably, it attracted derision from the many critics of the Restoration monarchy and satirists had a field day, linking the defeat forever to the perceived personal shortcomings – notably, the very obvious immorality – of King Charles II. In his *Last Instructions to a Painter,* Andrew Marvell conjured up a particularly devastating attack on the king. Having used the language of ravishing to describe de Ruyter's depredations in the river, he then used it to imagine Charles II, troubled by nightmares in the aftermath of the attack, dreaming that he was raping a naked and bound female embodiment of England. But the most devastating contribution to the making of this particular myth would not be published until over 150 years later. In his diary, still very much for his eyes only in 1667, the naval administrator Samuel Pepys reported a story of how 'the night the Dutch burned our ships, the King did sup with my Lady Castlemaine at the Duchess of Monmouth['s], and there were all mad in hunting of a poor moth'; a story that this essay will address directly in due course.[4]

The one positive note struck in the poetry penned in response to Chatham was an entirely different form of myth-making. One of the very few heroic incidents in the defence of the ships in the Medway was the valiant attempt by a Scottish soldier, Captain Archibald Douglas, to save the *Royal Oak*. Since the Restoration, Charles II had revived his grandfather's project for a political union between England and Scotland, but this was making little progress, due principally to virulent anti-Scottish sentiment among the English political elites and lower orders alike. Douglas's heroism – a Scot dying gallantly for England, in England, in a ship whose name was so closely associated with the king – inspired Marvell to pen *The Loyal Scot*, an expansion of a passage in the *Last Instructions to a Painter.* This attempted to turn Douglas into a mythic symbol of British national unity, but that is not the principal impression which readers now, and, quite possibly, then too, take away from the poem: instead, the most powerful imagery conveyed in *The Loyal Scot* is that of remarkably overt homoeroticism.

> As so, brave Douglas, on whose lovely chin
> The early down but newly did begin.
> And modest beauty yet his sex did veil,
> While envious virgins hope he is a male,
> His yellow locks curl back themselves to seek,
> Nor other courtship know but to his cheek.
> Oft as he in chill Esk or Tyne, by night,
> Hardened and cooled his limbs, so soft, so white,

Among the reeds, to be espied by him,
The nymphs would rustle, he would forward swim.
They sighed, and said, Fond boy, why so untame,
That fly'st love's fires, reserved for other flame?[5]

While Marvell and less gifted poets penned their verses, there was also a parallel attempt to downplay the seriousness of what had happened at Chatham. In one sense, Charles II and his court carried on as though very little had happened; indeed, in the immediate aftermath of the attack, the king and his brother James, Duke of York, adopted a triumphalist tone which would normally be associated with the victors, not with those who had just suffered an astonishingly humiliating defeat. John Roettier's medal issued to mark the Peace of Breda featured Britannia ruling the waves, one of her very first appearances in this context, and demonstrated Charles II's imperial ambitions with the legend *Carolus Secundus Pacis et Imperii Restitutor Augustus*.[6] Perhaps most remarkably of all, in September 1667, just three months after the events at Chatham, the new second-in-line to the throne, the Duke of York's newborn son, was christened with the name of Edgar, the tenth-century Saxon king who had supposedly first asserted the King of England's dominion over the seas.[7] This mood of defiance (or denial) found other outlets, too. The Earl of Castlemaine produced a staggering piece of revisionism, downplaying the Dutch success ('it was a million to one that this succeed'd'), minimising British losses, and even claiming that the *Royal Charles* was destined to suffer such a humiliating fate because it was originally built by Oliver Cromwell![8] However, Castlemaine had precisely the amount of credibility one would expect to be accorded a man who was given his title only because his wife was sleeping with the king, as Pepys' diary entry about the moth indicates. Ultimately, the most brazen attempt to minimalise the impact of the Medway action came in the first English biography of Michiel de Ruyter, published in c. 1681 (several years before the first Dutch equivalent). Despite the damage he had caused, de Ruyter was greatly respected in the British Isles: Pepys was impressed by the discipline he inculcated in his men, and Charles II offered him a knighthood. The events at Chatham in 1667 were therefore somewhat inconvenient, not to mention painful, for British audiences, so the anonymous biographer simply omitted them entirely.[9]

By the nineteenth century, Chatham was no longer a defeat to be derided in verse, or ignored as though it had never happened. In an age when the Stuarts were denigrated by historians as absolutists and crypto-papists who had slowed the inevitable advance toward Victorian parliamentary democracy, the Dutch invasion was proof positive of the utter degeneracy of the Restoration court. Pepys' diary was first published in 1825, and his meticulous recording of every scare story and second-hand rumour that he heard during the attack, including the 'moth myth', provided the Victorians with an irresistible picture of a truly corrupt regime: after all, to generations brought up on the heroism of Nelson at Trafalgar, the notions of English pilots leading the Dutch up the Medway, and English seamen aboard the Dutch ships shouting 'We did heretofore fight for tickets: now we fight for dollars!', were about as shocking a contrast as could possibly be imagined.[10] The degeneracy of Charles II's court became a byword even in such unlikely quarters as Middlesbrough, where in 1879 an anonymous letter writer attempted to defend the holding of balls during a time of economic difficulty by denying that those who enjoyed such activities 'were as dead to the wants of those around them as the courtiers of the second Charles, who danced while the Dutch were in the Medway and the people starving...'[11]

All of this fed into the second new myth about Chatham that also developed during the nineteenth and twentieth centuries, when it became a byword in Parliament and the press for the most humiliating national defeat imaginable. Above all, 'the Dutch in the Medway' became shorthand for national unpreparedness against invasion and tended to appear in speeches and newspapers during periods of 'invasion scares' or arguments about national defence. Consequently, it became a rallying call for those who advocated a strengthening of the armed forces, or for expenditure on particular branches of those forces; it could equally well support an argument for stronger coastal fortifications, or for having a stronger 'fleet in being' at sea. In 1850, for example, a letter writer to the *London Evening Standard* attacked Lord John Russell's government for spending too little on defence, described the events of 1667, and asked of Russell's ministers, 'with the means of defending the country placed within their hands, if they neglect of using them till too late, will they appear less culpable than Charles the Second and his corrupted court in the eyes of posterity?'[12] In 1887, on the 220th anniversary of the Chatham attack, one columnist observed that there is no reason in the world why any power which happens now to be as relatively strong upon the sea as Holland was two centuries ago should not make a dash into the Thames. If we were to go to war with a great power which possessed any navy to speak of – and France, Germany and Russia all have fine fleets now – many days would not elapse before the enemy (knowing of course very well how matters stand) would make an attempt to get into the river.[13]

Similar sentiments can be found in many other newspaper leader columns and letters pages, as well as in the works of 'navalist' historians, such as Alfred Thayer Mahan and A. J. Tedder.[14]

The First World War contained a number of incidents that could be compared to the Chatham attack, notably 'dastardly' German raids on British soil. This was first evident in the early months of the war in response to the bombardment of the east coast ports of Scarborough, Whitby and Hartlepool by the battlecruisers of the High Seas Fleet. On 17 December 1914, for example, the *Manchester Evening News* named the 1667 Chatham attack as the nearest parallel in history to the German raids and reminded its readers of the havoc the Dutch had wreaked. However, not all of the coverage of the raids made the same, relatively measured, comparisons. Hysterical reporting of the German raids in the British and, especially, the American press drew forth a response from one of the most distinguished historians of the age, A. J. Pollard, Professor of History at University College London and later the founder of the Institute of Historical Research, who wrote a lengthy letter to *The Times*, published on 19 December 1914. Pollard was particularly exercised by American suggestions that the raids demonstrated Britain's command of the sea to be purely nominal and proceeded to list the many occasions since 1066 when the British coast was 'not merely bombarded but invaded'. Chatham featured on the list, but so too did fourteen other enemy attacks from 1338 to 1797. 'If the raid on the East Coast disproves our command of the sea,' Pollard observed, 'then we have never possessed it'. Unfortunately, the reasonable and entirely correct judgements of historians like Pollard carried little weight against the torrent of hysteria being peddled by the popular press. For example, the Dutch attack on Chatham was recalled later in the war, too, as a (perhaps unlikely) point of comparison for Zeppelin raids. In July 1917, the *Daily Mail* thundered after one such attack that 'since the

Dutch burned Chatham [sic] 250 years ago, making mock of the miserable system of passive defence which the feeble English government of that age had organised with Stewart slovenliness, there has not been a more discreditable event in our military history than Saturday's raid'.[15]

During the 1930s, the memory of Chatham was sometimes deployed to criticise the government's policy of appeasement. In 1935, for example, Churchill's political ally Lord Lloyd warned that 'the British naval situation has never been so serious since the rag and tatter days of the Stuarts, which brought the Dutch up the Medway'.[16] Even in the late twentieth century, after two World Wars had added several new contenders to lists of 'worst British military disasters', the events of 1667 were still occasionally recalled in exactly the same way: the Suez fiasco of 1956 was described by the Labour MP George Wigg as 'the biggest humiliation and national defeat since the Dutch sailed up the Medway 300 years ago'.[17] The last occasion when the Medway attack was mentioned in Parliament, at least in this particular context, seems to have been in June 1991, when Lord Colnbrook used it to warn against the dangers of disarming too quickly following the collapse of the Soviet Union: 'Time after time we do this, generation after generation. It always costs us dear in the end.'[18] In one sense, his words were distinctly ironic. In his previous incarnation as Humphrey Atkins, Lord Privy Seal, Colnbrook had resigned following the Argentinian invasion of the Falklands in April 1982, a disaster compared to the Medway attack by some at the time and one undoubtedly caused in part by the announcement of swingeing naval budget cuts, as in 1667, by the government of which Atkins was a part.

The Medway attack has featured only rarely in English-language fiction and other entertainment media. One notable exception, though, was the novel *The Dutch in the Medway* by the mediocre but popular hack writer Charles Macfarlane (1799-1858).[19] First published in 1845, when concerns about the new French naval base at Cherbourg were increasing, *The Dutch in the Medway* was republished in 1897, when 'navalist' agitation was at its zenith. The Medway attack features briefly in the BBC's lavish 2003 mini-series about Charles II, *The Power and the Passion*, although the event itself takes place entirely offscreen: the Earl of Clarendon (played, somewhat disconcertingly, by the same actor who portrayed the Emperor in *Star Wars*) reports that the Dutch have launched a surprise overnight attack on Chatham, destroying 'the entire fleet' [sic] and thus forcing Charles II to sue for an immediate, humiliating peace. For those who did not blink and miss the relevant couple of lines of dialogue, the myth of the humiliation of a degenerate regime would have been reinforced.

***

In the Netherlands, too, the Chatham attack had a somewhat ambiguous legacy. Naturally, it was at first treated as a great national victory. The *Royal Charles* was displayed as an exhibit at Hellevoitsluis, the dishonoured royal coat-of-arms still adorning her stern (until they were taken down in November 1670 following a protest by Charles II); tourists carried away as souvenirs pieces of the ship. Her lantern was taken to Amsterdam as a trophy.[20] But the huge ship was far too large to be of any use to the Dutch navy in wartime and was quietly broken up in 1673. The controversial sternpiece was retained, though, and eventually became one of the most prized exhibits in Amsterdam's Rijksmuseum, where it still hangs.[21] So infuriated was Charles by this treatment of the ship that he had renamed after himself and his martyred father that (according to one, admittedly uncorroborated source), he authorised a daring 'commando' raid on Hellevoitsluis to retrieve her, but seemingly changed his mind at the last minute and cancelled the operation.[22]

When the third Anglo-Dutch war broke out in 1672, King Charles II's formal reasons for declaring war, and the pamphlets that were rushed out to support it, were perfectly clear on the principal cause. Naturally, the secret Treaty of Dover of 1670, by which Charles agreed to join Louis XIV in a war of annihilation against the Dutch, with victory to be followed in short order by the re-Catholicising of England, was not mentioned at all. Instead, the principal charge laid against the Dutch was that they had deliberately denigrated Charles II and his kingdoms, thereby diminishing their reputation in the world. This denigration was particularly apparent in medals and paintings, and a number of these that represented the Chatham attack were said to have caused Charles special offence. One was Christopher Adolfszoon's medal, produced for the States of Holland and West Friesland, ostensibly to commemorate the Peace of Breda. While there has been some disagreement over the symbolism displayed on the medal, and over its ultimate historical importance, Charles II certainly took offence at the expression *'mala bestia',* which he took as a reference to himself, and lodged a protest with the Dutch. As a result of this, the dies of the medal were broken and the surviving copies melted down. But even if it really was innocuous, an entirely new 'spin-off myth' grew up around the Adolfszoon medal: during the 1680s, the Thai ambassador to the court of Versailles was 'shown one medal which, we were told, had caused a war throughout Europe some fourteen summers before'.[23]

The Dutch produced some great art to commemorate the Chatham attack, but in their own way, these both contributed substantially to the myth-making surrounding the event and caused further offence to King Charles II. Take, for instance, Ludolf Bakhuysen's painting of the *Royal Charles* being towed from the Medway, which now hangs in the National Maritime Museum, Greenwich. This work shows the Dutch tricolour flying at the ensign staff, as it may well have done after the ship was taken; but it also shows the English royal standard flying from the maintop. This is pure invention on Bakhuysen's part. For one thing, it is very unlikely that the *Royal Charles* would have had her topmasts aloft (ships laid up 'in ordinary', as she was, generally took down their topmasts and yards), but for another, and above all, the royal standard was only ever flown, then as now, when the monarch was present in person. By showing the ship with the standard flying, Bakhuysen was sending out a powerful symbolic message. The ship and the king after whom she was named are effectively one and the same; there could be no more potent allegory of Charles II's humiliation than showing the *Royal Charles* being towed back to Holland with the royal standard flying. Debatably, though, even more offence was caused to the king by Jan de Baen's great picture of the apotheosis of Cornelis de Witt, which was hanging in the town hall of Dordrecht by June 1670 at the latest (Fig. 3.2).[24] This showed a victorious Cornelis, wreathed like a conquering Roman general, presiding over a view of the destruction being wreaked by the Dutch fleet in the Medway. Worst of all for Charles, the foreground of the picture depicted Sheerness Fort occupied by Dutch troops, and with the Dutch flag flying over it – a clear proof of a successful Dutch invasion, and a deliberate attempt to impugn the territorial integrity and national sovereignty of Charles II's kingdoms.

Taken together, these works of art had a powerful effect. The offence felt by the king, and by those who agreed with the war policy, was summarised by one pamphleteer who complained of 'the provocations of the Dutch by their pictures, medals and monuments (all public, and either authorised by the states or commonly tolerated) were such as would have justified a more early war'.[25] The king's reputation, it was argued, had also been diminished by the behaviour of the Dutch in foreign ports, where they were said to have boasted of crushing the English during the previous war; during a visit to Genoa, Jan van Brakel, who had led the successful attack on the Medway chain, hoisted beneath his Dutch ensign the colours that he had captured during the battle – the traditional sign of surrender and humiliation.[26] William de Britaine made the point that the Dutch affronts diminished Charles II in the eyes of both his subjects and his equals:

> The reputation of a prince ought to be as sacred as his person... contumely to a private person is but a private injury; but to a king, it's an affront to a whole nation; for the honour of the king is wound up with the safety and reputation of the people. It's not enough for a prince to be great among his own subjects, but he must carry a *grandezza* amongst kings...[27]

This picture of Dutch arrogance and downright rudeness was widely accepted, or at least, so some contemporaries believed. As the Earl of Arlington put it just after war was declared, 'It cannot be denied but the world is now generally convinced that *the provocations his Majesty hath exposed in his declaration to have received from the Dutch* do sufficiently justify the war he is making upon them' *[my emphasis]*.[28] Indeed, the inhabitants of Dordrecht evidently accepted the notion that the painting of 'The Apotheosis of Cornelis De Witt', hanging in their town hall, was one of the causes of the apocalypse that threatened to befall their country: in July 1672 the mob attacked the building and literally tore the painting to pieces, the same fate that befell its subject a few weeks later.[29]

Great historical events, such as wars, should have great causes, at least as far as many historians are concerned. The notion that a war could be launched because a head of state objected to the content of a few works of art – moreover, ones that did not even directly represent his own person – is hardly comprehensible to modern sensibilities. But many wars have begun for even more trivial reasons and a strong case can certainly be made for saying that the Dutch representations of the Chatham attack in medals and paintings went a long way toward deciding King Charles II to embark upon the third Anglo-Dutch war. As mentioned previously, Charles had many other reasons for war with the Dutch, notably his secret treaty with Louis

XIV.[30] But the medals and the artistic representations of Chatham were not mere pretexts, as has often been said: they cut to the very heart of Charles' royal status and pretensions, creating a set of myths so damaging, so deeply offensive on both the personal and public levels, that they could only be expunged by a new war, one with an avowed aim of nothing less than the utter destruction of the Dutch state.

***

Until at least the tercentenary of his birth in 1907, Dutch commemoration of Michiel de Ruyter and his achievements was conventionally reverential.[31] However, the twentieth and twenty-first centuries brought a new ambivalence to views of the great admiral and thus of his greatest triumph. Between 1940 and 1945, for instance, the occupying Nazi forces sought to turn de Ruyter and his achievements into a leitmotif for the encouragement of Dutch collaboration. A propaganda poster of 1943 referenced his brilliant defensive campaign in 1673 against a larger Anglo-French fleet with the slogan '1673-1943 *Steeds dezelfde vijand!'* ('always the same enemy'). Meanwhile, the bombastic *de Ruyter Kantata*, originally written in 1893 as a piece for children's choirs, took on a new lease of life under the Nazi regime, with huge performances taking place in 1942 and 1944; the chorus was drawn from the *Nationale Jeugdstorm*, the Dutch equivalent of the Hitler Youth.[32]

By contrast, the three-hundredth anniversary of the Chatham attack was commemorated in a more amicable way in 1967 as was the four-hundredth of de Ruyter's birth in 2007; the former saw Dutch warships visit the then still operational Chatham dockyard and the frigate *Fret* recreated the breaking of the chain by passing through 'a curtain of coloured water put up by firefighting tugs'.[33]

The 2015 film *Michiel de Ruyter*, starring Frank Lammers as the admiral, proved to be a huge commercial success, becoming the highest grossing Dutch movie of all time and being released in the English-speaking world as *Admiral: Command and Conquer.* Chatham was presented as the hero's one great unambiguous triumph, roughly half way through the film, even if it included the unlikely spectacle of de Ruyter himself leading Dutch marines in a shore attack on the British dockyard; thereafter, the admiral's career becomes increasingly entwined with, and compromised by, the complex politics of the Dutch state. However, the film was not universally acclaimed in its home country. The world premiere, at the Scheepvaartmuseum in Amsterdam, was picketed by protestors objecting to de Ruyter's undoubted involvement in the African slave trade.[34] His career, and the Anglo-Dutch wars as a whole, now feature much less prominently in the Dutch school curriculum: the entire epoch takes up no more than one or two lessons taught to 13-14 year olds, although it can be revisited in the equivalent of the sixth form years. Thus Dutch schoolchildren no longer learn the myth of Chatham that was taught to previous generations, where it was 'used by eager teachers to illustrate to their pupils the greatness of the Dutch Golden Age, emphasising how the Republic was strong enough to take on much larger England'.[35] A direct descendant of Admiral de Ruyter, who gives lectures in schools, reports that until the film raised awareness somewhat, the response from his children to his joke opening question, 'what do you think of when I say "de Ruyter"?', was 'chocolate sprinkles', a type of spread for sandwiches. But the Medway attack remains mythic within the Dutch Navy, especially in the *Korps Mariniers*, which sports it on its colour as its first triumph.[36]

***

In both Britain and the Netherlands, then, the myths surrounding what happened in June 1667 are rather less potent than once they were. In an age of terrorism and cyber-warfare, British MPs concerned about defence cuts are probably now unlikely to cite Chatham as a worst-case scenario. However, the Dutch attack had an unexpected renaissance during the 'Brexit' referendum campaign in June 2016, coincidentally on almost the exact 349th anniversary of the *tocht naar Chatham*, when a surreal 'battle' took place on the Thames between a 'leave' flotilla under UKIP leader Nigel Farage and a 'remain' vessel commanded by Bob Geldof: several journalists and 'Tweeters' were unable to resist a comparison with the events of 1667.[37] Even so, the 350th anniversary received rather less media and popular attention than the other two great calamities of the age, the Plague and the Great Fire of London.[38] But Chatham is an interesting example of how nations create myths around both victories and defeats: the British sought to downplay or deride what had happened in the Medway, while Dutch triumphalism proved counter-productive, and could be said to have been partly instrumental in triggering a new war which almost wiped the republic off the map during the *rampjaar* of 1672, 'the year of disasters'.

The other great myth that the British created around Chatham, that it was one of the worst defeats in the country's history – a myth created principally to further specific political ends during the nineteenth and twentieth centuries - also has dubious foundations. Indeed, closer examination of the evidence suggests something quite different, and in this respect, at least, the much-mocked Earl of Castlemaine was perfectly correct. For one thing, the attack could have been far worse: the Dutch could have destroyed the royal dockyard at Chatham, or the important timber yards on the Medway. True, they burned three great ships and towed away a fourth, as well as destroying a number of lesser ships (principally Dutch prizes). But ten other warships, including six Second Rates, survived. The Dutch could have sacked Rochester, and they could have moved further up the Thames to attack commercial shipping, which was what Charles II and his ministers certainly expected them to do. As it was, the economic impact of the Dutch attack was negligible: one estimate put the direct loss at about £20,000, and even if one added the replacement cost of the lost warships, it probably totalled some £200,000.[39] Contrast the burning of about 150 Dutch merchant ships in the Vlie anchorage during the previous year, an event known to the British as 'Sir Robert Holmes, his bonfire' and to the Dutch as 'the English fury', and which the 'trip to Chatham' was intended, at least in part, to avenge. Whatever one calls it, the damage done by this attack to the Dutch economy was substantial. The losses sustained were estimated at about 12 million guilders, or just over £1 million; this at a time when Charles II's annual revenue was some £1.2 million.[40] Furthermore, the material losses the Royal Navy suffered during the Chatham attack were made good in astonishingly short order, although many of the new ships in question were already under construction at the time of the attack. Thanks to the Medway and other losses during the war, when peace was signed in July 1667 King Charles II possessed only one First Rate man-of-war (the *Sovereign,* better known under her original name as the *Sovereign of the Seas*, which was at Portsmouth during the Dutch attack), along with seven Seconds. When the next war began, only four and a half years later, he could send to sea no fewer than seven Firsts (another was on order) and nine Seconds.[41]

In reality, the principal damage done by the Chatham attack was to the reputation, both contemporary and for posterity, of King Charles II and his court. In this sense, for much of the nineteenth and twentieth century, few things damaged the Stuart monarchy more, and enabled the 'Whig' charges against Charles to hold sway for so long, than the famous story about the moth.[42] But Pepys had this anecdote second-hand: his source was Sir Hugh Cholmley, a disillusioned Yorkshire Cavalier who was personally hostile to the laxity of the King's court and who, as a member of Queen Catherine of Braganza's household, would certainly have hated Barbara Castlemaine. Cholmley stated that the incident occurred on 'the night the Dutch burned our ships': in fact, the ships were burned during the afternoon of 13 June, so presumably Cholmley was referring to the evening of the same day. But Pepys failed to check the story against an unimpeachable source – namely, his own diary entry for that date. Had he done so, he would have found a fairly detailed account of Charles II's movements that gives a rather different impression of the king's actions. Both Charles and James were at Barking Creek at four in the morning, giving orders for the sinking of ships there in order to block any Dutch attempt to sail up to London (which they clearly and rightly regarded as a more important priority than trying to rescue the already calamitous situation in the Medway). Later that day, Pepys recorded 'the King and Duke of York up and down all the day here and there; some time on Tower Hill, where the City militia was; where the King did make a speech to them that they should venture themselves no further than he would himself'.[43] Therefore, it is very difficult to see how Charles II can reasonably be convicted of neglect of his royal duty on 13 June 1667.[44]

Even if the 'moth myth' is true, it can be interpreted in an entirely different way. On the night in question, the Dutch attack was causing hysterical panic in London. Assuming that the women of his court were as terror-stricken as the general population, the king's attempt to distract them with some harmless diversion can be regarded as a piece of remarkably shrewd psychology. In any case, it is very difficult to see what else Charles II could realistically have done during the evening of 13 June, even if he had stopped chasing the moth; and the news of the burning of the three great ships did not reach London until late that night, as Pepys noted.[45] Consequently, the pursuit of the moth only assumed significance in the light of hindsight. Thus Cholmley, a man with an obvious agenda, was judging Charles unfairly, assuming that the king should have reacted differently to a situation he simply did not know about – and when the military response to that situation was, in any case, in the charge of the commanders of the ground, who simply would not have had the time to send to the king for orders. The way in which Pepys recorded what Cholmley said to him has given the impression to posterity that Charles II went in pursuit of the moth *in the knowledge that his ships were burning*, in the manner of an entomological Nero; but as Pepys' own evidence proves, that was simply untrue. Thus, when all is said and done, the way in which posterity (in Britain, at any rate) has judged the events at Chatham in 1667, and, to a degree, the reputation of King Charles II in respect of them, essentially comes down to a myth of a moth.

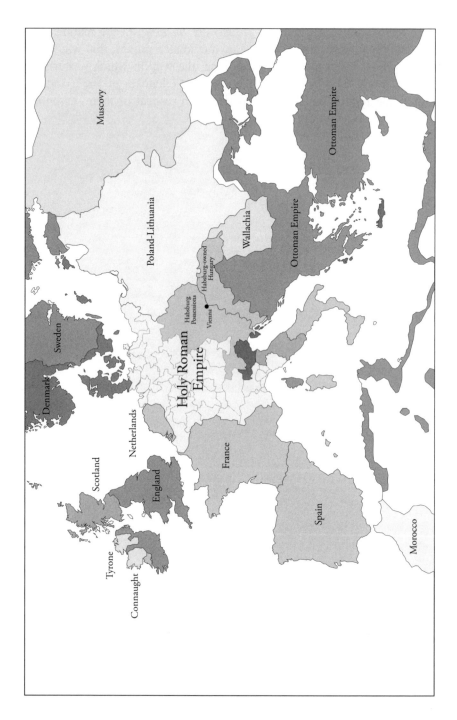

Muscovy

Ottoman Empire

Poland-Lithuania

Wallachia

Ottoman Empire

Habsburg-owned
Hungary

Sweden

Habsburg
Possessions

Vienna

Denmark

Holy Roman
Empire

Netherlands

Scotland

France

England

Spain

Tyrone

Morocco

Connaught

Chapter 4

Vienna 1683 and the Defence of Europe

Beatrice Heuser[1]

The Turks in Europe

Long before Mehmet II Fatih (the Conqueror) had fulfilled his forefathers'
dream – to take possession of the Golden Apple of Constantinople – the
Ottoman Turks had conquered what today is Greece, Bulgaria, and Thrace.
Adrianople – Edirne – had already been the capital of the Ottoman Empire
for almost a century before Constantinople fell in 1453, and the Bulgarian
cities which are now known as Plovdiv, Stara Zagora, Sofia, Ruse, Varna,
and Veliko Tarnovo, as well as Serbian Niš and Greek Thessaloniki had
already fallen to the Turks. But Mehmet's successors were still not content
with the vast empire he left them. They pushed on and on.

Even though he had slain Constantine XI, the last Eastern Roman
emperor to hold the City,[2] Mehmet, familiar with Western culture and
languages, wanted to see himself as legitimate successor to the Romans.
He and his successors knew that others also claimed the succession to
Rome: the Habsburg emperors of the Holy Roman Empire, ruling from
Vienna.

By the fifteenth century, most Ottoman Turks had turned from nomads
into farmers, but their urge to travel and conquer by the sword remained
a deeply ingrained cultural trait. From their Middle Eastern possessions,
they sought to encircle the Mediterranean. Riding south into Arabia they
began to conquer its southern shores, sweeping through Egypt and then
West along the Sea into the Maghreb. From Bulgaria and Greece, they
pushed further north and west into the Balkans, and north along the Black
Sea coast towards Crimea and modern Ukraine. Along with Bucharest,
Belgrade, and the coastal possessions of Genoa and Venice on the Aegean,
Vienna became a new target. Vienna, just as Constantinople before –
Kostantiniyye in Turkish – was now referred to by the Turks as the 'golden
apple' (*kızıl elma*),[3] ripe for the picking.

In 1529, Sultan Süleyman the Magnificent stood before the gates of Vienna. The siege did not last long: as winter set in early, the Ottoman forces withdrew after ravaging surrounding areas. But they held on to their many other conquests, consolidating their hold on the Balkans, the very name derived from a Turkish word for mountain. Still yearning for Vienna, they extended their conquests to Hungary, the South Slav lands, and the Greek islands.

Events leading up to the Turkish campaign of 1682/83

The scope and speed of Ottoman expansion had lost some of its momentum in the early seventeenth century, but had picked up again around 1660. It was mainly directed East, away from the Holy Roman Empire, after the Ottoman defeat at the Battle of Saint Gotthard in the Burgenland (today Szentgotthárd in Hungary) in 1664. Nevertheless, the Turks also still made further conquests in Europe, as far to the North as Nové Zámky (in today's Slovakia). While after Saint Gotthard, a twenty-year armistice was concluded, before this time was up, the two empires came to blows again over Hungary. A part of the Magyar-populated lands in the West was ruled by the Habsburgs; two principalities in the North and East were Turkish vassal states, while the southern parts were fully integrated into the Ottoman Empire as *vilayets*. A Protestant uprising in the Habsburg-controlled area under Imre (Emmeric) Thököly received Turkish support and he was recognised by the Sublime Porte as prince of Upper Hungary.[4]

Attempts in April and June 1682 by emissaries of the Emperor Leopold I to negotiate an extension of the armistice of 1664, due to expire in 1684, came to naught.[5] Instead of bringing news of peace, the emperor's emissaries had to report back preparations for war. A ritual gesture signalling an imminent expedition of some sort was made in Kostantiniyye in August 1682, when seven *tuğlar* – tall poles with horsetails at their top, the Turkish equivalent of banners – were erected at Topkapı Sarayı, the sultan's principal palace overlooking the Golden Horn, the Bosphorus and the Sea of Marmara. This was the first sign that Sultan Mehmet IV was planning a military campaign.[6] Soon thereafter, forces from Asia Minor (Anatolia) were concentrated at the Bosphorus and then, by the end of the year, moved into Europe to winter quarters in Edirne. On 2 January 1683 another *tuğ* was set up at Edirne, now definitely announcing war.[7] Rightly, the *Hofkriegsrat* or military council in Vienna began to worry about a possible invasion that year.[8]

On 31 March 1683, a force of 100,000 men moved out of Edirne, progressing via Niš to Belgrade, the 'White City'. Although Sultan Mehmet IV was only 40 years old, he decided to accompany his army only as far as Belgrade, where he handed over the command of his forces to his Albanian vizier, Kara Mustafa. He entrusted him also with the sacred green banner that is venerated even today as Prophet Mohammed's own in the Topkapı Sarayı. According to one tradition, Mehmet issued a formal declaration of war, addressed to the 'Caesar of Rome and the King of Poland' spelling out Mehmet's intention to track down both princes in Vienna where he intended to have them decapitated, without bothering to articulate any just cause on his side for this war.[9]

Poland was thus also seen as enemy by the sultan. The Ottoman and the Polish-Lithuanian empires had previously clashed over their conflicting interests in the northern Black Sea coast, which was held by the Turks. This moved the Polish King Jan III Sobieski to answer Leopold's plea for assistance when Vienna had received news of the incipient Ottoman campaign; on 31 March 1683 they concluded a pact of mutual defence against the Turks.[10] Leopold needed this support from a foreign power because, after a centuries of internal religious wars ending in 1648, the Protestant princes of the Empire were reluctant to pay the 'Turks' Penny', a tax levied for the defence of the Empire against Turkish onslaughts. In 1683, only Saxony, Bavaria, and Lorraine decided to send troops. Meanwhile Bourbon France, as usually pitted against the Habsburgs even if this meant supporting the Ottomans, stood by indifferently. In short, Christendom did not present a united front against the Turks.

The Siege and the Relief Battle

From Belgrade, the Ottoman Army or *ordu*, composed of units of several ethnicities including Tatars, Syrians, Albanians and Bosniaks, moved north into Hungarian territory. Charles V Duke of Lorraine, the brother-in-law of Emperor Leopold and commander-in-chief of his forces, unsuccessfully tried to distract it by besieging Nové Zámky. The Ottoman host, however, proceeded relentlessly, crossing the Rába, the border between Habsburg and Hungarian territory, on 1 July 1683. They sultan's soldiers or *askerler* were now in what it considered to be enemy territory and unleashed a great storm of destruction. Leaving behind lands ravaged by scorched earth tactics (which would later contribute to its own supply problems), they continued their march on Vienna. Unaware of the imminence of disaster, on

6 July, Emperor Leopold still went hunting. Only on 7 July did news reach him that the Ottoman host was now inexorably advancing on his capital. Panic ensued. The same night the emperor and his family decided to flee his capital, left under the command of Count Rüdiger von Starhemberg.

Meanwhile refugees from the surrounding countryside were pouring into the city. Some villages lying in the path of the Ottoman juggernaut had tried to defend themselves, mostly with catastrophic consequences. Many hamlets, small towns, monasteries and convents were destroyed by fire and their populations tortured, taken as slaves, raped and/or murdered; atrocities such as burning men alive, raping eight-, nine- and ten-year old children of both sexes and gang-raping girls and women were blamed mainly on the Tatars, who became known in Austria as 'runners and burners' (*Renner und Brenner*). The priest of Breitenbrunn wrote in his diary, 'My eyes no longer have tears to weep.'[11] Thus Nether Austria where the population had been decimated by the plague only four years earlier now lost another estimated 50,000 souls.[12] Peasants who themselves had taken up arms seeing the emperor's train pass by on its way to safety far from Vienna noted grimly that 'anybody might be an emperor in good times'.[13]

Having burnt, sacked, raped and plundered their way through the countryside to the south of Vienna, the sultan's *askerler* reached its suburbs on 13 July. On 14 July they began the siege which was to last until 12 September.

Like many cities, Vienna was founded at a strategic crossroads. It was built on a branch of the Danube, just to the south of the passage made by the river between the Wienerwald foothills of the Alps to the West and the mountain range which eventually runs into the Carpathians to the East. The city centre had been fortified after the previous Turkish siege of 1529. It was now surrounded by a glacis, ditches with scarps and counterscarps, bastions and small redoubts, all walls flattened *alla moderna*. Vienna lay far enough to the south of the foothills of the mountains for the Ottoman *ordu* to surround it on all sides except that of the Danube flood plains, by burning down the suburbs and surrounding villages. Turkish artillery proceeded to bomb the city from the positions around the fortifications which they had thus cleared of buildings. The sultan's engineers constructed trenches and mines outside the walls and bastions nearest to the main imperial palace, the Hofburg. By early September, the Viennese were starving and dysentery had spread due to overcrowding. Meanwhile the Ottoman engineers were close to bringing down the walls along the Hofburg; the Löbl Bastion was already crumbling above the tunnelling.

Eventually, on 11 September, Christian relief forces approached. Totalling somewhere around 70-75,000 men, these were composed of around 21,000 imperial soldier under the command of Charles Duke of Lorraine and a further 9,000 under Prince George Frederick of Waldeck, 11,000 Bavarians under the Bavarian Prince Elector Max Emmanuel, 10,000 Saxons under their King Johann Georg III, and 26,000 Poles and Lithuanians under King Jan Sobieski (Fig. 4.1). Smaller contingencies included Hanoverians, and Cossacks, the traditional enemies of the Tatars. They approached Vienna from the north-west, over the steep paths of the Wienerwald mountains, rather than straight from the north through the valley dug by the Danube, to catch the Ottomans by surprise.

Kara Mustafa may have had more than twice as many soldiers as the Christians, but accounts vary and seem to include units that had been left behind, or were merely counted as allies despite being far from Vienna (like Thököly's men). Moreover, the fighting strength of the Ottoman forces was reduced by self-inflicted shortages of food and fodder. They had with them many prisoners, captured Austrian peasants whom they had intended to sell as slaves. Not wanting to share their scarce food with them, they killed off many of them (especially the women – the Turkish camps were later described as littered with their bodies).[14]

On 12 September, fighting between the Christians and the Ottomans started at dawn with an attack by an Ottoman contingent under İbrahim Paşa, one of Kara Mustafa's subordinate generals. The relief forces had the advantage of coming from the higher ground of the mountain after which the battle would be named in German (Battle of Kahlenberg).[15] The Ottoman forces had well positioned guns, however, easier to aim upwards than downwards. Christian infantry and cavaly first clashed with the Muslim host in the Danube valley around Nussdorf on its western shore. From this point battle lines confronted each other diagonally in a line stretching from the Danube in the North-East down to the fields to the South-West of Vienna, always to the West of the city. The Imperial and the Saxon forces moved due south along the Danube. Jan Sobieski's Poles, shouting '*Jezus Maria ratuj*!' (Jesus and Mary save us), came down over the mountains to the West to clash with the Muslim host with their cries of '*Allah il Allah*'. The fighting continued until the late afternoon, when it became clear to Kara Mustafa that his forces had been defeated. Not wanting to let his animal menagerie fall into the hands of the *giaurs* (infidel), he had his pet ostrich decapitated, setting his parrot, cats, and rabbits free. The Polish king in turn did not order any serious pursuit of the Ottoman commander. He merely dispatched light cavalry to track him, presumably to remain informed of his whereabouts, lest he regroup his forces and return to the charge.[16]

Kara Mustafa retreated south, first, to the Rába river and Győr, and thence to Belgrade, where pitiless punishment awaited him for his failure. According to Ottoman practice, on the orders of the irate sultan, on Christmas Day 1683 Kara Mustafa was strangled by two executioners pulling ropes around his neck in opposite directions. This was recorded gleefully on a broadsheet illustration that soon made the rounds in the Habsburg lands.[17] His body was subsequently taken to Edirne for burial.[18]

Meanwhile the allies celebrated their victory, but not without some disagreement as to who could claim credit for the victory – Charles of Lorraine, celebrated by the imperial side; Jan Sobieski, celebrated by the Polish-Lithuanian commonwealth as the great defender of Christianity; or Starhemberg, who had organised the defence of Vienna itself throughout the siege (Fig. 4.2).

The Heroic Age and the Roll-Back of the Ottoman Empire

Nether Austria took years to recover from the devastation wrought by the Ottoman forces in this campaign. Many diaries and memoirs were published that recorded the cruelties of the sultan's forces and the suffering of the rural population, of some captives who later managed to escape, and of the Viennese. Local Austrian memories of the massacres, devastation, rapes and abductions continue to live on to our times, even if the occasional deserter from the Ottoman forces stayed behind and settled down.

For the Viennese elites who had largely fled the city, the stories of the massacres gradually receded, accompanied by the decline of the Ottoman threat. They gave way to light-hearted treatment of the subject of the Turk in European culture. Real or supposed Turkish motifs made their way into masques, fashion, architecture, and music, and the *tuğ*, in a variation equipped with bells, was adopted by Central European military bands as the *Schellenbaum*. Molière, writing well beyond the sultan's reach in Louis XIV's France, had in 1670 set the trend with a character disguising himself as an opulent Turkish ruler in his *Bourgeois Gentilhomme*. A century later, Mozart's *Abduction from the Seraglio* charmed Viennese audiences, and Turkish marches, less inspired by Turkish music than by the composers' vivid imaginations, abounded in the world of music. Turkish motifs were used cheerfully in art and architecture (Fig. 4.3).

VIENNA 1683 AND THE DEFENCE OF EUROPE

For the Austrian Habsburgs (and indeed for Europe)[19] 1683 was the turning point, the beginning of their 'Heroic Age' in which they undertook the liberation of swathe by swathe of south-eastern Europe from Turkish domination, appropriating it for themselves. Three years after the liberation of Vienna, following two sieges, Buda was snatched from the sultan's grip, then Belgrade in 1688. Charles of Lorraine thus managed to free Hungary (but bring it under the Habsburg yoke, as the Magyars would see it) and Transylvania was transformed from an Ottoman vassal state into one acknowledging Habsburg overlordship. Another series of campaigns under Prince Eugene of Savoy, the next-but one commander-in-chief of the Imperial forces who himself had taken a small part in the relief of Vienna in 1683, led to his spectacular victory over the Ottomans at Zenta in 1697 and the subsequent peace treaty of Karlowitz in 1699 which confirmed the territorial gains of the Habsburgs. The Turks temporarily reconquered Belgrade, but were pushed back again by Prince Eugene in the battles of Petrovaradin in 1716 and Belgrade in 1717. The latter was a great and decisive victory over the Ottomans which earned him the popular fame of a folksong composed at this very battle, and also confirmed the steady decline of the Ottoman Empire that would only end with the abolition of the Sultanate in 1922. In the intervening years, the Ottoman Empire lost one Balkan *vilayet* and client state after another, first to the Habsburgs, then to national independence movements that with the help of other great powers rose up against the Turks to establish their own states.

With the acquisition of Hungary and other lands that they wrested from the sultans, the centre of gravity of the Habsburg Empire shifted increasingly towards Europe's east and south-east. Especially after Napoleon forced Francis II to abdicate as Holy Roman Emperor in 1806 and to redefine himself as Austrian emperor Francis I, the need for a new identity and self-definition grew for Austria-Hungary. What united the peoples of the 'Danubian Monarchy' was their historic opposition against the Turks. The 'Heroic Age' of this opposition and the liberation of Christian lands from Muslim occupation were suitably celebrated with statues and paintings both in public places and private palaces.

When Austria was shorn of its Empire, and especially after its catastrophic merger with Austrian Adolf Hitler's *Third Reich*, Austria needed to re-invent its identity. Its new 'Sound of Music' image of peace-loving conservatives was first popularly presented in 1952 in a film financed by the Austrian government that was a plea to end its occupied status. The film was called *1 April 2000*. In the film, Austria's minister president asks for independence

51

(Austria was then still under allied occupation). For this cheeky request, as representative of Austria, he is put on trial by a world jury of 'Global Council'. In Austria's defence, the minister president evokes a number of episodes of Austria's history as evidence for its peaceful nature. A series of key events in Austria's history are passed review, in a narrative of Austrian history that in its deliberate selectivity would have delighted Ernest Renan.[20] The earliest explains the origins of the Austrian coat of arms, first acquired by the Duke of Austria who captured Acre from the Turks (!) during the crusades. Naturally, one of them was the siege and defence of Vienna 1683. At its end, the emperor Leopold is unable to pay his soldiers but discovers coffee (to the music of *The Abduction from the Seraglio*). Following his subsequent victories over the Ottoman host, Prince Eugene begs the emperor for permission to 'chase the Turk all the way back to Constantinople'. But the emperor is more interested in the arts and music and tells Eugene to let off because he needs the money to build new towns on the ruins of those devastated by the Turks. The film takes this as an excuse to lead on to Mozart and the matriarch Maria Theresia, and then delivering a potpourri of popular passages from operettas, while the members of the jury are placated by Austrian wine and exuberant Austrians in folk dress. At the end of the film, Austria is acquitted of the indictment of not being worthy of sovereignty and regains its independence. The defence against the Turks is thus shown as a key motif of Austrian national identity.[21]

While the Austrians celebrate their heroes Charles of Lorraine, Starhemberg, and later especially Prince Eugene of Savoy (all of whom appear in the film), after 1683 the Poles also cast themselves as saviours of Christianity, with their nation as 'bulwark of Christianity', their king as 'sword and shield of Europe'. Songs and poems as well as paintings and sculptures were dedicated to Jan Sobieski and his cult would live on in the following centuries, while from 1883 onwards, the date of the battle for the relief of Vienna was celebrated as a Polish 'national' [sic!] holiday.[22] But as we shall see, Austrians and Poles were not the only ones to claim the proud title of defenders of Christianity (or of Western civilisation).

Antemurale Christianitatis

It turns out that there is barely a nation in Europe which does not define itself in some sense as the defender of Christianity (or the civilised world) against pagan/heathen/infidel assaults in general or a particular attack by the forces of a pagan or Muslim or godless people. Already the Ancient

Greeks saw themselves as defenders of civilisation against barbarians (see chapters 3 and 4 of Volume 1). The (Christian) Roman Empire was attacked by Persians and Scythians, and beset by incursions from Vandals, Goths, and Huns, to which its western part finally fell. Until the barbarian invaders – especially Ostrogoths and Visigoths – converted to Christianity, the defence of the Roman Empire was tantamount to the defence of Christianity. The Christian Celts in Britain, left to fend for themselves against invading Angles and Saxons, bequeathed to posterity the legends in which Christianity was defended by King Arthur and his knights against these pagans (especially in the Battle of Baddon in 516).

No sooner had the Eastern Roman emperor Heraclius finally defeated the Persians in 627 at the Battle of Nineveh than Islam was born and with it the most fiercely and violently expansionist power the world had seen until then (the Mongols and Christians would later follow this bad example). The Spaniards, Portuguese and French as well as Italians see themselves as victims of (Arab) Islamic invasions and conquests which they finally reversed, in the case of Spain and Sicily only after centuries of Arab rule. The Battles of Tours in France (732) and of Las Navas de Tolosa in Spain (1212) are recognised beyond the confines of these nations as turning points in European history. For centuries, Spanish identity was defined by the *Reconquista* culminating in the Christian conquest of Granada in 1492 and eventually the expulsion of Jews and Moriscos from Spain.[23]

Meanwhile, the Germanic tribes of Central Europe had adopted Christianity and assumed a Roman inheritance, themselves driving back pagan Avars and Huns culminating in the Battle of the Catalaunian Fields of AD 451. The Eastern Roman Empire lost territory after territory to assaults by waves of Arabs and then Islamised Turkic peoples, until finally, only Constantinople itself with a small hinterland held out against the Islamic floods until it finally fell to Mehmet the Conqueror.

Set upon by the Turks, the peoples of the Holy Roman Empire as well as Bulgars, Hungarians, and South Slavs all saw themselves as last bastion of Christianity in a fight against the advancing Turks, whose victories and conquests were only checked by a Christian alliance in the naval battle of Lepanto in 1571. The princes of what today is Romania either came to an arrangement with the Sublime Porte or fortified their villages and churches against recurrent Ottoman assaults. While the Turkish siege of Vienna in 1529 had been unsuccessful, as noted above, the Ottoman rule over South-East Europe would last for centuries and was gradually rolled back only after the turning point of 1683. After the First World War, large-scale forced population resettlements moved Turks from Bulgaria and Greece to the modern Turkish state that emerged from the Ottoman Empire, and Greeks from Asia Minor to modern Greece. Yet even today, pockets of populations of Turkish extraction remain scattered across South-Eastern Europe, and some villages in Bulgaria still have all-Muslim populations where Turkish is the main language spoken.

In the context of Turkish expansion, the self-image as the *ante-murale* or *propugnaculum Christianitatis* (forward bastion or defences of Christianity) come into being in several East European countries. When Pope John Paul II visited the newly independent Croatia in 1994, its president Franjo Tudjman praised it as defender of Christendom. Indeed Pope Leo X had specifically called Croatia 'a firm shield and bulwark' of Christianity in 1519.[24] As a Pole, John Paul II would have known that his own country of origin claimed that title, as defenders against the pagan Turks, the Tatars, Ruthenians and Lithuanians, and against the Orthodox Russians as successors of the Mongol hordes of the great steppes, and later against Soviet Communism. Already King Casimir III the Great of Poland (1310-1370) begged for the support of the papacy for his defence of Polish lands against and eventually conquest of Ruthenia, making the case that the 'Kingdom of Poland, which is inhabited by the faithful, is located on the farthest borders of the Christians and because of this is more open to attack ... than other Catholic princes and others of the faithful.' Moreover, Casimir argued 'that the inhabitants of the kingdom are particularly faithful sons of the Church and dedicated to the defence, not only of the kingdom, but also of the faithful whether near or far ...' And thus 'the Kingdom of Poland, which is located near the perverse nations of unbelievers, is a defence of the faith which ought to be supported by subsidies.'[25] A century later, in 1444, the Italian humanist Francesco Filelfo wrote to King Władysław III Warneńczyk of Poland (who was also king of Hungary), 'All the nations and kings of Christendom pray God this day for your health and victory. ... Thou art a bulwark for the whole Christian Commonwealth.'[26] Appropriately, not having been able to secure victory, King Władysław would die that year in the battle of Varna against the Ottoman Turks, a Turkish triumph that cleared their way to the final siege and conquest of Constantinople. Nevertheless, the idea of Poland as defender of (especially Catholic) Christianity was reaffirmed by the crucial Polish contribution to the relief of Vienna in 1683. Later Poland cast itself as Catholic bastion against secular Communism when, in the 'miracle on the Vistula', Marshal Józef Piłsudski's armies beat back the Soviet forces in 1920, a victory which assured the newly found independence of Poland until the Second World War. It fitted this image that Poland, described by Poles as 'Christ Crucified' was several times the victim of collusion by non-Catholic powers to carve it up among them, most recently in 1939.[27]

Other European peoples also see themselves as chief defenders of Christianity in the fight against Muslim expansionism. The commemoration of the 600th anniversary of the Battle of Kosovo Polje of 1389 was marked by a large ceremony and mass rally in Gazimestan, Kosovo, where the Yugoslav President Slobodan Milošević addressed the crowds with the following words:

> Six centuries ago, Serbia heroically defended itself in the field of Kosovo, but it also defended Europe. Serbia was at that time the bastion that defended the European culture, religion, and European society in general. …
>
> The Kosovo heroism [of the Serbs] … has been feeding our pride and does not allow us to forget that at one time we were an army great, brave, and proud, one of the few that remained undefeated when losing [sic!].[28]

A decade later, however, Milošević had given up his appeal to pan-Yugoslav sentiments and Kosovo became the battleground for Serbs against the Kosovar Albanian independence movement: Kosovo, argued the Serbs, could not be given up as it was the holy ground on which Prince Lazar and his companions had shed their blood for Serbia.

Hungarians, too, claim to be the champions of Christianity. Mathias Corvinus (1443-1499), King of Hungary and Croatia, after defending his own lands launched a partially successful roll-back campaign against the Ottomans in Bosnia and for this was given the honorific title of '*Defensor Christianitatis*' by the Pope. In 1526, Hungarian troops fought and lost against Ottoman forces at Mohács which became a national site of memory and mourning. The Hungarian defence of Catholic Christendom was not constant, and occasions when the Magyars sought to come to an arrangement with the Turks triggered complaints. Previously called '*antemurale et Christianitatis clypeus*' (shield), Hungarians had now become traitors, wrote Johannes Cuspianus, the physician of Emperor Maximilian I.[29] Treason also in 1683, when the Thököly rebellion permitted the Ottomans to use Nether Hungary as a transit area to move against Vienna. These are episodes that do not fit the heroic image of the defenders of Christianity.

The modern Greeks are also prominent examples of this self-image. As nationalism became a political force in Europe, they were the first in the early nineteenth century to rise up against the Ottomans, not in support of the claim to a throne by one of their princes, but in quest of a nation-state. Classicists throughout Europe lent them their emotional and at times physical support, as in the case of the British poet Byron. Artists who saw in the Greek revival a rebirth also of Europe's classical traditions celebrated their uprising and brought their suffering to the civilised world's attention. Most famously perhaps this is captured by Eugène Delacroix in his painting of the Third Siege of Missolongi and subsequent slaughter of its inhabitants by the Turks in 1826.

The Swedes equally see themselves as last bastion of civilisation, in their case against Russian barbarism. The Battle of Poltava of 1709, in which a Swedes were defeated by the Russians, marks for them the decline of the enlightened Swedish Empire and the rise of Russia (and later the Soviet Union) (Fig. 4.4). The Russians in turn saw themselves as victims of the (Muslim) Mongols, who ruled them for centuries, and in the nineteenth and early twentieth centuries, as defenders of Christendom against the Turks (Fig. 4.5).

Indeed, for centuries the identity of Europe was inextricably linked with the defence of *Christendom* (*Christianitas,* the Christian world, the term more commonly used) against pagans and, more important still, Muslims. The (Muslim) Selçuk Turks conquered the Eastern littoral of the Mediterranean in the eleventh century and suppressed Christian worship to an extent which the Arabs had not. This was the trigger for the crusades, Pope Urban II's call to come to the defence of Christians in an area which had once been part of the Christian world, the Christian Roman Empire. Any pan-European, pan-Christian identity was nurtured by a common fear of Islamic expansion, the main Other against which European identity has crystallized. Even anti-Soviet propaganda in the Cold War occasionally likened the forces of the Red Army not only to Communist atheism but also to (Muslim) 'Mongol Hordes' (Fig. 4.6). It thus cast Communism not only in the role of atheist adversaries of Christendom, but also pointed to the Central Asian Republics (as the Nazis had done in their propaganda posters) to conjure up the image of an alien threat to the Christian Occident – around which European integration was constructed.

In short, Europe as a whole, and several particular nations, have constructed their collective identity around the Turkish component of a larger Islamic threat.

The Return of the 'Turkish Threat'?

In his excellent study of the siege of Vienna and its aftermath, historian Andrew Wheatcroft illustrated the fading trope of the Turkish threat in Austria in the later eighteenth, nineteenth and the early twentieth centuries. Relations between the Hofburg and the Sublime Porte improved as the Turks were pushed back, little by little, and one south-east European people after another fought to establish an independent nation-state (never entirely satisfactorily, in view of the colourful chequer-board mix of ethnicities). From about the mid-nineteenth century, both Vienna and Kostantiniyye began to see Russia as a common enemy, and began to see their enemy's enemy as their own potential ally. This culminated in their formal alliance in the First World War, which nevertheless resulted in the end of both empires.

Within the Habsburg Empire, Muslim subjects – mainly Slav-speaking Bosniaks – had been an exceptionally well integrated religious minority. Loyal to Vienna, they offset the (Orthodox) Serb influence in the region, and the influence of the increasingly feared (Orthodox) Russian Empire.[30] Yet in the 1990s they would become victims of Serb persecutions, culminating in the massacre of Srebrenica in 1995, explained by the Serb perpetrators as a revenge for Turkish deeds centuries earlier.[31] Further to the East, old traumas still caused new horrors centuries later with the massacres inflicted on each other by Christian and Muslim communities in Bulgaria in the 1870s, and in the Balkan Wars of the early twentieth century.

Then, in the second half of the twentieth century, there was a peaceful influx of Turkish guest workers into Austria, West Germany and other West European countries, at the invitation of governments wishing to offset domestic blue-collar labour shortages. This rekindled old memories of a Turkish threat, and 'a fresh Battle for Europe' was construed by opponents of this influx 'as a direct continuation of the old Battle for Europe'.[32] As Wheatcroft has rightly argued, this particular mass migration of Turks into Europe, welcomed by the Turkish Republic as an opportunity to export its surplus of unskilled manpower to Western Europe, of course has nothing to do with the expansionism of the Selçuk, the Mamluk, and then the Ottoman Turks, or indeed the Ottoman Empire. Old patterns of aggressive Turkish expansionism are recognisable, however, in Turkey's last conquest of 1974 when it invaded Cyprus and set up a Turkish state in the north. It was quickly followed by an exportation of surplus Turkish population from Anatolia to Cyprus which does link it to the general pattern of Turkish demographic explosion, abundance of unskilled workers and youth bulge.

That the guest worker project was poorly conceived, not thought through, and subsequently mishandled badly, so that instead of resulting in temporary labour movements it led to large families came to settle permanently, is undeniably the fault of the governments of the receiving countries. But what is equally undeniable is that this great movement of populations – which in absolute numbers of people with Turkish passports and their offspring now living in Europe now probably exceeds the numbers of Turks who at any one time lived in the European parts of the Ottoman Empire – has led to Turkish culture and Islam reaching areas neither had ever previously attained on a significant scale.

At times, poor education of the original migrants and resistance to integration on both sides of the population have resulted in a disappointment of many immigrants' social ambitions. Even some second-generation Turks in Europe – who still speak Turkish amongst themselves – are frustrated in their career hopes. When resurgence of Islamic religiosity, economic crisis and generally high unemployment are added to this mix, social tensions can arise. That in such a context, there should be the perception of a creeping Islamisation of Europe is hardly surprising, nor that it would be instrumentalised in local politics.[33]

Unease about Muslim immigration in all forms is especially strong in those areas of Europe that were once under Ottoman rule or vassals of Kostantiniyye and that are now among the poorest in Europe. Under Ottoman occupation all non-Muslims were treated as second class citizens paying punitive taxes; this added to their craving for independence from the Ottoman Empire. In view of the multi-ethnicity of Eastern Europe, however, none of them ever managed to achieve the ideal of pure monolingual 'nation-statehood'. Given European collective memories, enduring ethnic heterogeneity, and the self-identification of Europeans as against the Turks or Muslims, the siege of Vienna of 1683 remains emblematic of European identity to this day.

When in 2010, the German President, Christian Wulff, tried a different approach, asserting publicly that 'By now, Islam belongs to Germany', 63 per cent of Germans polled disagreed. Thomas Petersen, an analyst of German opinion polls of 2015, thinks that this is not the result of a rejection of individual Turks, or hostility to the Turks as a people. It does however, he argues, show a significant confusion between 'Turks' and non-Turkish Muslim refugees and migrants, just as speaking about 'Turkish forces' in the battle for Vienna 1683 was a shorthand for a multi-ethnic but mainly Muslim army under a Turkish sultan. In his article on German attitudes in 2015 towards the Syrian (!) immigration crisis, Petersen concludes:

> The centuries of controversy between Europe and the Orient have left a deep mark in the history of mentalities. ... [T]he notion that the world of Islam and the West are cultural antitheses is deeply anchored in the subconscious of the [German] population. Nothing united the Germans more in the times of their deepest confessional conflicts of the seventeenth century as the alarum cry, 'The Turks are standing before Vienna'.

As we have seen, this is not true: the siege of Vienna took place a generation after the end of religious conflicts in Central Europe, and the components of the Holy Roman Empire, not to mention other Western parts of Europe, demonstrated little solidarity when the city was to be defended. Nevertheless, this narrative fits the myth. Petersen rightly continues: '"The Turks", and with them the entire world of Islam, were always "the other"'.[34]

Chapter 5

Culloden 1746: Six Myths and their Politics

Beatrice Heuser[1]

The battle of Culloden, fought near Inverness on 16 April 1746, has ultimately become an example of a benign descent from politically loaded myths into historization. The National Trust of Scotland (NTS) built a new visitor centre there in 2007 which is an outstanding example of historically faithful documentation of the different positions taken in this last of the Jacobite Rebellions by eyewitnesses and actors. There were Scots on both sides, but also Irish mercenaries fighting for a higher religious cause and French money, Frenchmen, Englishmen, Flemings, and German Hanoverians. This new centre provides an excellent introduction into the complexity and international dimensions of this conflict. At the same time, it inspires nothing but sadness for suffering and the waste of life in this last battle on Scottish soil on the sodden moor of Culloden. The equally praiseworthy NTS publication on the battle and the battlefield of 2014, year of a referendum on Scottish independence (in which the unionists prevailed), warns its readers up front that where Culloden is concerned,

> propaganda merges with history and fact with fiction. Many believe that Culloden was a war [sic] between Scotland's Highlanders and Lowlanders; others hold that it was a battle between the Scots and the English. Some believe that the Jacobite army was little more than an unruly rabble, while others consider that Culloden was the direct cause of the Highland clearances. Yet none of these is true.[2]

These different beliefs stem from a number of myths that were forged around the Jacobite Rebellions in general and Culloden in particular: between 1746 and 2014, Culloden gave rise to several narratives constructed to serve diverse political and cultural agendas, but also fashions and interests of their times.

FAMOUS BATTLES

Culloden: Background and Battle

The Jacobite Rebellions, especially that of 1745 ('the '45') have been described too well and extensively elsewhere for it to be necessary here to provide more than the briefest of summaries.[3] Around 1700, probably no more than 30 per cent of the population of Scotland spoke Gaelic, and these lived mostly in the north and north-west of Scotland. Gaelic speakers were mainly Catholic, while Protestantism went along with the southern and north-eastern Scottish dialect of English (Lallans) which had been widely spoken for several centuries, especially in the cities. Scotland was thus both linguistically and religiously a heterogeneous society.[4] Moreover, Scots had a long tradition of bellicosity, well-practised in several centuries of border warfare with England, and especially during the Scottish Wars of Independence of 1291-1327. When independence came to an end through the union of the two crowns, Scots directed their martial spirit outwards: in the Thirty Years' War more than half the mercenaries raised on the British Isles were Scots,[5] even though there were three to four times as many Englishmen as Scots in the British isles.

The Glorious Revolution in 1688, and then the Hanoverian succession in 1714, brought war back to the British isles in the form of the Jacobite Revolts ('Jacobite' after the 'old' Stuart pretender, James Stuart, the younger Catholic brother of the last two Stuart queens: James VIII by Jacobite reckoning).[6] The uprising of 1715 was defeated, but thirty years later, James's son, Charles Edward Stuart, the 'Young Pretender' (Fig. 5.1), staged a further uprising by taking advantage of the Austrian War of Succession (which had global dimensions, as we shall see). At this point Hanoverian forces were tied down in the Low Countries: at Fontenoy in May 1745, the French had inflicted a humiliating defeat on Hanoverian forces under Prince William Augustus, Duke of Cumberland, younger son of Hanoverian King George II of Scotland and England (Fig. 5.2). The king himself resided at Hanover at the time, so the moment seemed auspicious for the Scottish Catholics to challenge the Hanoverian rule of Britain. Aged 25, Charles secured the support of King Louis XV of France, who gave him his Irish mercenaries (the Wild Geese), some French soldiers, and two ships (one would be lost *en route*).

Thus on 23 July 1745 the remaining ship, carrying the prince, reached the Hebrides island of Eriskay, and Charles proclaimed (presumably with an Italian accent as he had been born and raised in Rome): 'I am come home'. As 'the Young Chevalier' reached the mainland and made for Scotland's capital, Edinburgh, he gathered around him Catholic clan chiefs and other Stuart supporters on his way.

In the following months he had a series of military successes, especially at the Battle of Prestonpans near Edinburgh on 20 September 1745, where, impressively, Charles with fewer than 3000 infantry, but no heavy cavalry or artillery, defeated a Hanoverian army of c. 2400 men that included cavalry and six cannon. Thirteen-hundred of the Hanoverian troops were taken prisoner, 300 lost. This battle was a last triumph of the 'highland charge' tactics which relied on shock and awe rather than fire power.

From Edinburgh the Jacobites moved south. Carlisle, Lancaster, Preston, and Manchester fell to them; on 4 December the Jacobites entered Derby, deep in English territory, thus signalling that Charles was not content to claim merely the Scottish crown for his father. Charles expected reinforcements from France, and indeed in October some French ships defied the Royal Navy to bring supplies to Montrose and Stonehaven on the East Coast of Scotland. The British government was so worried that it decided to move Dutch soldiers to Britain, despite their engagement in the Netherlands with the French (this redeployment enabled France to capture Antwerp, Mons, Charleroi and Namur). By contrast, the Royal Navy managed to intercept en route, destroy, or turn back, a number of other French ships that set out to supply the Jacobites; also a small Armada promised by Bourbon Spain never arrived in Britain.[7]

The Jacobites were themselves torn over the question of whether to go further south to challenge London. In the end they followed Lord George Murray's counsel to retreat north of the Scottish border as wintry weather with frost and snow had hit the Midlands.[8] Meanwhile, new forces had arrived to strengthen the Hanoverian side and by 17 January 1746, the Jacobites encountered a second Hanoverian army near Falkirk, a key point on the narrow waist of Scotland and gateway to the north. Charles had around 8000 men, the largest force he could field during the entire campaign. The Hanoverians had around 8500, so the armies were equally matched. Again, impressively, the Jacobite army triumphed. Nevertheless, in the following two months, the Jacobites relinquished the isthmus and as spring approached – as usual, late in Scotland – they withdrew to Inverness, in the vain hope of receiving further French supplies by sea. They were disappointed as the French had decided to prioritise an expedition to America to free Louisbourg which had fallen to the British in 1745.

As none of the foreign relief forces got through and supplies ran low, the Jacobite forces dwindled. In mid-April 1746, Hanoverian troops under Cumberland were closing in on Inverness; they included three Scottish loyalist infantry regiments.

The battle that the Jacobites gave at the Pretender's insistence – after further disagreement between him and Lord George Murray about the time and place – was ultimately about the defence of Inverness, both as a stronghold and as gateway to help from France. When the forces met on 16 April, Charles had about 5000 men, mostly poor tenant-farmers from the Highlands following their chiefs, plus the Irish (Catholic) mercenaries. The men were exhausted from a forced march, as they had made an abortive attempt to encircle the Hanoverians in the night of 15 - 16 April. Moreover, they had not eaten for more than 24 hours when they went into battle in the early afternoon on a cold day on Drumrossie Moor near Culloden House, where the prince had enjoyed the warm hospitality of local supporters. The battle began under incessant rain and sleet, when the Jacobites fired twelve cannon, aiming badly, causing little damage. They fired their muskets, mostly once only, as further supplies of bullets were still with their baggage train in Inverness. Abandoning their muskets, the Jacobites then tried to charge the redcoats in their traditional way; given the uneven, slippery, boggy ground, there must have been many sprained ankles and falls, and the charge can hardly have unfolded as intended. Cumberland had 9000 men, all well fed, well-dressed and well-seasoned soldiers. His artillery fired volley upon volley into the advancing Jacobites, mowing them down in swathes. Captain Thomas Davis, an officer in Cumberland's forces, recorded:

> The action with cannonading and all did not last above half an hour in which about 1500 of the rebels were killed and 700 taken prisoners … It is very certain that the proportion of their officers killed is great.[9]

As another officer on the Hanoverian side commented:

> [T]he rebels were … put to flight, and when we marched on to pursue them I never saw such dreadful slaughter we had made lying as thick as if they grounded their arms and our men gave no quarter to them; I reckon two thousand of them killed in the field besides full a thousand killed in the pursuit by the horse and dragoons with a great many of their chiefs.[10]

By contrast, the Hanoverians only lost 50 dead and 259 wounded.[11]

Cumberland had a reputation to restore after his defeat at Fontenoy. Just before the battle of Culloden, he had published ostensible evidence that the

Jacobites had been given orders not to make any prisoners, i.e. to kill all soldiers and not to accept surrenders. He took this as excuse to apply exactly that practice himself. The retreating soldiers were slaughtered, and in the bloody frenzy, the Hanoverian troops also killed civilians they met on the road to Inverness.[12] Here, too, figures vary; about another 3500 Jacobites or Jacobite supporters in the area were taken prisoner, of whom 120 were executed, almost 1000 deported to the colonies, over 200 otherwise exiled. Around 1300 were freed after initial arrest.

Hanoverian punishment of the rebels did not stop there. In 1746, a Disabling Act was passed: highlanders were henceforth forbidden to wear arms, play bagpipes, wear highland dress (kilts and tartan); offenders would be imprisoned or deported to the colonies. The cultural discrimination this implied became highly mythogenic. Nevertheless, as Jeremy Black has rightly noted, the punishment meted out at the rebels was far from unusual at the time[13] – since Antiquity, rebels were treated in such fashion, quite unlike adversaries seen as legitimate, who would be allowed to leave the field of battle carrying their arms and with colours flying.

'The Butcher Cumberland' could now ride into London triumphant, and was celebrated accordingly: Handel composed the famous 'Conquering Hero' aria in *Judas Maccabaeus* on his return. Bonnie Prince Charlie himself got away, however. As Captain Davis noted, 'The Pretender is gone to the hills, with some of the rebels. This is very certain that of the 9000 rebels there is not 1000 of them left together, parties are out after him…'. Supposedly at one point in his long Odyssey of the following months, Charles, dressed in women's clothes, was helped to escape Hanoverian controls by the brave Flora Macdonald. In September 1746 he set sail, first for France, and ultimately for Rome where he died an unromantic old man.

Myth 1. The original Hanoverian anti-Catholic take on the rebellion

In early eighteenth century Europe, nationalism was still confined to a few countries and there, rooted in particular rivalries (especially the Anglo-French and the Anglo-Scottish). By contrast to Central Europe, religions strife had not disappeared from the British Isles as is so often claimed for post-1648 Europe in general. The Glorious Revolution with the Catholic-Protestant contest at its core was living memory, and the Protestant Hanoverians had only ruled for three decades. Old fears of Popish plots and Bourbon French aspirations to universal monarchy were still alive. The novelist Henry Fielding issued a call to arms in a pamphlet published on

3 October 1745, after the Jacobite victory at Prestonpans, when rumours predicted their descent into England. Fielding denounced Prince Charles as an invader, his Scottish Highlander and Irish supporters as 'Savages, who, as they inhabit as barren a Country, have the barbarous Manners of *Huns* and *Vandals*; and like them, would by their Swords cut their Way into the Wealth of richer Climates.' A few days later, in another pamphlet, he described them, accompanied by their Catholic priests, as 'liker to a Legion of Devils than of Men', for Catholicism was to him a 'dreadful Religion indeed'.[14]

Just after Christmas 1745 – the rebels had already withdrawn from England to Scotland – the Rev. Gibbon Jones, Rector of Sudburgh and Oreford in Suffolk, preached an emblematic sermon, warning Protestants that the Jacobites aimed to bring back that Catholicism,

> *the Abhorrence of which every good Man should carry with him in his Breast in these Days of Rebellion, and Disturbance; a Rebellion calculated to introduce Popery, and Arbitrary Power; to make us the Dupes of Rome, and the Vassals of France. To avoid therefore the Imposition of such a Religion, it behoves very wise Man to exert himself in the Cause of true Holiness, and native Liberty; ...*

He then went on to praise the United Kingdom in which 'Prince and People are so uniformly blended; where the Prince murmurs not at the Liberty of the Subject'. He extolled 'the Happiness of a limited Monarchy'.

> *But let us suppose, that the young Italian Desperado, with his Levee of Scotch Prostitutes and Bravos, should succeed, what must be the Consequence of such a Revolution? Must not Anarchy usurp the Seat of Royalty? Must not wild Confusion be substituted in the Place of Order? And must not arbitrary despotick Power be introduced in the Room of limited Government?*[15]

For contemporaries, the '45 thus formed a clear part of the older religious struggles that had marked British politics and society since Henry VIII's break with Rome and of the political struggles between monarchs and parliament which had culminated in the War of the Three Kingdoms. Apart from that, the '45 was a dynastic quarrel akin to the Hundred Years' War or the Wars of the Roses, a war over who should be the legitimate successor to the last Stuart monarchs. It was not or at least not primarily perceived by contemporaries as a *national* struggle. But the dynastic and the religious motivations, clearly the main driving factors of the Jacobite insurgencies themselves, were all but squeezed out of collective memory by later takes on this story.

Myth 2. The Effects: Ethnocide or integration of Northern Britain?

The slaughter of the Jacobites at Culloden and of soldiers and putative supporters, and the deportation of survivors to the colonies would resonate for centuries. Yet after these initial excesses, after the Disabling Act and the undeniable efforts to change some aspects of Scottish Highland culture (the populations of Glasgow and Edinburgh had long stopped wearing kilts), the Hanoverians found a creative way to deal with the martial Scots: they recruited them into their armies in special units were they were allowed to wear their kilts and play their bagpipes.[16] The creation of the Black Watch regiment, made up of Highlanders, predated the '45: it had been founded in 1739, and survived the '45. Then in 1757 the Frasers Highlanders Regiment was founded, under Simon Fraser who had actually fought on the Jacobite side at Culloden: his father had been executed for his Jacobite affiliation. Jacobite rebels, especially 'Highlanders', were thus converted into useful soldiers for the Hanoverian Empire's wars.[17] General Wolfe, Hero of Quebec 1759, who had also fought at Culloden, but on the Hanoverian side, wrote about his Highlanders:

> I should imagine that two or three independent Highland companies might be of use; they are hardy, intrepid, accustom'd to a rough country, and no great mischief if they fall. How can you better employ a secret enemy than by making his end conducive to the common good?[18]

The Disabling Act was revoked in 1782, and henceforth Scottish soldiers fought wherever the Union Jack led them. As Linda Colley has shown, it was above all the Scottish element in the armed forces which made these British and helped crucially to forge a British national identity in the Napoleonic Wars.[19]

There were few intellectuals in Scotland at this stage who would have defended the Stuart cause – indeed, they saw the integration into Britain as 'Northern Britain' as progressive and desirable.[20] The Hanoverian rulers' social engineering of Scotland was hugely aided by the Highland Clearances and the pull to the burgeoning industrial centres of the south which transformed Scotland by relocating its population: away from the less fertile northwest, towards the cities, or to the colonies. Sheep farming on a much larger scale became more profitable with the introduction of sturdier, 'winter-proof' black-faced and Cheviot sheep. The advent of the Industrial Revolution and the woollen mills made possible the production of woollen cloth on an industrial scale , and also large-scale exports. These were reasons enough for land owners to expel tenants and turn farming land into grazing land. As noted at the beginning, these Highland Clearances are often described as consequences of the aftermath of Culloden[21] – even though there really is little if any link between the two. These measures on the part of individual Scottish landlords which followed in the decades *after* the punitive measures of the Hanoverians took on a momentum of their own and a causality quite separate from the last Catholic uprising.[22]

While the Highland Clearances were seen by members of the Scottish élite a sensible step away from the poverty of the small subsistence farming pattern of large parts of Scotland, the tenant-farmers who were thus pushed off the land saw this as even worse than their struggle for survival had been hitherto. They described the following century as the time when 'sheep ate men'. In their collective memory – and in that of Scottish emigrants who would settle in the colonies, and in that of their descendants – the Disabling Act and the Highland Clearances would become conflated, and would be interpreted as ethnocide, i.e. the deliberate destruction of a culture and a way of life. This is the second narrative of the '45; it would live on to our times.

Myth 3. The Romantic Myth

The third is the Romantic myth. Already during the '45 itself, several leading Hanoverians, including Cumberland himself, curiously called it a 'romantic expedition'.[23] This perception of the campaign was seized upon by poets and authors who developed some sort of detached nostalgia for the Scotland that was lost forever. European elites of the late eighteenth century, among them the Scots, often embraced such a form of historical nostalgia to build up their own self-esteem as that of a *Kulturnation* to rival the predominant French (and to some extent English) culture in Europe, and the crushing heritage of Antiquity and of the Italian Renaissance. In the mid-eighteenth century, secret societies sprang up, which at their gatherings would toast 'the King across the

Water' from glasses engraved with Jacobite motifs (of which a fair collection is on display at the NTS Visitor Centre and across Scottish stately homes). Against this background, *the* Scottish romantic poet par excellence, Robert Burns (1759-96) wrote about 40 years after the battle of Culloden that it meant a

> Fareweel to a' ou Scottish fame,
> Fareweel our ancient glory!
> Fareweel ev'n to our Scottish name
> sae famed in martial glory![24]

Wrongly so, as we have seen, as thanks to the British colonial empire Scottish martial glory was about to become known globally.

But the real impact of the romantisation of 'the '45' came from an early battlefield tourist, Sir Walter Scott. (We need not delve here into 'the invention of the Highland cult (or the kilt) by Sir Walter Scott, the invention of Sir Walter Scott by George IV', as *Punch* put it,[25] or the great Hanoverian-Highland reconciliation in 1822 supposedly engineered by Scott.) Scott visited Prestonpans, site of Charles' Stuart's astonishing victory, and then wrote the novel *Waverley, or 'tis sixty years since* (1814). In a 'Postscript which should have been a preface', he commented:

> There is no European nation which, within the course of half a century, or little more, has undergone so complete a change as this kingdom of Scotland. The effects of the insurrection of 1745 – the destruction of the patriarchal power of the Highland chiefs, the abolition of the heritable jurisdictions of the Lowland nobility and barons, the total eradication of the Jacobite party, which, averse to intermingle with the English, or adopt their customs, long continued to pride themselves upon maintaining ancient Scottish manners and customs – commenced this innovation. The gradual influx of wealth, and extension of commerce, have since united to render the present people of Scotland a class of beings as different from their grandfathers as the existing English are from those of Queen Elizabeth's time.

Yet it was with a nostalgia that Scott noted the passing of the '"folks of the old leaven," who still cherished a lingering, though hopeless, attachment to the house of Stuart.' Scott saw them as having been particularly loyal, with a special sense of faith, hospitality, worth, and honour.[26]

The first of Scott's *Waverley* novels deals directly with 'the '45'. Its narrative boils down to one in which our hero, having taken part in Bonnie Prince Charlie's uprising, has to choose between the charms of the Catholic, Jacobite heroine Flora MacIver and the Protestant Rose Bradwardine, and finds that the family of the latter will help him to escape persecution for his Jacobite leanings; he opts for Rose and his future in a happy Hanoverian state, leaving the Jacobite cause behind him.

After the tremendous success of the *Waverley* novels – illustrated not least by the fact that the main railway station of Scotland's capital was named after them – Scott returned to this theme in a later novel, *Redgauntlet,* the plot of which turns on a fictional third Jacobite rising in 1765, which is nipped in the bud, with all the romance and heroism characteristic of Scott's books.[27]

Victorian painters also embraced the romantic myth of the '45 and the passing of the Highland tradition. Queen Victoria's court painter and sculptor Edwin Henry Landseer (1802-1873) invented the cult of the stag that still adorns cheap wall hangings from Istanbul to Hong Kong. Upmarket hotels feature prints of his paintings such as one of the Highland chiefs returning from the hunt, turned into a popular print by T.A. Prior. On the socially conscious side we find Sir John Everett Millais' *The Order of Release 1746,* painted a century after Culloden: a young woman carrying a child hands over the said order of release to a guard to free a kilted Jacobite, one assumes, who is clearly ashamed – the spectator is left wondering whether this is because of what the woman had to do to obtain his order of release. (Sabine Volk-Birke speculates that this would have involved self-abasement; the sketch for the painting depicted a purse rather than the letter, and bore as title *the Ransom*). The painting was first exhibited at the Royal Academy in 1853 and was so popular that a guard had to be detailed to deal with the crowds.[28] A more straightforwardly saccharine rendering of the theme – now available as mobile phone cover – is William Ewart Lockhart's 1899 painting of young lovers: the girl attaches a white rose to the beret of her kilted young man, the Jacobites' sign of recognition.[29]

Besides novels and paintings, many poems, but also many songs were dedicated to the exiled prince. A traditional song the author of which is unknown is probably among the earliest: here a little bird sings of its woe for the persecuted prince, a refugee in tempest-swept 'hills and valleys'

'Wae's me for Prince Chairlie'. Perhaps most famously, Sir Henry Boulton (1859-1935) composed the Skye Boat Song at the end of the nineteenth century, when Scottish nostalgia was in full swing. Curiously, the image of the bonnie prince is that of a weak boy in need of comforting and protection: the boat carries 'the lad who's born to be king/over the sea to Skye'. The song addresses the fugitive prince:

> 2
> Though the waves leap, soft shall ye sleep,
> Ocean's a royal bed;
> Rocked in the deep, Flora will keep
> Watch by your royal head.

The horrors which the battle held for the others is depicted in stark contrast with this nursery scene:

> 3
> Many's the lad fought on that day,
> Well the claymore could wield;
> When the nicht came silently lay
> Dead on Culloden's field.

> 4
> Burned are our homes, exile and death
> Scatter the loyal men...

Indeed, most of Scotland's popular and world-famous songs seems to revolve around the Young Pretender. In one he is either named directly or alluded to, most weirdly, perhaps, as 'my bonnie moorhen'.[30] Elsewhere he is named openly, 'Charlie is my darlin, my darlin, my darlin,/ Charlie is my darlin, the young chevalier'. Many 'would fecht for their Charlie' and 'die for their Charlie' ('I hae but son'), and several have the motive of sailing 'O'er the Water tae Charlie', including the famous 'Come o'er the stream Charlie, dear Charlie, brave Charlie'.[31] Even along the bonnie, bonnie banks of Loch Lomond, where we find a verse dedicated to 'braw Charlie Stewart, dear true, true heart' who 'Like the weeping birk on the wild hillside' looked so 'gracefu' ... in dejection'.[32]

The fate of individual soldiers was also commemorated: 'The Highlander's Lament' is the song of the exiled clansman: 'My country is ravaged, my kinsmen are slain,/ my Prince is in exile and treated with scorn,/ My chief is no more, he hath suffered in vain...'.[33] The widows, too, are remembered, as in 'Lady Keith's Lament', and 'The Highland Widow's Lament' for a husband who was 'the bravest man' and was 'mine'

> Till Charlie he came oer at last,
> Sae far, tae set us free,
> My Donald's arm it wanted was
> For Scotland and for me. ...
> My Donald and his country fell
> Upon Culloden field.[34]

Curiously, along with a series of other songs and poems, the Skye Boat song ends with the expression of the hope that the prince will return:

> Yet ere the sword cool in the sheath
> Charlie will come again.

We see here and in other songs parallels to King Arthur, the Once and Future King, and Emperor Frederick I Barbarossa in the *Kyffhäuser*, as the ideal monarchs who will return from death, in analogy to Christ, with the repeated refrain, 'Will ye no come back again?'[35] (More Scottish songs commemorating the Jacobite rebellions can be found in the 1959 TV production *A Song for Prince Charlie*, 'A story of the Stuart rising of 1745, told in song against a background of the enduring Scottish landscape", sponsored by the Drambui liqueur company.[36])

Returning to the bookshelves, Sir Walter Scott's blockbusters set the pattern for a series of novels published throughout the following two centuries, extolling the special virtues, the modesty and yet sincere nobility of the Jacobite clans and especially of their heroic leaders. Take, for example, Robert Louis Stevenson's *Kidnapped*, first published in 1886, an adventure novel aimed at an adolescent readership that revolves around events in the aftermath of the '45. The young hero on his flight from his evil brother meets a likeable former Jacobite, forced to flee to France; he and the Jacobites generally are here presented as courageous and gallant. A generation later, John Buchan made his contribution to the genre. In his *Midwinter*, a Scottish Jacobite incongruously spends the winter of 1745/1746 in the Cotswolds, trying to foil a treacherous plot to betray a Jacobite network, so as to rescue the lady of his heart, an English Jacobite enthusiast, while coming repeatedly across Dr Samuel Johnson. The hero is of noble yet impecunious origins, but gallant through and through.[37] D.K. Brooster's *Jacobite Trilogy*, the first volume of which was published in 1925, and which inspired its adolescent readers well until the end of the century, was written in much the same spirit: a young Englishman who is sent up north to pacify Scotland, is captured by Jacobites in a skirmish, and discovers that a their leader is a true gentleman, nurses his wounds, treats him with great respect, and although living on a remove Highland farm, has learned books in French and Latin on his shelves.

Other adventure stories would merely echo the Jacobite theme and ethos, thus for example Bram Stoker's *Lady of the Shroud,* published in 1909. The hero of the story, an orphan [living in the present] of good Scottish stock by the name of Rupert Sent Leger, whose family have fallen upon hardship on account of a love-match, suddenly receives the generous support of a distant relative, to which the young hero replies: 'By Jove, sir, this is history repeating itself.' An ancestor of his benefactor had 'laid his sword before Prince Charlie. ... Don't imagine, sir,' he modestly adds, 'that I am thinking myself a Charles Edward.' But, he concludes, 'The whole thing ... seemed to take me back to the days of the Pretender.'[38] Towards the lower end of the quality spectrum, this genre merged with that of 'Kailyard' literature, indulging in fantasies of 'merrie auld Scotland'.[39]

Then came the cinema. The first (eponymous) film about *Bonnie Prince Charlie*, a silent movie, was released in 1923 and unsurprisingly gives a similarly romantic picture of events,[40] as does its re-make of 1948, starring David Niven, directed by Alexander Korda. Niven's stellar acting and impeccable English diction (!) contrasts here with the harsh Germanic rasp of the voices of King George II and Cumberland. Niven of course does not have Charles' baby-face, but the visual images of lochs and glens framed by thistles and sword tick all the boxes of Scottish kitsch.[41] Documentaries and other films followed.[42] The Scottish historian Peter Womack commented insightfully,

We know that the Highlands of Scotland are romantic. Bens and glens, the lone shieling in the misty island, purple heather, kilted clansmen, battles long ago, an ancient and beautiful language, claymores and bagpipes and Bonny Prince Charlie – we know all that, and we also know that it's not real. Not that it's a pure fabrication: on the contrary, all the things on that rough-and-ready list actually exist or existed. But the romance is not simply the aggregate of the things, it is a message which the things carry.[43]

Bottom line, far from marking the end of Scottish culture as Robbie Burns feared, the standard clichés of Scottish culture as we know them today owe a very great deal to Culloden, and the wrong but romatic Jacobites.

Marketing the Myth

With Culloden, the Scottish Highlands became a symbol for something eminently exportable, just as the Scots themselves had been exported, deported or had of their own volition emigrated to the colonies. Scotland became a fashionable destination for holidays when Queen Victoria discovered it for herself and her family, and historical mass tourism was invented in the nineteenth century, after it had been confined to elites and to the Grand Tour of France and Italy and a few other bits of the Continent in the seventeenth and eighteenth. There was cultural tourism and battlefield tourism: the end of the nineteenth century was the golden age of battle monuments.

The National Trust for England, Wales and Ireland was founded in 1895; the National Trust for Scotland (NTS) followed suit in 1930 and immediately turned the battle sites of Bannockburn, Glencoe and Culloden into sites of memory.[44] Interestingly, even then, Scottish Heritage USA contributed sizeable funds to the purchase of the land.

It is the quest for heritage and roots in North America and Australia which resulted in massive tourist flows to Scotland, especially since the 1970s. In 2012, the United Kingdom, according to the UK Tourism Alliance, was the 'sixth largest international tourism destination ranked by visitor numbers', following France, USA, China, Spain and Italy, and the 'the seventh largest international tourism destination ranked by visitor expenditure', following the same countries, this time headed by the US, plus Germany.[45] In 2011, of the 2.345 million visitors to Scotland, 566,000 came from the USA, Canada, and Ireland.[46] In search of roots, many of these like to see themselves as descendants of romantic clans, and travel back laden with placemats, woollens, badges and key-rings with tartan patterns and clan name inscriptions. These they can show off in the annual gatherings of their clans in Denver, Colorado or Kansas City. They give the feeling of belonging – if not to an elite, then to a big family, as the (for our purposes randomly chosen) website for Americans with the surname 'MacDonald' suggests, with its curiously contradictory branding, 'The world-wide web home [!] of Clan Donald, USA'.[47] In 2004, New York invented the tradition of a 'Tartan Day' (apparently with support from the Scottish Minister for Finance, to 'calm fears in the US about the outbreak of foot-and-mouth disease in the United Kingdom').[48]

Riding on this trend, Scottish woollen mills and whisky breweries have long added touristy shops to their factory sites, where anything Scottish is sold from kilts, plaids and knitted jumpers to whisky, quaichs, miniature dirks and brooches with Celtic motifs made of sterling silver, Caithness glass, sporrans, and clan symbols. Walker's shortbread biscuit tins over the years were quite tastefully designed around several late Victorian paintings of Bonnie Prince Charlie (Fig. 5.3). Likewise, Scottish castles, whether privately owned like Lord George Murray's Blair Castle, or owned by the NTS, are key to marketing Scottish tourism. The website of Blair Castle thus woos visitors with the words:

> The historic story of Blair Castle and the Dukes of Atholl will take you from Mary Queen of Scots to the English Civil War, from Lord George Murray and the Jacobite cause to the disaster [sic!] of Culloden, and from the Isle of Man to Queen Victoria's love affair with the Scottish Highlands and her presentation of Colours to the Atholl Highlanders.[49]

In all this, and especially in the 'biscuit-tin kitsch' (Matthew Dziennik), Culloden and Bonnie Prince Charlie are clearly major selling points.[50] Even today, Scots in Scotland but more still their foreign descendants might melancholically down their whisky with Jacobite toasts, thereby supporting the Scottish liquor industry.

Myth 4. The Nationalist Myth

But Culloden is not just an international myth connecting Scotland with the Celtic, i.e. non-English parts of the Anglosphere. Culloden in its Romantic rendering became a central building bloc of Scottish identity. And as such, or in reaction to a general feeling of being marginalised within the United Kingdom and distinct in political views and socio-economic needs, Scottish nationalism (or one should better say patriotism, see below) has grown substantially in the early 2000s, as the rise of the Scottish National Party demonstrates. (see Tables 5.1 and 5.2 below)

Table 5.1: UK General Election Results for Scotland (* = Scottish Unitary or Parliamentary Elections)[51]

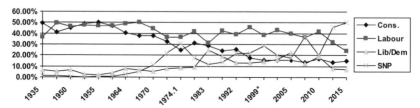

Scotland's separate history and traditions are often invoked in this context. As historian Malcolm Chapman has argued:

> The 'Forty-Five occupies an enormously important place in the Scottish historical consciousness, … We might … wonder that a relatively minor rising should have come to occupy such an important place. The battles were fought over a constitutional issue that had been irrevocably decided a century before. The military engagements were none of them great or glorious, and might be expected to fade into comparative insignificance before, say, the civil wars of the [seventeenth century] or the Napoleonic wars … [T]he enterprise was without any great chance of success, and … the constitutional threat was not nearly as great as history has made it. The 'Forty-Five might have appeared to history … as regrettable, unfortunate, unnecessary, and pointlessly bloody, and it might … have fallen into historical obscurity. Instead, it has become one of the few dates in the historical calendar that is commonly remembered …[52]

In this sense, Culloden is 'manufactured history', as Malcolm Chapman and Colin Kidd have observed.[53]

The narrative of Culloden as being a last battle defending Scottish independence against absorption and domination by the English was the hallmark of the NTS's mid-twentieth century narrative of the significance of the battle. In 1965, the NTS published a guidebook informing the reader that

> Culloden was to prove the final defeat of an ancient race [sic!]; the race which gave its name to the country, the race which won independence for Scotland at [the battle of] Bannockburn [in 1314], and a race which was now doomed. The Celtic Scot had at long last been conquered by the Anglo-Saxon.[54]

Like its guidebook, the NTS's earlier Culloden Visitor Centre built in 1970 focused on the history of the

> original Scots, those Gaelic-speakers from Ireland who settled here and gave the country their name. A civilised race [sic!], they brought Christianity and founded our royal dynasty. Under Bruce, they fought against the English for the sake of their independence, and later, after the Union, resisted by many, they have contributed in remarkable fashion with soldiers and settlers to the formation of the British Empire overseas. In short, it is THE STORY OF THE GAEL [sic!] – of a minority that continues to exist, the culture, poetry, songs and cloths of whom – but regrettably not the language – are regarded as the characteristic image of Scotland both at home and abroad.[55]

Thus Culloden was turned into a clash between Gaelic-speaking Scots and English oppressors. We find this falsification of the story (which leaves out the Scots on the Hanoverian side and all other ethnic components) in American author Diana Gabaldon's novel series *Outlander* (the first published in 1991).[56] *Outlander's* recent British-American TV adaptation goes one step further: it pits noble (albeit a little rough and unwashed) Scots not against Englishmen, but against the *British*, as the Redcoats are called throughout (!), and the Scots rant against the *British* occupation of their country. The '45 is told as though it were the Irish Easter Rising of 1916: Britons are the foreign occupation force in a Gaelic-speaking, Catholic country, the Irish 'identification friend or foe' pattern more familiar to Americans.

In the 1990s this ethnic myth lost much of its traction in Scotland, to the point where pressure grew to change the contents and layout of the Culloden visitor centre quite fundamentally.[57] This may well be due to the publication of a series of scholarly works of historiography about the campaign, to better and more objective school teaching which made it more widely known that Scots had fought on both sides at Culloden, and that more Scots had benefitted from the union with England in the century after Culloden than had suffered.[58]

At any rate, there is good evidence that Scottish nationalism is generally not racist: polls have shown in recent years that Scottish National Party members are more concerned about self-defined identification and solidarity with Scotland than by 'Gaelic roots' or Scottish ancestry. An opinion poll among SNP members conducted in 2007 came up with the following results: [59]

Table 5.2

How important is … to be truly Scottish?	Very (3)	Fairly (2)	Not very (1)	Not at all (0)	Mean (0-3)
To have Scottish ancestry	24%	32%	27%	17%	1.6
To have been born in Scotland	33%	30%	22%	15%	1.8
To live in Scotland now	48%	32%	15%	6%	2.2
To have lived in Scotland for most of one's life	28%	37%	26%	9%	1.8
To be a Christian	12%	13%	19%	56%	0.8
To respect Scottish political institutions and laws	59%	34%	5%	2%	2.5
To feel Scottish	78%	18%	3%	1%	2.7
To be able to speak English, Gaelic, Scots.	39%	34%	17%	10%	2.0

Even among SNP members, passive descriptors (ancestry, place of birth) are less important than active descriptors – one's own attitude towards Scotland. This makes Scottish nationalism – or one should perhaps better say patriotism – inclusive, civic, revolving around acts of self-identification and not biological pre-determination.[60]

Myth 5. The Socialist Myth

Scottish patriotism is thus not far away in its values from traditional Scottish Socialism, which has its own myth of Culloden. This is most famously narrated by Peter Watkins, in a TV-film commissioned by the BBC, made on a shoestring budget, broadcast 1964. Watkins' *Culloden* is a fascinating experimental film, a grainy black-and-white television docu-drama and a landmark of its genre, in which we are given the illusion of following a war correspondent onto the battlefield to interview the combatants, impersonated by amateur actors. The commentator emphasises that most Scots followed their lords due to a system of clan loyalty and economic dependence which ruled out any opting out of this clash of the lairds. Linguistic differences are underscored to mark the class differences: the lords speak with English accents, lower down the social hierarchy, the sub-tenants speak with Scottish accents, and at the lowest social levels, the subtenants of the subtenants who own at best a 'share in a small potato patch measuring thirty feet', and the cotters (servants of the subtenant), owning 'nothing', speak only Gaelic. They would not even have understood their lords who did not speak their language. Charles Edward Stuart, a little surprisingly sporting a thick French accent, is portrayed as a thoroughly selfish coward, who – along with his chief supporters – has no qualms about sacrificing his cold and hungry followers on the battlefield while fleeing at the first reversal of fortune.

Part of this narrative is also one of the poverty which hit Scotland supposedly only after the turning point of the '45. The old clan system is put in a straight line of continuity with the exploitation of the lower by the upper classes that went on to the Highland Clearances, mass emigration of Scots either abroad or to the nineteenth-century slums of Glasgow and Paisley where industry but also poverty sprouted, conditions which so impressed Friedrich Engels. The narrative then moves to the twentieth century, the decline of manufacturing and with it, the Scottish economy. In a play contrasting the late twentieth-century the oil boom (benefitting the few, it is argued) with the decline of Scotland's industry, the left-wing playwright John McGrath in his play – later turned into a film – *The Cheviot, the Stag, and the Black, Black Oil*[61] sums up this narrative:

> we're going to be telling a story. It's a story of what's been happening, here, in the Highlands. ... *It begins, I suppose, in 1746 with Culloden and all that* [my emphasis]. The Highlands are a bit of a mess; speaking or singing the Gaelic language is forbidden, the wearing of the plaid is forbidden. For sixty years the people put up with the oppression by the law, the soldiers, the landowners, and the poverty of the soil, many thousands emigrated, leaving sadly behind a browbeaten, starving people.[62]

This passage, cast as a foundation story, thus elevates Culloden to the lofty category of origin or foundation myths.[63]

The poem "No gods and precious few heroes", by Brian McNeill, goes in the same direction. It mocks politicians' profession to be 'proud to be Scottish' on the basis of 'the glories of our past', while McNeill regards 'the pride and the glory' as 'just another bloody lie …they use to keep us all in line.'

> *Refrain*
> For there's no gods & there's precious few heroes,
> but there's plenty on the dole in the land o' the leal [loyal].
> And it's time now to sweep the future clear o' the lies
> of a past that we know was never real. …

The third verse homes in on Culoden, asking

> … will we never hear the end
> of poor bloody Charlie and Culloden yet again,
> though he ran like a rabbit down the glen,
> leavin' better folk than him to be butchered?
> Or, are you sitting in your council house, thinking o' your clan?
> Waitin' for the Jacobites to come and free the land?
> Try goin' doon the broo [unemployment bureau] wi' a claymore
> in your hand
> and count all the princes in the queue![64]

Culloden, in this narrative, is thus an example of the exploitation of one class by another, to which the exploited submit out of ignorance. The Socialist narrative thus stigmatizes the nationalist and the romantic myths as the opium of the people, keeping them in passive submission to this exploitation.

Myth 6. The Myth of Moral Victory in Defeat

But the Scottish attachment to Culloden can also be explained in a sixth way: there are cultures in the world which revel in their own glorious defeat. The Serbs are among them, as are the Poles, and so, clearly, are the Scots. Scottish heroes tend to have come to a sticky end – think of *Braveheart*, William the Wallace,[65] or of Rob Roy, who can hardly be counted among the victors of History, and of Mary Stuart.

The ultimate analysis of this tendency is provided by *The Punch Short History of Scotland*, which notes the Scottish proclivity to 'claim a crushing defeat as a romantic landmark of history':

> 'Catastrophe struck in 1603 when James [VI] became King of England [as James I]. For almost a century the fight against England seemed pointless ... At last the Stuarts ... fled from England and Scottish History could start again. ... [While] The '15 was a washout – the Old Pretender arrived too late for the best defeats – but in the '45 the Young Pretender was a smash hit from the finish.
>
> As Scotland has not been invaded or defeated by England in modern times, Scottish History can be said to have come to an end, though there have been half-hearted attempts to see Scotland's perpetual failure in the World Cup as a romantic tragedy. The Scot is now a quiet kilted gentleman dreaming of past disasters in the hillsides...'[66]

What more evidence could one want of the benign descent of the memory of Culloden into political insignificance?

Yet many a moral victory has been won in defeat. Britons in general tend to confuse war and sports, and we can find this confusion well reflected in the traditions of Scottish football fans. We might look there for our final explanation of the myth of Culloden as one of moral victory in defeat. What do Scots sing if their team wins? 'Here we go, here we go, here we go'. What do they sing if their team loses? 'Here we go, here we go, here we go'.

Quod erat demonstrandum.

History, however, is a story without end. There is another song one hears, especially at rugby matches where the Scots have performed somewhat better in recent years, on the whole, than at football. Composed only in the mid-1960s by Roy Williamson, it is called 'Flower of Scotland'. It has gained dramatically in popularity even more recently, in the last thirty years or so. Its popularity rose along with that of the Scottish National Party, the re-establishment of a Scottish Government in Edinburgh in 1999 with powers over domestic issues, and a renewed movement aiming for total Scottish independence from Westminster (including also defence and foreign affairs).

Hailed as the 'unofficial Scottish national anthem', 'Flower of Scotland' celebrates, not a romantic defeat, but a Scottish victory: the Battle of Bannockburn (1314). But that is another story, another famous battle with its own myths.

Chapter 6

Waterloo 1815 – the Battle for History

Alan Forrest

The Battle of Waterloo, which was fought on 18 June 1815 in fields to the south of Brussels, was, even by the standards of the Napoleonic Wars, a cruel and murderous encounter.[1] Its outcome was not a foregone conclusion. As Wellington's Anglo-Dutch army lined up against Napoleon's French on the morning of the battle, the two sides were more or less evenly matched with around 70,000 men apiece; some on the Allied side approached the battle with caution, even despondency; and the Emperor's decision to engage with Wellington's forces cannot be dismissed as foolhardy. But the day did not go well for the French. Wellington's careful reconnaissance of Mont Saint-Jean and his familiarity with the site brought rich dividends. Heavy rain and clawing mud persuaded Napoleon to delay his attack for nearly two hours until the earth dried out sufficiently to move his heavy cannon and that delay would prove fateful. French assaults up the slope towards where the Allies were dug in were repeatedly repulsed; and Wellington's outposts at the farms of Hougoumont and La Haie Sainte held out stubbornly and impeded Napoleon's attacks. Ney proved yet again that he might be the 'bravest of the brave', but he lacked tactical acumen and too easily threw caution to the winds. Napoleon's communications system repeatedly broke down, most especially with Marshal Grouchy and the French force which had left in pursuit of the Prussians after Ligny two days earlier. As a consequence, the balance of the battle changed dramatically and, when Wellington was joined by Blücher's Prussians at around 5 in the afternoon, the French found themselves heavily outnumbered. The last hours of the battle turned into an unremitting slaughter and by the end of the day Napoleon's army had been destroyed, unable either to regroup or to continue the campaign. The adventure of the Hundred Days, and with it the dream of a French empire in Europe, was over.

Thousands of soldiers were taken prisoner as the bedraggled remnants of what would be Napoleon's last army straggled back across the border into

France. The death toll in the battle was chillingly high, particularly as it had been fought during a single day in a confined space, within easy access of the civilisation of a European capital city. In the course of the fighting Wellington's army suffered around 16,200 killed, wounded and missing; the Prussians over 7,000; and French casualties were even higher, with some 31,000 killed or wounded, and thousands more taken prisoner.[2] Waterloo was not an elegant battle, a test of tactics or a testimony to chivalric values. It was a bruising, bludgeoning encounter between two armies that were determined to fight to the death, seemingly regardless of casualties and of the degree of suffering incurred. If the French lost, they lacked nothing in courage: in the words of one British soldier, Edward Cotton of the 7th Hussars, 'at Waterloo we had to contend against soldiers of undaunted spirit, full of enthusiasm and careless of life'.[3] On the following morning the battlefield was strewn with the bodies of the dead, the air pierced with the cries of the wounded and heavy with the stench of death. If Waterloo was an undoubted victory for the Allies, it was a victory that was gained at a terrible price in human life.

A European site of memory

This chapter is not really about the battle as such, but about how Waterloo has been remembered over the two centuries since 1815, and how it has entered the national myths and narratives of the countries involved.[4] From the moment when news of the battle was announced, it was greeted with competing emotions ranging from mass enthusiasm to ill-concealed despair. Some of these memories were official ones, recorded in political tributes, in street names, columns and monuments, celebrated in public ceremonies and endorsed by all the pomp and majesty of the state. But Waterloo also created a powerful popular memory in several of the combatant nations, a memory in which the present linked to the past and in which the letters and memoirs of survivors played a significant part. This memory was, of course, subject to considerable political manipulation as both states and their citizens struggled to come to terms with the politics of the post-war world; small incidents were magnified, tales of bravery invented.[5] But its continued existence can be seen in popular culture, in poems and ballads, in folk song, and in everyday language: it is not only Napoleon who has 'met his Waterloo'.[6] For the bicentenary of the battle in 2015, the centrepiece event was a massive re-enactment at Waterloo itself, involving 6,200 re-enactors from across the world, along with 330 horses and 120 cannon.[7] Waterloo retains, in other words, an appeal and a poignancy that few battles before the twentieth century can match, an appeal which the nations involved in the battle have tailored to their own history, their own particular narrative.

The dates of decisive battles can quickly be transformed into public holidays or dividers in the public calendar. It is here that we encounter the notion of the battlefield as a *lieu de mémoire*: a point of reference for those who had lived through the battle, and a source of pride and of identity for future generations. Interestingly, though, battles appear somewhat unevenly in the (admittedly often very subjective) choices of *lieux de mémoire* made by Pierre Nora and his colleagues in their studies of France and Germany. It is striking how the French choices focus on regimes, institutions and political symbolism, rather than battles, and it is surely significant that, during the Napoleonic bicentenary, France has found it difficult to commemorate, let alone to celebrate, Napoleon's battlefield triumphs.[8] The bicentenary of Austerlitz, for instance, created a polemical outburst in France, with neither the President, Jacques Chirac, nor his prime minister electing to attend.[9] In contrast, in their work on 'days of commemoration' (*Erinnerungstage*) in German memory, Etienne François and Uwe Puschner came up with four battles – not all victories – from the nineteenth century alone: Jena/Auerstedt, Leipzig, Sedan, and – most significantly from the point of view of this chapter – Waterloo.[10] This is worth underlining because it has not always been clear that Waterloo has loomed very large in German national memory, even in the nineteenth century, when Leipzig occupied a much more prominent place in public perception. But then Leipzig was a battle fought on German soil, in the outskirts of a German capital city, blighting German civilian lives with plague, fever and disease in the weeks and months that followed the actual fighting.[11] For Prussia, particularly, Leipzig was a landmark and it continued to be celebrated as such: the moment when other German rulers had united behind Prussia to defend German Central Europe against a foreign invader. Throughout the nineteenth century Leipzig continued to be one of the foundation myths of the new Germany[12], until, in 1913, its centenary was marked by the construction of the huge and militaristic monument to German nationalism in Leipzig itself, the *Völkerschlachtsdenkmal*.[13] There would be no equivalent place for Waterloo in German national mythology.

Indeed, if we judge by the intensity of public celebrations in the years following 1815 we can see very different roles being ascribed to Waterloo in the national narratives of the countries whose troops were engaged in the battle. In what became modern Germany the impact of the battle was clearly very different between the north and the south, and between Prussia, where the importance of Blücher's role was understandably emphasized, and Hanover, which underlined its loyalty to the British Crown and cherished the memory of the King's German Legion (the KGL).[14] The monumental sculpture of two north German cities tells its own story in this regard. In Rostock there stands a statue to Blücher as the city's favourite son, placed strategically in front of the city's university; in Hanover the square used for military drills and displays in the nineteenth century was named the *Waterlooplatz*, distinguished by the proud military column standing at its heart. Here the men of the King's German Legion would continue to train and parade until Victoria became Queen and Hanover's dynastic link with Britain was broken in 1837. On the battlefield itself the only memorial to the Prussians who fell is a relatively modest monument designed by the sculptor Karl Friedrich Schinkel and inaugurated in 1819. In post-1945 Germany, too, there has been little appetite for grandiose public celebrations of Waterloo. As Jasper Heinzen has shown, the public celebrations in 1965 were largely confined to Hanover, with tributes restricted to their Hanoverian ancestors, the men of the King's German Legion who had fought and died in the battle. Waterloo was largely ignored in the rest of the country; it was excluded from the national narrative and was abandoned to what Heinzen calls a 'regional memory tradition'.[15]

The Dutch created their own narrative of the battle, and it is a dynastic narrative rather than a national one, emphasising the part played by the young Prince William of Orange, who had been present at Waterloo and had commanded the Dutch troops in Wellington's army. For supporters of the House of Orange and to Dutch patriots after 1815, he was a Dutch national hero who had been wounded in the battle that had liberated Holland from the threat of a Napoleonic restoration. For them the principal importance of Waterloo was in confirming Napoleon's defeat and guaranteeing the political solution agreed the previous year in Paris, whereby Belgium had been incorporated into an expanded Kingdom of the Netherlands. Yet his claims to heroism may seem slender. William quickly recovered from what some dismissed as a light graze on the shoulder. And his part in the fighting had not been particularly distinguished; in Wellington's somewhat acerbic view, 'the Prince is a brave young man, but that's all'.[16] But it was the prince that Holland chose to celebrate, whether in Jan Willem Pienemann's life-size painting of *The Battle of Waterloo* (the largest single canvas in the Rijksmuseum in Amsterdam) or in the Lion Mound which was erected by the Dutch on the Waterloo battlefield in 1826, at the place where their prince had spilt his blood to defeat Napoleon (Figs. 6.1 and 6.2).[17] And it was as such that Waterloo found its place in Dutch - and especially in Orangist - mythology. [18]

Britain and Waterloo

Memories of great battles are often wreathed in nostalgia as they become a central part of a nation's patriotic narrative, a heroic moment in a victorious past. Waterloo, like Trafalgar before it, has risked being engulfed in this kind of narrative. It was portrayed as the moment when Britain took on the greatest army Napoleonic France could muster and defeated it, so soundly, indeed, that Napoleon never again posed a threat to Britain's shores or to Britain's imperial glory. Some will add that it was one of the proudest moments in the history of the British army and of the regiments that fought there, and that Wellington's tactics drew on the particularly British strengths of defensive grit and resilience. But this narrative is somewhat mythical, since the British were a minority of the Allied troops on the battlefield; Peter Hofschröer has even argued that it was more a German than a British victory.[19] Waterloo has always been put to good use by patriots and nationalist propagandists. For nineteenth-century Britons it was the final pulverising victory in an Anglo-French rivalry for power and empire that had produced heroes on both sides, from Fontenoy to the Heights of Abraham and from Yorktown to the Nile. It was also the last great battle between these two warring nations, ushering in a period of international collaboration and heralding the years of the Entente Cordiale.[20] Like other countries which have suffered relative decline on the world stage, a substantial segment of the British public seek solace in a past that seemed always more glorious, more representative of what they regard as true British values. As one writer has pertinently phrased it in the context of the recent campaign against Britain's membership of the European Union, it is 'snorting a line of that most pernicious and debilitating Little English drug, nostalgia', part of a desire to 'shuffle back to a regret-curdled inward-looking yesterday'.[21]

But why was Waterloo celebrated so effusively in Britain? What was it about this battle that distinguished it from the many others in which British troops had been involved across the centuries or lent it to such strong identification with what were taken to be supremely British military qualities? At first glance it might seem a strange choice. Waterloo was a decisive battle, certainly, in that it finally effaced the last possible revival of a Bonapartist France and exiled the former Emperor to the island of Saint-Helena in the South Atlantic. But it was in many ways a codicil to the great campaigns that had preceded it – including the war in the Peninsula in which Britain had played a major role. The Napoleonic Wars had already ended with Napoleon's first abdication and exile to Elba in 1814. The Congress of Vienna had set out the basis of a new balance of power in Europe. The Waterloo Campaign of 1815 followed on from the major conflict, a united response by the Allied powers to Napoleon's escape from Elba and his charm offensive on the French people. The allies – including Austria and Russia who lay further to the east with some 350,000 troops between them – were determined to stop Napoleon's advance and refused any compromise with him. It is difficult to see how – with or without the battle at Mont Saint-Jean – the campaign could have resulted in anything other than a French defeat. Yet it is Waterloo that was turned into a British military myth. Regiments took enormous pride in including Waterloo among their battle honours. The Waterloo Medal, uniquely in the history of Britain's military, was awarded to every soldier who had fought in the battle.[22] Siborne's model of Waterloo, ordered and paid for by Parliament in the 1830s to celebrate a great British triumph, was deliberately made to show the state of the battle before the Prussian regiments arrived on the scene, in order to emphasize the specifically British character of the victory.[23] The battle created the phenomenon of mass battlefield tourism – and collecting, which was closely associated with it.[24]

Britain's principal concern – and it started in 1815, in the days following the announcement of the victory in London – was to claim Waterloo as a victory for British arms. This was done partly to attract popular enthusiasm for the government of the day, partly to contribute to Wellington's own reputation. Wellington was hailed as the military genius who had planned the battle and chosen the spot he would defend, before going on to outwit and then destroy Napoleon. Among the officers who served under him were heroes and martyrs, men like Lord Uxbridge and Thomas Picton and Alexander Gordon, who had shown exemplary courage in combat and either gave their lives in the battle or left limbs on the battlefield. Wellington's Waterloo Despatch, sent within hours of the battle, emphasised the national nature of the victory, offering his Allies – Belgians and Dutch, Hanoverians and especially Prussians – passing praise but underlining the centrality of Britain's own military effort.[25]

Fig 1.1: Liberty Leading the People
Painted in 1830 by Eugene Delacroix (1798-1863).
(*Erich Lessing/Art Resource, NY*)

Fig 1.2:
Verdun Memorial, France.
(*DBG Heuser*)

Fig 1.3:
Memorial of Grunwald, Poland.
(*DBG Heuser*)

Figs 2.1-3: The discovery of the Spanish Fleet opposite the Lizard
Anthony Oakshett (1955-)
(*Parliamentary Art Collection WOA 7123*)
The English Fleet pursuing the Spanish Fleet against Fowey
Richard Burchett (1815-1875)
(*Parliamentary Art Collection WOA 2954*)

Drake takes De Valdés's Galleon, the Lord Admiral pursues the Enemy
Anthony Oakshett (1955-)
(*Parliamentary Art Collection WOA 7124*)

Figs 2.4-6 The Engagement of Both Fleets against the Isle of Portland
Anthony Oakshett (1955-)
(*Parliamentary Art Collection WOA 7125*)
The Sharpest Engagement against the Isle of Wight
Anthony Oakshett (1955-)
(*Parliamentary Art Collection WOA 7126*)

English Fireships dislodge the Spanish fleet before Calais
Anthony Oakshett (1955-)
(*Parliamentary Art Collection WOA 7127*)

Fig 3.1:
Stern carving from the *Royal Charles.* (*Rijksmuseum, Amsterdam*)

Fig 3.2:
The Apotheosis of Cornelis de Witt, with the Dutch Raid on the Medway in the background.
Copy after Jan de Baen
(*Rijksmuseum, Amsterdam*)

Fig 4.1:
Sketch for a statue of Jan Sobieski, now at the Villa Willanow, Warsaw. (*Author's Collection*)

Fig 4.2:
The Victors of Vienna, 1683, from a nineteenth-century history book. (*Author's Collection*)

Fig 4.3:
A nineteenth-century mosaic on a house in Vienna.
(*DBG Heuser*)

Fig 4.4: The Battle of Poltava 1709
Eighteenth-century etching.
(*Author's Collection*)

Fig 4.5:
Russian poster
I. M. Mashistov,
Moscow, Издатель:
И. М. Машистов, Москва,
(*Кузнецов - Krasnoyarsk Museum of Regional Studies*)

Fig 4.6:
Christian Democratic Union of West Germny,
election poster of 1949: 'NO, therefore [vote]
Christian Democratic Union'.
(*Konrad Adenauer Stiftung Archiv für Christlich-Demokratische Politi via Wikimedia Commons, CC BY-SA 3.0*)

Fig 5.1:
Prince Charles Edward Stuart.
(*Author's Collection*)

THE HIGHLANDERS MEDLEY, or THE DUKE TRIUMPHANT.

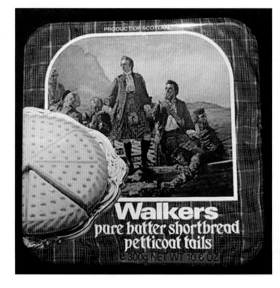

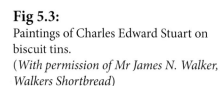

Fig 6.1: Construction of the Butte des Lions
Marcellin Jobard (1792-1861)

Fig 6.2: Vue générale du champ de bataille de Waterloo
H. Gerard
(*Rijksmuseum, Amsterdam*)

Lith. de Gerard, à Bruxelles.   Déposée à la Direction le 1er Septembre 1842.

Vue Générale du Champ de Bataille de Waterloo 18. Juin 1815.

A general view WATERLOO of the Field of Battle 18th June 1815.

Fig 7.1:
Equestrian Statue of General Robert Lee, Gettysburg.
(*Georg Schild*)

Fig 7.2:
Equestrian Statue of General George Gordon Meade.
(*Georg Schild*)

1863

NORTH CAROLINA

TO THE ETERNAL GLORY OF THE NORTH CAROLINA
SOLDIERS, WHO ON THIS BATTLEFIELD, DISPLAYED
HEROISM UNSURPASSED, SACRIFICING ALL IN SUP—
PORT OF THEIR CAUSE. THEIR VALOROUS DEEDS
WILL BE ENSHRINED IN THE HEARTS OF MEN LONG
AFTER THESE TRANSIENT MEMORIALS HAVE CRUM—
BLED INTO DUST.

THIRTY TWO NORTH CAROLINA REGIMENTS WERE IN
ACTION AT GETTYSBURG JULY 1, 2, 3, 1863. ONE CON
—FEDERATE SOLDIER IN EVERY FOUR WHO FELL HERE
WAS A NORTH CAROLINIAN.

THIS TABLET ERECTED BY THE NORTH CAROLINA DIVISION UNITED DAUGHTERS
OF THE CONFEDERACY

Fig 7.3:
North Carolina marker at the Gettysburg battlefield.
(*Georg Schild*)

Fig 7.4:
South Carolina marker at the Gettysburg battlefield.
(*Georg Schild*)

THAT MEN OF HONOR MIGHT FOREVER KNOW
THE RESPONSIBILITIES OF FREEDOM,
DEDICATED SOUTH CAROLINIANS STOOD
AND WERE COUNTED FOR THEIR HERITAGE
AND CONVICTIONS. ABIDING FAITH IN THE
SACREDNESS OF STATES RIGHTS PROVIDED
THEIR CREED. HERE, MANY EARNED
ETERNAL GLORY.

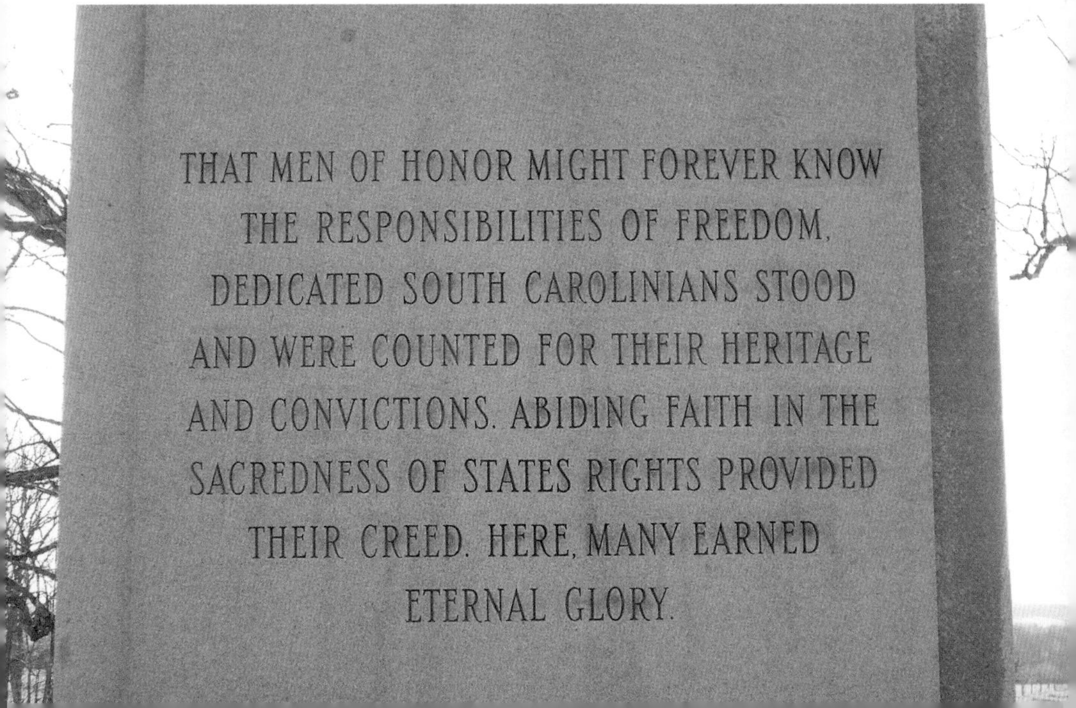

Fig 8.1:
The Anglo-French Memorial at Thiepval.

Fig 8.2:
A Cheshire Regiment's trench at the Somme, 1916.

Fig 8.3:
Battle of the Somme, 1916. British soldiers advancing under cover of gas and smoke. This photograph was taken by a captured prisoner. (*HIP/Art Resource, NY*)

Fig 8.4: The War
Triptych, oil on wood, by Otto Dix (1891-1969)
(*Erich Lessing/Art Resource, NY*)

Fig 9.1:
A scene from *Hunde, Wollt Ihr Ewig Leben* (dir. Frank Wisbar, 1959).

Fig 9.2:
A scene from *Stalingrad* (dir. Joseph Vilsmaier, 1993).

Within days its significance was being described in hugely inflated terms, in the press, by political leaders, and in parliament. The Foreign Secretary, Lord Castlereagh, expressed the national mood as well as anyone when he reminded MPs that Napoleon had been called 'the greatest Captain of his age'; in defeating him Wellington had shown exceptional prowess, to the extent that his achievement was 'of such high merit, of such pre-eminent importance, as had never perhaps graced the annals of this or any other country till now'.[26] It was by the use of such unrestrained hyperbole that Britain's national myth of Waterloo was created and sustained. But behind it lay another, more surreptitious truth. Even for the British, Wellington's reputation as a conqueror was not made by him alone; it reflected the fascination of the British for the man he had defeated, a despot and a usurper, no doubt, in English eyes, but still a military genius, a god of war - and after Waterloo, a British prisoner banished into exile. When he no longer threatened Britain, Napoleon was recreated as a victim of the would-be despotism of British ministers.[27]

Waterloo would be celebrated by poets and writers from Robert Southey to Walter Scott.[28] It became an iconic battle for the Victorians, the last of those traditional battles of the eighteenth century which the new industrial technology now threatened to sweep away. For some it also represented an older, more aristocratic style of warfare, one where officers were gentlemen, drawn from the gentry and the county nobility. Wellington was seen as belonging to that class, a member of the Anglo-Irish aristocracy, at home among the landowning nobility, whether in London or Dublin or Brussels. The myth of Waterloo draws on such social stereotypes in the importance it attaches to courtly etiquette, the gallantry shown to ladies, the social round of the British expatriate community in Brussels, and – perhaps especially - Wellington's attendance, along with most of his officers, at the Duchess of Richmond's ball on the eve of the battle. It was a fitting image of the entanglement of army and civil society, all distinctions blurred as the aristocracy and the officers' mess came together on the eve of the fighting. These were a reflection of that other persistent stereotype, the playing fields of Eton, where, the English upper classes liked to believe, the army and its values had been honed in preparation for war and the defence of the realm. For the Romantics, and especially Byron, it represented something more exciting, 'war with the frisson of sexual adventure'.[29] Made famous first by Byron's *Childe Harold's Pilgrimage*, and later by Thackeray's *Vanity Fair*, the Duchess of Richmond's Ball was the very stuff of English mythification.[30]

'The Greatest Captain of his Age'

The French, stunned by the totality of their defeat, could not fail to acknowledge the importance of Wellington's role in the battle. Even Napoleon, looking back on his military career on St. Helena, accepted that Wellington had won a resounding victory, though he could not hold back from remarking that 'his glory is utterly negative, his errors immense'.[31] He would also claim, a little spuriously, that Wellington acted against his country's interests in choosing to engage in the battle at all. In Napoleon's eyes, it was Wellington who had elected to fight at Waterloo on 18 June, a decision that 'went against the interests of his country and against the general war plan that had been agreed by the Allies'. The Allies had agreed to oppose Napoleon with the massed forces they had assembled, Austrians and Russians as well as British and Prussians. 'He violated all the rules of war', the Emperor argued. 'It was not in the interests of England, which needs so many men for its armies in the Indies and its colonies in America… to expose itself with such lightness of heart to a murderous struggle that could have cost her the only army she possessed'.[32] Here Napoleon was wrong. Wellington understood how important it was for Britain to play a central part in Napoleon's downfall in order to gain a privileged position in the diplomacy that would follow. In deciding to fight at Waterloo he was thinking beyond the battlefield. His instincts were keenly political. His career had been launched in the highly political atmosphere of British India; he went on to serve as ambassador to Paris, would replace Castlereagh at the Congress of Vienna, and would go on to be prime minister of his country. It is not accidental that Castlereagh played such a significant part at Vienna, or that Wellington was given overall command of the army of occupation that was sent into France. Throughout, the continued balance of power in Europe had been one of his principal concerns.[33]

In the first glad morning of victory the British public was unrestrained in its praise for Wellington. He was given a country house in Hampshire, Stratford Saye, as a token of the gratitude of the nation.[34] Statues were erected in his honour across England and the Empire. Cities proudly named streets, squares and bridges to commemorate a hero, and that in a nation where naval heroes usually commanded centre stage; the number of naval officers who were buried in St Paul's Cathedral is surely testimony to the standing in which the senior service continued to be held. But 1815 was unquestionably Wellington's moment. Huge crowds cheered him in the streets. And the Duke's reputation was such that he stood above calumny and vilification. In 1816, a charge of libel was brought by Lady Frances Caroline Wedderburn Webster against the proprietor of the *St James Chronicle*, Charles Baldwin, after his paper published allegations of her adultery with Wellington while he was visiting wounded soldiers in Brussels. The case achieved widespread publicity because of Wellington's standing and his status as 'Europe's Liberator', as Baldwin knew it would do. But Wellington's celebrity was also Baldwin's undoing. The court agreed with the plaintiff that the hero of Waterloo was 'above the reach of such slander', and ordered him to pay damages to Webster of £2000.[35] In 1816 that was regarded as appropriate punishment for bringing Wellington's name into disrepute.

Wellington's popularity did not endure, however, and the fact that he elected to pursue a political career after returning to civilian life fundamentally altered his relationship with history. He soon found himself reviled in caricatures and in the press as public opinion turned against him and he became associated with a cold, aloof rural conservatism that fitted poorly with the public mood. The massacre by the Salford Yeomanry of a number of demonstrators in a peaceful crowd at Manchester's St Peter's Fields in 1819 set the tone for much of the decade that followed, when Wellington – one of the most diehard opponents of the Great Reform Bill – became widely hated, especially in the radical North, where he was seen as unsympathetic to the needs of commercial society and coldly aloof from the interests of ordinary people.[36] His greatest victory, on the other hand, continued to be an object of national pride, sustained both by the state and by private initiatives. Subscriptions were raised to build columns and statues across the country and around the Empire; the Church of England invested in Waterloo Churches for the new urban working class;[37] even the monarchy got involved, opening the lavishly patriotic Waterloo Chamber at Windsor Castle. Overall, more fuss was made of this battle and of Britain's victory in 1815 than of any other land battle of modern times – though it is, of course, arguable that Britain (and England in particular) continued to value the navy more, and to take greater pleasure in naval victories. England remained at heart a sea-faring nation: since the time of the Armada the navy had been central to England's identity as well as critical to her defence. At times when soldiers had been feared and distrusted as 'the scum of the earth' (and it is Wellington's description), the public looked to their 'honest tars' to protect them from foreign invasion. Unlike Arthur Wellesley, a product of the Anglo-Irish gentry, Nelson was a true Englishman, Norfolk born and bred. Like Leipzig for the Germans, Trafalgar retained a special place in English hearts.[38]

Waterloo in the Celtic Lands

But Waterloo had another use, and it was one that the British government had particular reason to value at this time. It could portray quite dramatically the unity of the United Kingdom at a time when smouldering discontent – in Scotland after the 1745 Jacobite Rebellion, in an Ireland still reeling from the savage repression of the 1798 rebellion by the United Irishmen. Both countries were over-represented in the British army during the Napoleonic Wars; and both played their part at Waterloo, though perhaps not to the degree that was subsequently claimed. Of the thirty-nine British regiments present on the battlefields, only eight were Scottish, and Scots made up rather less than one-fifth of the troops engaged in the action.[39] But the Waterloo of popular legend placed far more emphasis on the part that Scottish regiments contributed to the battle, and during the 1820s and 1830s the popular image of Waterloo would become increasingly dominated by kilted Highland soldiers, heroically idealized in paintings like Lady Butler's *Charge of the Scots Greys* and reproduced since on 1,000 tins of shortbread. Scottish writers, not unnaturally, tended to emphasise the Scottish dimension, and to distinguish the role played by Scots from that of other regiments. More significantly, the British government had no reason to dissent, seeing the shared patriotism kindled by Waterloo as a tool with which they might hope to mould a more truly United Kingdom out of its constituent parts. It is surely no accident that some of the earliest public monuments to the battle were first mooted in parts of the Empire where patriotism was least assured, like Montreal and Dublin. Waterloo had become another means of creating British identity in areas where it was weakest; and in the troubled social climate of the post-war years there would be a discrete Celtic dimension to Waterloo commemoration – and to the ways in which the Waterloo myth was used and presented.[40]

A Glorious Defeat

If the different Allied powers had to decide how to present a victory to posterity, theirs was a simple task compared to that faced by the French. How could they hope to commemorate a crushing defeat which had not only obliterated France's army, but had brought about regime change and a loss of territory, restoring the widely-hated Bourbons for a second time in as many years and destroying all hope of establishing a French empire on the European continent? How could they integrate into the national narrative a battle that had resulted in Napoleon's exile, a huge bill in reparations, and an army of occupation that saw Russian and Prussian soldiers policing Paris?[41] What myths would be needed to veil the extent of the disaster and make Waterloo more palatable to public opinion? And could these be maintained distinct from the Bonapartist myth, a deep nostalgia, especially in military circles, for the person of Napoleon himself?

For many Frenchmen Waterloo would always remain as Victor Hugo so famously described it, that '*morne plaine*', engulfed in the mist and drizzle of a Belgian morning, where the Imperial adventure finally ended and the dream of glory was lost. They could not deny that he had been defeated, but dwelt instead on the glorious manner of that defeat, on the courage of his soldiers, on his unquenchable thirst for victory. Barely had the sound of battle ceased than representations began to appear, in words and images, proclaiming it a 'glorious defeat' – the image of the battle that survived throughout the nineteenth century, finding new expression under the July Monarchy, the Second Empire and the Third Republic until it had become a basic trope of French history and an essential plank in Napoleon's legend. French schoolchildren learned to shed tears over Waterloo, to share the moment when greatness and melancholy converged.[42] Defeat added an element of tragedy to what was built into an epic of modern times. There was something deeply saddening about the solitude of his final years, a man who had reigned over most of a continent confined to a rocky island with seagulls for company. But, though Napoleon divided French opinion and in 1815 aroused the anger of conservatives and legitimists for what they saw as a lawless and unnecessary return – for there was no basis in law for his return from Elba or for the Hundred Days - French historians and public figures have found it difficult not to express their admiration for all that he had achieved. 'His fall was huge, in proportion to his glory', noted General de Gaulle.[43] And, when he then surrendered to the British in hope of greater clemency than he could expect from the Bourbons, there was a quiet understanding. Caricatures at the time had mocked him, of course, some calling for him to be tried for treason and executed as an outlaw. But history has been more relenting. 'His decision to surrender to his conqueror', in the view of Dominique de Villepin, merely 'shows his greatness'.[44] It added to, rather than detracted from, the Napoleonic legend. And if his military ambitions had ended in calamity, both for his regime and his country, many, especially in France, would continue to believe that it was Napoleon who won the battle for history.

French memory of Waterloo has been dominated by two images of courage and defiance, images that serve to confirm the concept of a glorious defeat and helped, in highly a romantic age, to stoke a growing cult of Napoleon, in France and beyond. The two are, of course, linked, images of abiding courage in the face of defeat and adversity. Waterloo had not been a shameful rout that would fill those who fought there with a sense of humiliation. It had been, in Wellington's own words, 'a damned close-run thing', a battle which the French had come close to winning, a battle, moreover, that had been illuminated by acts of outstanding courage in the pursuit of victory which would be remembered long after the sun had gone down on the battlefield. The heroic defence of the last squares of the Old Guard, and the famous, if almost certainly apocryphal, verdict of General Cambronne that 'the Guard dies and does not surrender', would live long in nineteenth-century lore, giving Waterloo a unique place among Napoleon's battles.[45] Balzac, Stendhal, Victor Hugo and even Walter Scott were dazzled by the person of the Emperor and by the scope of his military ambition, and through their writings a new generation would come to share the experiences of their elders. Nor were they immune from sadness over what occurred at Waterloo, the decline and fall of the last of the eighteenth century's Great Men. In their poems and novels they would contribute powerfully to Napoleon's myth.[46]

Waterloo remains for many the battle that finally rid Europe of Napoleon, who was in turn portrayed as a tyrant, a usurper and a warmonger, whose success would spell disaster for the rest of Europe. Napoleon certainly lived by war – that much is surely true. But what he brought to the countries he conquered was not all bad. There was, of course, exploitation on a huge scale, economic exploitation through taxes and requisitions, human exploitation through conscription. But he also brought institutional change and modernization, whose influence often lingered on long after the armies had left. Napoleon was a man who thought beyond the battlefield, a soldier-emperor who dreamt of being a new Alexander or a new Charlemagne, bringing governance and justice, education and the rule of law, to the lands he conquered.[47] And in much of central and eastern Europe, the countries he invaded had never enjoyed any liberties, any access to the suffrage, any human rights. To them Napoleon brought ideas that had been born in Revolutionary France, ideas that benefited their citizens and would go on to inspire future generations across the continent. In Poland, Napoleon's

Grand Duchy of Warsaw brought the people undreamt-of freedoms that would be remembered, long after his death, with gratitude and even affection.[48] Not everywhere would he be demonized as an ogre or a tyrant. Even in Britain, among the myriad responses to the battle in the year that followed, Philip Shaw can comment that 'it is a curious aspect of modern culture that Waterloo is best remembered as a tragic defeat rather than as a glorious triumph'.[49]

It would prove a powerful image, and an enduring one. Even in his moment of defeat, Napoleon continues to dwarf Wellington in the memory of the general public. The tourists who flock to the battlefield visit it as the place where Napoleon fought his last battle. And where nineteenth-century writers and artists led, twentieth-century film-makers have followed, dazzled by the memory of the Emperor. The sumptuously-filmed *Waterloo* of Sergei Bondarchuk (1970), with Rod Steiger as Napoleon, was loudly applauded in both Moscow and London, but failed at the box office so disastrously that it caused Stanley Kubrick's intended mega-project on Napoleon to be abandoned by the studio.[50] Cinema audiences proved singularly partisan where Napoleon was concerned. English cinema-goers resisted the glorification of the Emperor, while French viewers appeared especially sensitive to any denigration of a national hero. Indeed, in 1940 even the wartime love story *Waterloo Bridge*, with Vivien Leigh and Robert Taylor, was released in France under the more discreet title of '*La valse dans l'ombre*'.

For some, the Bicentenary provided the excuse they were looking for to rekindle past animosities. A right-wing French deputy, Jacques Myard, went so far as to suggest in 2015 that we should really see Waterloo for what it was - a French victory. For, he declared, it saw 'the start of the myth and the glorification of Bonaparte', not just in France but across the world. 'We should not listen to the English', he added, with calculated provocation. 'It was a victory. And that is all there is to it.'[51]

FAMOUS BATTLES

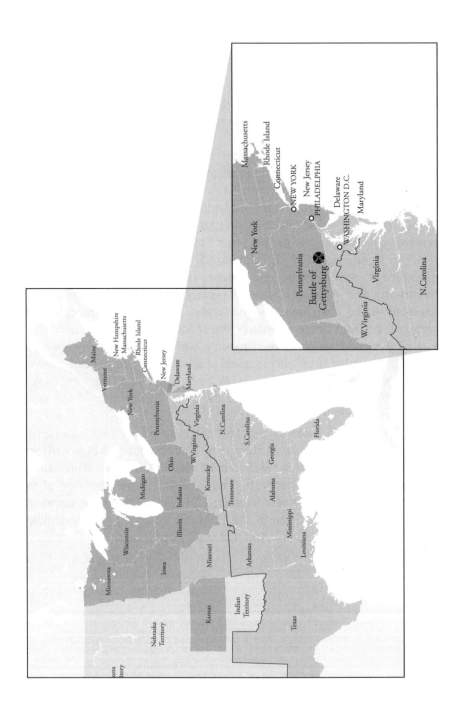

Chapter 7

Gettysburg, 1863, and American National Identity

Georg Schild

This uniting of North and South in a renewed American nationalism was a fine thing, to be sure, but all too often it was characterized by forgetting what the war had been about.

James McPherson, *Hallowed Ground*
(New York: Crown, 2003), p. 45

In early July 1863, two years into the American Civil War, two large armies faced each other in the small southern Pennsylvania town of Gettysburg. There was the Union army, officially called the Army of the Potomac, commanded by General George Gordon Meade, and the Army of Northern Virginia, led by the legendary Robert E. Lee. Their engagement in Gettysburg was one of the largest and bloodiest battles of the war. Roughly 90,000 Northerners faced 70,000 Southerners. Of these 160,000 men, some 44,000 were killed, wounded or taken prisoner.

The battle of Gettysburg is still very much alive in the American collective memory because it was so bloody and because Southern mythology claims that the Confederates had almost won the confrontation due to their superior virtue and exceptionally brave fighting abilities. And if they had won Gettysburg, perhaps they could have also won the war and their independence. The Gettysburg battle is one of the few cases where the defeated came to dominate the historiography of the confrontation. Southerners turned the defeat into a mythological struggle. Such a reframing of the narrative came at a price, however. In the collective memory of the Southern states, the causes of the war have been almost completely eradicated. Fighting for secession and for maintaining slavery did not fit into a post-war societal discourse of bravery and eventually, national unity.

Secession and War

The American Civil War is arguably the most thoroughly researched topic in all of human history. There are numerous eyewitness accounts of many of the battles, and generations of historians have gone over every detail of the confrontation. There is an agreement about the basic course of events during the Civil War and including the battle of Gettysburg. The war commenced in the spring of 1861 after eleven Southern states had declared their secession from the Union. There can be no doubt that slavery was at the heart of that decision. The Southern states feared that a majority of northerners would sometime in the future declare slavery unconstitutional and would thereby undermine the economic basis of the Southern way of life. Faced with the choice of preserving slavery or maintaining the union, Southern whites chose the former. President Abraham Lincoln, who had been elected to office in November 1860, rejected the notion that states had a right to secede. In his inaugural address of March 1861, he declared unequivocally that 'the Union of these States is perpetual.[1] He let the Southerners know that he would not interfere with the institution of slavery where it existed. They had nothing to fear if they stayed in the Union. But Lincoln left no doubt that he would be willing to resort to war to maintain national unity. He also insisted that the federal government would maintain control over all military installations in the South, including Fort Sumter in Charleston harbour. When the Confederates bombarded the Fort on 12 April 1861 and forced its commandant Major Robert Anderson to surrender, the people in the North were so outraged that Lincoln was able to lead united Northern states into a civil war.

Initially, the war went poorly for both sides. By the fall of 1862, after a year and a half of fighting, the Union had not achieved victory over the Confederacy despite an overwhelming technological, industrial and demographic superiority. The Union twice tried to capture Richmond, the capital of the Confederacy, but was forced to retreat on both occasions in July 1861 after the disastrous First Battle of Bull Run and a year later after the so called Peninsular Campaign.

The war was not going much better for the Confederacy, either. Since the summer of 1861, the Southern states faced wave after wave of invading Northern troops. By the fall of 1862, the Confederates had barely been able to defend their own territory. They lost control over much of the Mississippi river, effectively splitting the Confederacy into two halves. The battles had been costly in terms of human losses and the destruction of valuable infrastructure.

While most of the fighting occurred in the South, there were two noteworthy Confederate attempts to invade the North. In the fall of 1862, taking advantage of the Union defeat in the Peninsular Campaign, Lee marched his troops into Maryland and faced a Union army at the battle of Antietam. Even though the Maryland campaign ended in defeat for the Confederacy, Lee's army moved into Pennsylvania again the next year and fought the battle of Gettysburg. At first glance, this strategy of carrying the war north again appears counterintuitive. In their own minds, the Southerners waged a defensive war. They had seceded from the union (which they believed they had every right to do) and fought a defensive war against invading Northerners. This strategy was successful to a certain extent; the union army had not achieved a decisive victory during the first two years of the confrontation.

Nevertheless, General Lee strongly argued in favour of invading the North because he believed that the Southerners could never gain their recognition as sovereign states by just fending off union troops. The South had to intensify the fighting in order to increase the cost of continuing the war for the North to levels that were unacceptable to the Union public. Such a strategy should resemble that of General George Washington in the Revolutionary War of 1775 through 1783. Washington had never defeated the British army, he had only through crucial victories at Saratoga and Yorktown managed to convince King George III and his cabinet that victory in America would come at unacceptable costs. Lee had something similar in mind. He believed that if Southern armies would continue to raid Maryland and Pennsylvania and threaten Washington and Philadelphia, the Lincoln administration might conclude that it was more expedient to end the war rather than be stuck in a perpetual conflict with an enemy who steadfastly refused to give up.

There is a debate among historians whether Lee's strategy could ever have worked. Historians Scott Bowden and Bill Ward defend Lee's invasion plans as the South's 'last chance for victory'; a 'series of engagements [somewhere north of the Potomac river] culminating in a resounding Southern victory might prove so politically damaging to the Lincoln administration that Confederate independence would be substantially closer or realized.' Other historians criticize Lee's strategy. Historian Alan Nolan pointed out that Lee wasted his most precious and irreplaceable military commodity during the two Northern invasions: soldiers. The high death rates that the South experienced in Antietam and Gettysburg weakened the Confederacy and forced Lee to sue for peace in the spring of 1865.[2]

Every military strategy rests on certain assumptions about how the opponent will react when he is attacked. The South repeatedly erred in predicting Northern responses. The secession decision itself did not lead to Northern calls for military action. It was only the shelling of Fort Sumter that hardened Northern attitudes toward the South. Lee's assumption that the North would abandon the war effort when faced with a Southern invasion appears as wishful thinking. Lincoln even used the beginning of the Gettysburg campaign to call for more volunteers in the fight against the Southerners. Against this background, the invasion was doomed from the start. And Southern commanders continued to make mistakes.

The Battle of Gettysburg

The Gettysburg campaign began in early June 1863, when two columns of Confederate troops started moving north up the Shenandoah Valley. It is not known where Lee wanted to go. Most likely his plan was to capture Harrisburg, the capital of Pennsylvania, establish a strong defensive position there and wait for the Union to attack him. Fighting from a fortified defensive position was Lee's favoured tactic. Such a plan, however, rested on certain assumptions. The Confederate army had to move deep into Pennsylvania almost unopposed by Northern armies in order to create a bridgehead. However, General Meade learned about the Southern march north as soon as it started. After briefly conferring with President Lincoln whether to attack the Confederate capital Richmond or pursue the invading army, Meade started chasing Lee. When Lee realized that his original plan would not work, he concentrated his army in the vicinity of the town of Gettysburg. Meade followed him. With two large hostile armies in close proximity, a confrontation was only a matter of time.

The battle began almost by chance in the early morning hours of 1 July 1863 when two scouting parties from the union and confederate armies met west of town. The resulting exchange of gun fire attracted more and more units and eventually forced Lee and Meade to fight a major battle in Gettysburg. German-born Union General Carl Schurz later described the fighting of the first day: 'About four o'clock, the attack by the enemy along the whole line became general and still more vehement. Regiment stood against regiment in the open fields, near enough almost to see the white in one another's eyes, firing literally in one another's faces. The slaughter on both sides was awful.'[3]

From Lee's point of view the sudden beginning of the engagement was most unwelcome news because it denied him the option of carefully choosing a suitable defensive position from where to await an attack. However, the Confederate troops were successful at first and were able to force the Northerners to withdraw to elevated positions south of town where they built a strong defensive line. This retreat was 'more or less disorderly,' as Schurz put it, 'the streets being crowded with vehicles of every description, which offered to the passing troops exceedingly troublesome obstructions.'[4]

In the afternoon of the first day of the battle, Lee told General James Longstreet, the commander of his 1st Corps that he planned to attack the Union army's defensive positions. Longstreet disagreed with that plan and quoted Lee as saying: 'If the enemy is there to-morrow, we must attack him.' To that Longstreet replied: 'If he is there, it will be because he is anxious that we should attack him – a good reason … for not doing so.' Longstreet urged Lee to change his plan and move past the union position toward Washington and 'force [Meade] to attack us in such position as we might select.' Longstreet went on to describe their conversation and concluded that Lee would not abandon the idea of an attack the next day. He added that Lee was excited; the battle fought on the first day had given him a 'taste of victory.'[5]

British military observer Colonel Arthur Freemantle who spent the Gettysburg campaign in the Confederate camp recorded some deliberations in the evening of the first day: 'At supper this evening, General [James] Longstreet spoke of the enemy's position as being "very formidable." He also said that they would doubtless entrench themselves strongly during the night. The Staff officers spoke of the battle as a certainty, and the universal feeling in the army was one of profound contempt for an enemy whom they have beaten so constantly, and under so many disadvantages.'[6]

Fighting on 2 July began late in the day. In the morning, Lee conferred with his generals. It was only around 11am that he gave his final orders. Generals Richard Ewell and Longstreet were to attack the union flanks. There is a very vivid description of the attack of 2 July in the New York *World*:

> Until six o'clock the roar of cannon, the rush of missiles, and the bursting of bombs filled all the air. … About six o'clock p.m.

silence ... was permitted ... to dwell upon the field. Only the groans
– unheard before – of the wounded and dying, only a murmur, a
warning memory of the breeze through the foliage; only the low
rattle of preparation of what was to come embroidered this blank
stillness. Then, as the smoke beyond the village was lightly borne
to the eastward, the woods on the left were seen filled with dark
masses of infantry, three columns deep, who advanced at a quick
step. ... The battle ... grew fearful. Standing firmly up against the
storm, our troops, though still outnumbered, gave back shot for
shot, volley for volley, almost death for death. Still the enemy was
not restrained. Down he came upon our left with a momentum that
nothing could check. The rifled guns that lay before our infantry
on a knoll were in danger of capture. General Hancock was
wounded in the thigh, General Gibbon in the shoulder. The Fifth
Corps ... went into the breach with such shouts and such volleys
as made the rebel column tremble at last. ... The rebel's camel's
back was broken ... His line staggered, reeled, and drifted slowly
back, while the shouts of our soldiers, lifted up amid the roar of
musketry over the bodies of the dead and wounded, proclaimed
the completeness of their victory.[7]

The Southern attack on 2 July was unsuccessful. Nevertheless, Lee decided
to renew the attack on 3 July. Around 1 p.m., Southern artillery opened
fire on union positions. Union canons responded in kind. At 2.30 p.m., the
Confederates attacked the centre of the union troops. 13 000 soldiers under
the command of General George E. Pickett marched one mile over an open
field toward union troops that stood behind a stone wall. The attack was
repulsed within thirty minutes.

Pickett's charge, as it has become known, has been described by
contemporaries, by generations of historians, and by numerous fictional
writers looking for inspiration. In the 1993 movie *Gettysburg*, based on
the novel *The Killer Angels* by Michael Shaara, Pickett's charge takes place
almost in real time. Soldiers marched through open fields and meadows
in straight lines making them easy targets for Union artillery and infantry
attacks.

There have been bitter disputes among leading Confederate politicians and
military officers why the battles of 2 and 3 July failed. Foremost among those
who criticized Lee's plan was General Longstreet: 'The battle [of Gettysburg]
was not made as I would have made it. My idea was to throw ourselves

between the enemy and Washington, select a strong position, and force the enemy to attack us. So far as is given to man the ability to judge, we may say, with confidence, that we should have destroyed the Federal army, marched into Washington and dictated our terms. … I cannot help but think that great results would have been obtained had my views been thought better of.'[8]

Longstreet wrote in his memoirs *From Manassas to Appomattox* that he had told Lee that the Confederates needed at least 30,000 soldiers for the attack on the Northern defensive position on the third day. They only had about a third of that number available. Still, Lee ordered the attack, and Longstreet had the duty to inform his division commander Pickett that he had to move ahead and lead the charge. Longstreet described the scene in his memoirs:

> General Pickett rode to confer with [General] Alexander, then to the ground upon which I was resting. … Pickett said, 'General, shall I advance?' The effort to speak the order failed, and I could only indicate it by an affirmative bow. He accepted the duty with seeming confidence of success, leaped on his horse, and rode gaily to his command.

Later Longstreet described the brutal consequences of the attack:

> Confederate batteries put their fire over the heads of the men as they moved down the slope, and continued to draw the fire of the enemy until the smoke lifted and drifted to the rear, when every gun was turned upon the infantry columns. The batteries that had been drawn off were replaced by others that were fresh. Soldiers and officers began to fall, some to rise no more, others to find their way to the hospital tents. Single files were cut here and there, then the gaps increased, and an occasional shot tore wider openings, but, closing the gaps as quickly as made, the march moved on. The Divisions of McLaws and Hood were ordered to move to closer lines for the enemy of their front, to spring to the charge as soon as the breach at the centre could be made. The enemy's right overreached my left and gave serious trouble. … General Lee and the corps commander were there, but failed to order help.[9]

Longstreet concluded that 40,000 men 'could not have carried the position at Gettysburg. The enemy was there. Officers and men knew their advantage, and were resolved to stay until the hills came down over them. It is simply out of the question for a lesser force to march over broad, open fields and carry a fortified front occupied by a greater force of seasoned troops.'[10]

Table: Losses of the Battle of Gettysburg

	Union	Confederacy	Total
Killed	3,155	2,592	5,747
Wounded	15,029	12,709	27,738
Missing or taken prisoner	5,365	5,150	10,515
	23,549	20,451	44,000

Source: U.S. Department of War: *War of the Rebellion: A Compilation of the Official Records of the Union and Confederate Armies* (*OR*), 128 vols (Washington, DC, 1889-1901), vol. 27, pt. 1, p. 187; *OR*, vol. 27, pt. 2, p. 346.

Badly beaten and having suffered thousands of casualties, the Confederates retreated back to Virginia. Never again were they able to mount a serious offensive in the North. While the years 1864 and 1865 saw some of the most brutal fighting of the war, few observers could harbor any doubts that the North would eventually emerge victoriously. Even an apolitical observer like Scarlett O'Hara was told the hard truth when Ashley Wilkes remarked to her: 'Yes, Scarlett, I think the Yankees have us. Gettysburg was the beginning of the end.'[11]

The Divided Legacy of the Civil War

At first glance there is very little in the history of the battle of Gettysburg that invites mythmaking. The Northerners had to fight a desperate defensive battle on their own soil and were forced out of town on the first day of the confrontation. Something similar can be said of the Confederates. In retrospect, they did everything wrong. Lee attacked a strong Northern defensive position and in doing so wasted many soldiers' lives. After the war, the South was doubly embarrassed. They lost a war that was fought for an immoral objective. How can such a defeat be turned into a myth?

Northern and Southern mythology about Gettysburg and the Civil War developed along different tracks. Initially, the Northerners were not shy about letting the Southerners know what they were fighting for and who won the war. At the dedication of the Gettysburg cemetery in November

1863, the main speaker Edward Everett asked his audience to consider 'what would have been the consequences to the country, to yourselves, and to all you hold dear, if those who sleep beneath our feet, and their gallant comrades who survive to serve their country on other fields of danger, had failed in their duty on those memorable days.'[12]

Union troops took command of the South and made sure that slaves were freed in accordance with the thirteenth amendment to the constitution. A generation after the end of the Civil War, more accommodating views about Gettysburg, the war and the creation of a new and better America appeared. The earliest spokesman for such a view may have been President Lincoln. When he spoke at the dedication of the Gettysburg cemetery following Everett's address, he interpreted the war not as a conflict to eradicate slavery, but as a confrontation for democracy and for the creation of a better and stronger America. He talked about a 'great task' that remained before all Americans, 'that from these honored [sic] dead we take increased devotion to that cause for which they gave the last full measure of devotion - that we here highly resolve that these dead shall not have died in vain - that the nation, under God, shall have a new birth of freedom, and that government of the people, by the people, for the people, shall not perish from the earth.'[13] Lincoln's words were vague, however. What exactly did he mean when he talked about a new birth of freedom? Slavery as a dividing issue between North and South was not explicitly mentioned. People in the North and in the South could interpret his words according to their own interests and desires.

The South developed a peculiar way of remembering the Civil War that has become known as the *Lost Cause*. It was history written by the losers of the conflict, trying to get their version of events into print. According to historian Gary W. Gallagher, the proponents of the *Lost Cause* sought to justify their pre-war way of life, to find something positive in an all encompassing failure, and to provide future generations of white Southerners with a 'correct' narrative of the war.[14]

Lost Cause proponents used two angles to give the Civil War and the Gettysburg narrative a new direction. The first element of the mythmaking-strategy began almost as soon as the war was over. Southern politicians such as President Jefferson Davis wrote lengthy books in which they claimed that the war was not fought for slavery but that it was a states' rights fight: 'The truth remains intact and incontrovertible, that the existence of African servitude was in no way the cause of the conflict, but only an incident. In the later controversies that arose, however, its effect in operating as a lever upon the passions, prejudices, or sympathies of mankind, was so potent that it has been spread, like a thick cloud, over the whole horizon of historic truth.'[15] Southern writers claimed that they were the true followers of Jeffersonian democracy that rejected the idea of a strong federal government in favour of strengthening states and local communities.

Slavery, some Southern writers believed, was in fact alien to the South and was forced upon it, first by British kings and then by northern speculators who sought the greatest profit from growing cotton most cheaply. A report of the history committee of the Confederate veterans published in 1907 absolves the South from all responsibility for slavery: 'The South was ... in no sense responsible for the existence of slavery within its borders, but it was brought there against its will.' Southerners had made numerous efforts to abolish slavery and 'it is the almost universal belief now that these efforts would have succeeded gradually, but for the harsh and unjust criticisms of the Southern people by some of those at the North.' The South blamed the North for forcing slavery upon the South and for making it impossible to abolish it.

There was, however, one Confederate document that appeared to contradict this idea. In February 1861, Confederate Vice President Alexander Stephens called slavery the 'cornerstone of the Confederacy.' Stephens based his views on the belief that 'the negro is not the equal of the white man.' The 1907 report asked: 'Isn't this fact recognized as true to-day in every part of this land?' The report charged Northerners with hypocrisy: they were responsible for slavery, they made gradual emancipation impossible, and they treated blacks in the new United States with the same sense of racial inferiority as the Southerners had treated their slaves a generation earlier.[16]

The second element of the mythmaking-strategy focused on the battle of Gettysburg and, more precisely, on Pickett's Charge of 3 July. The journalist and Southern propagandist Edward Pollard described the charge in his 1866 book *The Lost Cause* as an act of heroism:

> Pickett's division proceeded to descent the slope of hills and to move across the open ground. The front was thickly covered with skirmishers; then followed Kemper's and Garnett's brigades ... The five thousand Virginians descended the hill with the precision and regularity of a parade. As they reached the Emmitsburg road, the Confederate guns, which had fired over their heads to cover the movement, ceased, and there stood exposed these devoted troops

to the uninterrupted fire of the enemy's batteries, while the fringe of musketry fire along a stone wall marked the further boundary of death to which they marched. No halt, no waver. ... Steadily the Virginians press on. The name of Virginia was that day baptized in fire, and illuminated forever in the temple of History. There had been no such example of devotion in the war.[17]

For Pollard, even Lee's retreat after the lost battle was an act of superior military ability: 'The field was covered with Confederates slowly and sulkily retiring in small broken parties under a heavy fire of artillery. There was no panic. Never did a commanding general behave better in such trying circumstances than did Lee. He was truly great in disaster.'[18]

In Southern mythology, the defeat became a necessary precondition for the Southern soldiers to prove their virtue in the face of an overwhelming enemy force. In 1883, writer John C. Kensil wrote the poem 'Battle-field of Gettysburg, After Twenty Years' that glorified the charge:

Then, charging all along our lines, beneath that July sun,
The back-bone of Rebellion broke, and Gettysburg was won.
And when the smoke had rolled away, 'twas a sickening sight indeed,
For Pickett's line was swept away by the smoking guns of Meade.
'Twas a gallant charge – a forlorn hope – and well may history say:
'No grander charge the world had seen than Pickett's charge that day.'[19]

As historian Carol Reardon put it, 'in the immediate post-war years, the gallantry and sacrifice of the Confederate infantry on July 3 gave Southerners some much needed heroes to help ease the pangs of defeat and, in some ways, to validate and represent all that was right about the Lost Cause.'[20]

While Southerners praised themselves for their bravery in the war, they left out any consideration about the causes for which the war was fought. This was most striking in the early twentieth century with the publication of Thomas Dixon's novel *The Clansman* (1905) that was made into a hugely successful movie under the title *The Birth of a Nation* (1915, director David Wark Griffith). The novel and the movie reinterpreted the war and its consequences. It was no longer a good war to liberate an enslaved population but a conflict that allowed a group of rude and uncivilized blacks to have a say in government affairs. Another less known example of this reinterpretation of the war in the early twentieth century was LaSalle Corbell Pickett's book *The Bugles of Gettysburg* (1913). LaSalle Corbell Pickett, General Pickett's widow, made it her life's task to turn her husband into a war hero. She sought to convince the reader that the charge of 3 July should not be remembered as a defeat but as an act of valor:

> Pickett's men started on their death-march. They moved out from the forest calmly and steadily as if drawn up for a grand review. Two great armies watched them in admiring awe. Over on Seminary Hill the man on the gray horse looked on at the costly sacrifice the South was making for its cause. On Cemetery Height the men in blue were silent, watching the majestic scene. The rhythmic motion of the thousands of tramping feet had so taken possession of Garnett s imagination that he seemed to have been for ages walking in that solemn procession. The resounding tramp, tramp, tramp filled all the world. Garnett's gaze was fixed on the Commander far away in front, leading his men into the flames of battle with an air of chivalrous lightness and grace such as he might have worn had he led them in picturesque procession to enliven a festal day. He marveled over the daring that could enable a man to maintain a poise like that at the open door of death. He thought of what he had heard a commanding officer say: 'Give George Pickett an order and he will storm the gates of hell.'[21]

A generation after Dixon and Corbell Pickett, Southern writer William Faulkner turned Gettysburg into one of the most crucial events defining the modern American South. In his 1948 novel *Intruder in the Dust*, he wrote:

> For every southern boy fourteen years old, not once but whenever he wants it, there is the instant when it's still not yet two o'clock on that July afternoon in 1863, the brigades are in position behind the rail fence, the guns are laid and ready in the woods and the furled flags are already loosened to break out and Pickett himself with his long oiled ringlets and his hat in one hand probably and his sword in the other looking up the hill waiting for Longstreet to give the word and it's all in the balance, it hasn't happened yet, it hasn't even begun yet, it not only hasn't begun yet but there is still time for it not to begin against that position and those

> circumstances . . . that moment doesn't need even a fourteen year-old boy to think This time. Maybe this time with all this much to lose and all this much to gain: Pennsylvania, Maryland, the world, the gold dome of Washington itself.[22]

While the South used tales of Gettysburg heroism to overcome the defeat in the Civil War, the North came to understand the battle as a necessary precondition to turning the old Union into a new Nation. The climax of Civil War revisionism was reached during the 50th anniversary of the battle of Gettysburg. In his address on the battlefield in July 1913, President Woodrow Wilson reinterpreted the war not as a conflict to divide the country, but to bring it closer together: 'I need not tell you what the Battle of Gettysburg meant. These gallant men in blue and gray sit all about us here. Many of them met upon this ground in grim and deadly struggle. Upon these famous fields and hillsides their comrades died about them. In their presence it was an impertinence to discourse upon how the battle went, how it ended, what it signified! But fifty years have gone by since then, and I crave the privilege of speaking to you for a few minutes of what those fifty years have meant. What have they meant? They have meant peace and union and vigor, and the maturity and might of a great nation. How wholesome and healing the peace has been! We have found one another again as brothers and comrades in arms, enemies no longer, generous friends rather, our battles long past, the quarrel forgotten—except that we shall not forget the splendid valor, the manly devotion of the men then arrayed against one another, now grasping hands and smiling into each other's eyes. ... Come, let us be comrades and soldiers yet to serve our fellow-men in quiet counsel, where the blare of trumpets is neither heard nor heeded and where the things are done which make blessed the nations of the world in peace and righteousness and love.'[23]

Twenty-five years later, President Franklin D. Roosevelt addressed the veterans during the 75th anniversary of the battle of Gettysburg and said 'all of them we honor, not asking under which Flag they fought then – thankful that they stand together under one Flag now.' Wilson and Roosevelt completed the path that Lincoln had devised: Americans should not remember a war that divided a union, but one that forged a nation.[24]

A modern visitor to the Gettysburg battlefield notices statues and plaques pointing out the bravery of soldiers from the North and the South. Among the multitude of statues on the Gettysburg battlefields are two equestrian statues of Generals George Gordon Meade (dedicated in 1895, above) and

Robert E. Lee (erected 1917, below). Lee's statute is taller, but Meade's is displayed at a more prominent place. (Figs. 7.1 and 7.2)

The soldiers of each Southern state are being honoured by stone monuments that refer to the valor, heroism, and glory of the soldiers from each state. The plaque for the North Carolina soldiers reads as follows (Fig. 7.3):

NORTH CAROLINA
To the Eternal Glory of the North Carolina
Soldiers. Who on the Battlefield Displayed
Heroism Unsurpassed. Sacrificing all in Support of their Cause. Their Valorous Deeds
will be Enshrined in the Hearts of Men Long
after these Transient Memorials Have Crum-
bled to Dust.

This is the inscription on the South Carolina marker (Fig. 7.4):

That Men of Honor Might Forever Know
The Responsibilies of Freedom.
Dedicated South Carolinians Stood
And Were Counted for their Heritage
And Convictions. Abiding Faith in the
Sacredness of States Rights Provided
Their Creed. Here Many Earned
Eternal Glory.

Equestrian statues and state and regimental markers do not distinguish between aggressor and defender and do not refer to the causes of the war in any way. A visitor to the Gettysburg battlefield who had no prior knowledge of the American Civil War will leave the field in utter confusion about a war fought between two heroic armies for no discernible cause.

The battle of Gettysburg left a deep impact on American public culture. Few works question the causes of the conflict. Instead there is an attempt to fictionalize events to make them fit preconceived notions. One of the features authors emphasize was the joint suffering of Northern and Southern soldiers. MacKinley Kantor's 1934 novel *Long Remember* used a vivid language to describe what happened to soldiers in wartime when he describes preparations for a battlefield amputation: 'An invisible broth, the smell of perspiration and unwashed bodies and fresh blood, saturated the rooms. The surgeon and his assistants kept the library door closed – that was where they did awful things, that was where they had the tubs and dishpans, and where the yells came from.'[25]

The movie *Gettysburg* (1993, directed by Ronald F. Maxwell) presents an epic confrontation of heroic soldiers and officers. There is no reference to the causes of the conflict. Slavery is only mentioned in passing. In one scene, a Confederate prisoner of war asks a Union officer why the Northerners have attacked the South. The officer replies that they have done so in order to liberate the slaves and to preserve the Union, 'to free the slaves of course. And to protect the Union.' Both men were standing up for what they believed to be right. 'All characters in the film have noble reason to take part in the fighting,' as historian Jeffrey M. Parrotte points out. 'With all of these causes presented in equal light, it is nearly impossible to choose which characters are supposed to represent good and which are supposed to represent evil.'[26]

In 2003, Newt Gingrich and William R. Forstchen published *Gettysburg: A Novel About the Civil War*. Gingrich, an historian and member of the American House of Representatives from 1979 to 1999 for a Georgia district, is the author of a number of historical novels. In *Gettysburg* they present a contrafactual version of events. Their hero is Robert E. Lee. The novel begins with an inner monologue in which Lee ruminates about his values, desires and virtues. According to Gingrich and Forstchen, Lee suffered from hero worship by his soldiers: 'They make me too much a statue of marble, he thought. I have already become a legend to them. Legends can create victory. Convince your men that they can win, convince the enemy they cannot win, and the battle is half decided before the first shot is fired.' In Gingrich's and Forstchen's version of events, Lee did not order a straight assault on the Union troops, but bypassed them and defeated them in the (fictional) battle of Union Mills. The Confederates had won the battle but not yet the war.

> Typical of most newspapers, the news was distorted or simply untrue. The lead story declared that the Army of the Potomac was totally destroyed. That was not true. Three corps, the Third, Fifth, and Eleventh, had gotten out with some semblance of command structure intact. Yes, the victory was complete, but still, their total annihilation, another Cannae or Waterloo, had eluded him.

Lee had hoped that the battle of Gettysburg would end the war. 'It had not, though this campaign was a triumph beyond any ever achieved by Confederate arms.'[27]

In 2012, Ralph Peters, a former US-Army officer presented yet another Civil War novel entitled *Cain at Gettysburg*. Peters is interested in a realistic portrayal of the life and travails of soldiers in the nineteenth century. There are swarms of insects that make the soldiers' life miserable, the officers swear and everyone suffers from the all encompassing smell of the dead and of excrements. On the evening of 2 July, General Meade met his commanding generals in a small room: 'A single candle lit the room where Meade's corps commanders gathered. The shanty stank of sweat and tobacco, of ill-digested meals and burned gunpowder. Every man was exhausted, but the mood was far from despondent.' Peters was not impressed with the way the Confederates conducted the war. In a final scene he described that the British observer Col. Arthur Freemantle relieved himself among a stand of trees thinking to himself: 'As an officer, he had nothing to learn from these American amateurs. No English general would even order his infantry to attack en masse across open fields in the face of entrenched modern weapons. It just wasn't done.'[28]

Conclusions

The battle of Gettysburg today has taken on a double meaning for the United States. It was initially an important engagement in the Civil War. Some historians are of the opinion that the South was never closer to victory than in the afternoon of 3 July when Pickett's men advanced toward union soldiers along Cemetery Ridge. What if they had overwhelmed the defenders and had moved on to Harrisburg, Philadelphia or Washington? The Northerners almost certainly would have continued the fight until they had won. But perhaps the Confederates were too strong after all and the people in the North had become weary about sending their young men in a bloody war for an abstract legal principle.

Gettysburg has also assumed a second, mythical dimension. Since 1865, every generation of Americans has re-interpreted the Civil War 'to support its own ideological agendas' as historians Alice Fahs and Joan Waugh put it.[29] For veterans of the Union Army, the war stood for the fight between good and evil. The South sought to compensate its defeat by stressing the valour and virtue of its troops.

Remembering the battle of Gettysburg has assumed almost a life of its own. Americans remember heroism on all sides but leave out inconvenient details such as the goals of the warring parties in the confrontation. The U.S. Military Academy in West Point even honours its former superintendent Robert E. Lee – a man who had violated his oath to the United States, who had turned his gun against the Union and was responsible for the death of many thousands of people - by naming a building after him.

Chapter 8

Busting the Myths of the Somme 1916

Mungo Melvin[1]

Introduction

On the 100th anniversary of the beginning of the Battle of the Somme (1 July 2016), British newspaper headlines were dominated by one story – the back-stabbing of one 'brexiteer' or Brexit-supporter, Boris Johnson, by another, Michael Gove, during the race for the British premiership, following the national referendum on membership of the European Union (EU) on 23 June. Due space was nevertheless found to reflect on the sacrifice of the fallen of the Somme. The *Daily Mirror*, for example, reminded its readers of their suffering, and that 'many of the men who died did not have the vote and their suffering played a part in obtaining rights and freedoms we should cherish'.[2] Putting such polemics aside, the irony of a narrow majority of the British electorate voting to leave the EU almost 100 years after the Somme, on whose foreign field – the rolling chalk lands of France's Picardy – so many hundreds of thousands of Britons (and their comrades from the Dominions) fought and fell, was entirely lost.

The centennial reportage of 1 July 2016 reflects the national grand narrative and associated mythologies of the deeply controversial battle of the Somme in 1916. Traditionally, it has been described as a heroic, largely *British*, rather than a coalition struggle. Furthermore, it was a battle that had to be fought, whatever the cost, even if it were to prove, as historian A. J. P. Taylor claimed in 1963, 'an unredeemed defeat'.[3] A generation earlier, in 1940 when Britain found itself once again at war with Germany, Arthur Bryant lamented the loss of the 'very flower of England' in 'the great slaughter of the Somme'.[4] For the centenary in 2016, the Royal British Legion produced an interpretational 'toolkit' to explain the battle, declaring:

> The Battle of the Somme was fought at such terrible cost that it has come to symbolise the tragic futility of the First World War.

Its first day of conflict remains the bloodiest day in the history
of the British Army and it was felt deeply at home, in particular
in those towns and villages which had raised Pals battalions and
suffered terrible losses.[5]

Such wording only serves to accentuate the popular received wisdom of
the Somme as an unmitigated disaster, confirming A. J. P. Taylor's view
that the battle 'set the picture by which future generations saw the First
World War; brave helpless soldiers; blundering obstinate generals; nothing
achieved'.[6]

'Setting the picture' is code for the establishment of a British myth,
a 'sacred story', to employ the sociological description of Bronislaw
Malinowski (the noted inter-war professor of anthropology at the London
School of Economics), who defined a myth, inter alia, in terms of that
which 'expresses, enhances and codifies belief'.[7] Although much of this
scholar's work focused on ethnography and the study of early societies,
popular myths – as opposed to idle tales or manifest falsehoods (what is
now being termed as 'fake news') – continue to feature in the modern world
and find widespread resonance. As cherished perceptions and perspectives,
they contain far more than a grain of truth. Those of the First World War
and the battle of the Somme are not exceptional. As a 'special class of
stories,[8] they can become statements of national faith and identification –
not only as we like to see ourselves, but also as to the manner in which we
commemorate in solemn ritual the sacrifice of the fallen and extol their
virtues of valour and commitment to present-day generations.

This chapter attempts to address some of the peculiarly British
misconceptions concerning the 1916 Somme offensive. The first concerns
the myth that the 'battle' was effectively lost on the first day, when nearly
20,000 British troops of Kitchener's New Army volunteers were killed
in action or died of their wounds. In fact, the *campaign* on the Somme
continued for another 140 days until 18 November 1916.[9] At this stage of
the First World War, the British Army consisted of a medley of formations
and units of various types – by no means were all soldiers members of the
New Army. The first conscripts arrived in France during the course of July
1916 to refill units that had been badly smashed up on the first days of
the fighting at the Somme.[10] Secondly, most British accounts of the battle
exclude the very significant French contribution (Fig. 8.1), a historical
distortion that is reinforced by overly concentrating on the events of 1 July
1916 (when the British proportion of the fighting was much larger than

that of the French) at the expense of the major engagements that followed during a protracted campaign. Thirdly, while popular British accounts accentuate British incompetence – particularly during the crass blunders of 1 July 1916 – far less attention is paid to the German defensive skill. Jack Sheldon and Andrew Macdonald provide honourable exceptions.[11] While British historians such as John Terraine, Paddy Griffith and Gary Sheffield have largely exposed the first myth, they do not examine the French contribution in any detail.[12] These authors, however, suggest that the British Army's experience of the Somme prompted the innovative 'learning curve' that ensured ultimate victory in 1918.

The First Day of the Somme

The British Army that attacked on 1 July 1916 was composed of pre-war professional regulars and reservists; part-timers of the Territorial Force who had volunteered for overseas service; and the growing cohorts of Kitchener's New Army.[13] Many of the new recruits were concentrated in so-called 'Pals' or 'Chums' battalions – 'bands of brothers' drawn from a particular place, workforce or sporting fraternity who had signed up together. Of the thirteen infantry divisions which went 'over the top' on that fateful day, four were regular, two territorial and seven New Army.[14]

The first day of the Somme in 1916 was not the first bloodletting of the New Army, as is commonly supposed. Three New Army divisions fought during the Gallipoli campaign of 1915: the 10th (Irish), the 11th (Northern) and the 13th (Western) Divisions. At the battle of Loos, the British Army's first large-scale offensive on the Western Front, which opened on 25 September 1915, the 9th and 15th (Scottish), among the six British divisions which attacked, suffered appalling casualties. So too did the 20th and 24th Divisions, which were badly handled on the second day, and the 12th (Eastern) Division later in the battle. No fewer than forty-five Scottish battalions were involved in the battle of Loos. Thus for many Scottish communities, tragedy struck already a year before the Somme.

Martin Middlebrook's best-selling *The First Day on the Somme* (1971) provided much impetus for the popular fascination with this, the bloodiest day of the battle of 1916.[15] The severe losses of the New Army battalions, including the Northern English Pals, triggered deep public remorse in 1916 and continue to evoke emotions today. Many of these units were involved in a series of entirely fruitless attacks on 1 July 1916. Such miserable failures served to accentuate the stereotypical gap between the brave volunteers and their supposedly incompetent generals, as portrayed on stage (1963) and on film (1969) in 'Oh What a Lovely War!' and in the BBC television series of *Blackadder Goes Forth* (1989). Middlebrook's analysis provides weight to the perception that the New Army formations suffered disproportionally. Of the thirty-two British battalions that suffered more than 500 casualties (representing approximately half their strength) on 1 July 1916, no fewer than twenty were from Kitchener's New Army. Of the remaining twelve, seven were Regular, four were Territorial Force and one was from the British Empire.[16]

Gary Sheffield describes the experience of the 31st Division (part of VIII Corps) on 1 July 1916 in its abortive operation to capture the fortified village of Serre on the left flank of General Sir Henry Rawlinson's Fourth Army. Commanded by Major General Wanless O'Gowan, this 'Pals formation *par excellence*', in Sheffield's words, comprised 'battalions from the industrial towns and cities of northern England: Bradford, Leeds, Barnsley, Durham, Halifax, Accrington; four battalions from Hull (Commercials, Tradesmen, Sportsmen and the aptly named T'Others); and the Sheffield City Battalion'. The two attacking infantry brigades (the 93rd and 94th) 'immediately walked into heavy fire'.[17] Only a handful of men managed to reach Serre before they were either killed or captured.

The figures hide infinite personal and communal pain. The 31st Division lost 3,593 men, the 31st Division's right neighbour to the south of Serre, the 4th Division, 4,692, and to the immediate south, the 29th Division took even worse losses in its attack towards Beaumont Hamel: 5,240 men, and all that on the opening day of the Somme offensive. Of the 34th Division, which comprised the 101st, the 102nd Tyneside Scottish and the 103rd Tyneside Irish Brigades, no fewer than 6380 men fell.

In contrast, the most effective British divisional attacks of 1 July 1916 were carried out by the 'Immortal' 7th Division (XV Corps), a regular formation that had fought with distinction at First Ypres and at Loos, which captured Mametz; and by two New Army divisions (the 18th and the 30th of XIII Corps), who took their objectives near and at Montauban.[18] Although a detailed analysis of the reasons for the relative success on the right flank of the Fourth Army's attack as opposed to the left (VIII Corps) and centre (X and III Corps) goes beyond the scope of this chapter, all three divisions concerned benefited from good training and inspired leadership – particularly in respect of the 18th Division commanded by Major General Ivor Maxse.

The significant losses of these three 'successful' divisions (7th, 18th and 30th, with 3,410, 3,115 and 3,011 casualties respectively) in the south of the British sector at the Somme demonstrate that there were few cheap wins to be scored on the Western Front when fighting the German Army. Where the British attacks stalled or were beaten back, representing the majority across the battlefront, a failure to cut the wire, and to suppress or destroy the German machine-gunners and artillerymen represented the root causes. The general inability to exploit local successes merely compounded the sense of frustration and failure, however heroically the initial assault was conducted. The experience of the 36th (Ulster) Division, which took in gallant action the Schwaben Redoubt, Thiepval, on the left flank of the X Corps attack, but could not hold this objective, is a case in point.

Had the operations in the centre and north by III, X and VIII Corps achieved successes comparable to those of XV and XIII Corps, then it might be argued that the appalling losses suffered by the British Army on 1 July 1916 would have been more acceptable. Any such cold logic of gain versus pain, however, cannot obscure the fact that the casualty rate incurred by the British on that fateful day at the Somme was far too high for any army, however brave, to sustain. Yet the shocking toll of the first day – 52,470 officers and men, of whom 19,240 were killed and 35,493 were wounded – was wholly exceptional; such 'freak' losses never recurred during the remainder of the offensive. Facts, however, often spoil a good story. Writing of the Leeds Pals, who lost 528 officers and men on 1 July 1916, journalist Jayne Dawson declared to the readers of the *Yorkshire Evening Post* nearly a century later that 'the carnage was repeated the next day, and the next, and for every day after that until four mad months had passed'. Her account of the Leeds Pals continued:

> Their coats were mud-sodden, their legs were protected only by the inadequate cloth wrappings of the soldier's uniform. In their hands they clutched rifles they would never use, for in moments a storm of bullets had cut through their soft clothes and weary bodies, and they were dead. Our young Leeds men were not so much beaten as wiped out. At 7.20 a.m. with fearful, pounding hearts, they began to run blindly at their enemy. By 7.30 a.m. a city of mothers had lost their sons, wives were widows and children fatherless. [19]

Although the experience of the Leeds Pals was unexceptional on that first day, the battle was not abandoned. The British Army fought on for a further four and a half months, which would appear to compound the futility.

119

Hence such accounts serve for many as damning 'proof' of the failure of British strategy and the inadequacy of the British Army's generalship at the Somme, if not for the First World War as a whole.[20]

John Terraine, perhaps the greatest British myth-buster of the First World War, offers some interesting statistics that challenge the popular view of the Somme (1 July – 18 November 1916). Of the five major battles fought by the British Army during the period 1916–1918, it represented the *second-lowest* casualty rate (2,950 a day), with Third Ypres of 1917 (Passchendaele – another byword for tragedy and futility) the lowest (2,121). The greatest daily loss occurred during the opening weeks of the German offensive of 1918, the 'Kaiser's battle'. Over the 41-day period of 21 March – 30 April 1918, the BEF in defence, delaying battle and retreat lost 239,793 men, representing 5,848 men a day. Hence contrary to popular myth, offensive actions are not necessarily more expensive than defensive ones.[21] If there is one enduring lesson of war, typically, whatever the type of operation, whether successful or unsuccessful, battle does not come cheaply when fighting a well-equipped and well-led opponent.

Three further points stand out from any comparative analysis of the first day of the Somme in 1916. First, the failures of the British attacks at Serre, Beaumont Hamel, Thiepval, La Boisselle and Fricourt fit the myth of 'unredeemed defeat' far better than the relative gains scored at Mametz and Montauban. Secondly, if the memorialisation of the battlefield provides any indication, it would appear that the fate of a northern Pals battalion generates more interest today than that of a regular or territorial unit. The fallen of whatever origin, nationality or ethnicity, surely remain 'equal unto God'. Thirdly, as John Terraine stresses, the British had 'no monopoly of catastrophe' in 1916. For example, during the opening week of the Russian Brusilov offensive (4–10 June) on the Eastern Front, the Austro-Hungarian Army lost a staggering 280,000 men, equating to 40,000 a day.[22] None the less, the near destruction of so many Pals battalions on 1 July 1916 represents the most compelling and enduring story of the Somme specifically and of the First World War generally from a British perspective. As historian Peter Simkins observed in 1991, 'The slaughter of Britain's citizen soldiers on the Somme was a major psychological shock and is still planted deep in the nation's collective folk memory'.[23] For France and Germany, memories of the terrible sacrifices at the battle of Verdun, which had reached its 132nd day on 1 July 1916, evoke similar feelings.

The Forgotten French Army of the Somme

Designed at the outset as a joint Franco-British offensive, the envisaged French contribution immediately north, and to the south, of the river Somme was progressively reduced as the battle of Verdun took its toll. Commencing on 21 February 1916, the fighting at the 'Mill on the Meuse' consumed increasing numbers of French formations. What originally had been conceived as constituting the predominant Allied attack at the Somme became a supporting one to the British; by early June, the French role had been 'reduced to covering the British right'. Furthermore, in late May the French had already demanded a sustained effort by the British in order to wear down the Germans if a 'decision' (meaning a decisive victory) were not obtained during the opening phase of the battle. In this case, the French commander-in-chief, Marshal Joseph Joffre, anticipated a 'protracted struggle', involving a 'long battle of attrition … until the enemy was weakened beyond recovery'.[24] Bearing in mind that the Somme offensive represented by far the biggest concentration of British effort to date on the Western Front, both British and French expectations of success on the eve of battle were high, perhaps unduly so.

On 1 July 1916, five French divisions of the Sixth Army attacked, representing well less than half of the British employment of troops that day.[25] By the end of the offensive, however, the French had committed no fewer than forty-four divisions to the Somme campaign, only eight fewer than the British total of fifty-two.[26] Until the appearance of William Philpott's seminal, prize-winning work, *Bloody Victory* (2009), however, no serious British military historian had paid anything like sufficient attention to the role of the French Army at the Somme.[27]

There is a distinct pattern in many of these British accounts. Typically the French are mentioned as mere adjuncts in accounts that seek to explain why the British Army lost so many men on the first day, and then continued to fight for so long despite the enormous casualties incurred. The cost of 419,654 killed, wounded and missing appears vastly disproportional for the relatively small gain of terrain made – an advance of 11 kilometres. In contrast, the actions of the French, who lost 204,000 men during the course of the campaign, appear but incidental to this story, except where they lie along the boundary between the two armies. Thus British readers should be forgiven for gaining the mistaken impression that the battle of the Somme was largely a British-German affair. Yet it is surely significant that the greatest advance made on 1 July 1916 by any British formation (and for the least casualties) was that by the 89th Brigade, which attacked on the right flank of the 30th Division (XIII Corps) alongside the 39th French Division (XX Corps). French heavy artillery had helped smash the German defenders of Montauban. Hence local battlefield success here stemmed from Allied co-operation.

By the close of the Somme campaign on 18 November, the French frontage and the area of ground gained since 1 July roughly equalled those of the British. For the majority of the fighting, both nations contributed two field armies apiece: the British, the Fourth and Fifth; the French, the Sixth and Tenth. Hence the campaign was much more of a partnership of Entente arms than might be supposed from a cursory glance at the events of 1 July 1916. Quite simply, without the British Army there would have been no battle of the Somme; but without the very important French contribution, the campaign could never have been sustained for so long and with such destructive pressure on the out-numbered and hard-pressed German defenders.

William Philpott has done the historiography of the First World War generally, and of the Somme specifically, an enormous service in addressing the French role in the campaign and reassessing the strategic impact of the Allied offensive as a whole. Unlike any other British military historian to date he has taken the pains not only to describe the character of the three armies involved (British, French and German), but also to narrate and analyse French operations in unprecedented detail. Apart from describing the French attacks of 1 July and the remainder of that month, Philpott devotes considerable attention to the actions of the French Sixth and Tenth Armies from August 1916 onwards, commanded by generals Marie-Émile Fayolle and Joseph Alfred Micheler respectively. By then, the river Somme acted as the French inter-army boundary with the Sixth fighting to the north and the Tenth to the south. Marshal Ferdinand Foch coordinated the operations of both armies.

In Philpott's view, Micheler is the 'forgotten commander of the Somme'.[28] Yet the forces the French general commanded were considerable: from September 1916, no fewer than six infantry and one cavalry corps, representing fourteen infantry and three cavalry divisions. Of these formations, ten infantry divisions attacked on 4 September on a seventeen-kilometre front towards the Santerre plain. Far away from British sight and mind, and on a divergent axis to the attacks of the French Sixth and the British Fourth and Fifth Armies, other British accounts of the Somme neglect this operation almost completely. Although not a stunning success, largely due to an insufficient concentration of heavy artillery (ironically repeating the British failure of 1 July), Micheler's attack added to the cumulative pressure on the German defenders.

The Sixth Army, which had supported Tenth Army's attack, staged its own major operation north of the Somme in mid-September. On a narrow frontage north of the Somme, Fayolle concentrated three corps in an attempt to break the Germans' third and final position, and to turn the German defences and vital logistics hub of Péronne. Launched on 12 September, the attack took 6 kilometres of the German line; at the furthest extent of the advance at Bouchavesnes, French troops had advanced a further 3 kilometres beyond. Yet the German defenders were able to seal off this penetration, and no French operational breakthrough occurred. None the less, the French gains on both sides of the Somme during the first two weeks of September 1916 were significant.

On the German side, Colonel Fritz von Lossberg, appointed on 3 July as chief of staff of the German Second Army, and later of the First Army on 19 July 1916, became the mastermind of the German defence during the Somme campaign. Commenting on the loss of Bouchavesnes, Lossberg described the French attack there as 'strong and deeply echeloned'. The capture of Bouchavesnes marked the high water mark of the French operations north of the Somme; significantly, the village is graced with an imposing statue of Marshal Foch. The French effort here and to the south of the river, however, continued for two further months. In particular, Sixth Army's prolonged and intense fight for the fortified village of Sailly-Saillisel from October to early November 1916, almost totally ignored by British historians, remains worthy of study. This action represented the 'anticlimactic finale' of Sixth Army's offensive at the Somme.[29]

Meanwhile, the Tenth Army mounted a series of attacks throughout October, making slow and slim territorial gains against a determined German 'active' defence that bent, springing occasionally back in counter attack, but did not buckle. While cumulative fatigue across the British, French and German armies mounted, combat in the mud of Picardy continued until the third week of November. This fact begs the question as to how the Germans were able to continue fighting for so long in an unforgiving attritional battle when confronting superior Allied forces, both in terms of men and materiel. British mythology fails to explain this apparent paradox.

The Beaten German Army of the Somme?

Although Lossberg assumed responsibility for the coordination of the German effort shortly after battle was joined, others deserve the credit for planning and conducting the German defence that withstood the first Allied assault on 1 July 1916, particularly in the British sector. The first advantages the Germans enjoyed in preparing their defence were of terrain and time. Having failed to exploit beyond Albert in October 1914, they chose to step back a short distance and select a dominating series of positions (such as the Thiepval spur), well suited for the fighting of a defensive battle. Largely speaking, the Germans enjoyed good observation over their opponents; conversely, the Allies often had to attack uphill. Secondly, the Germans were able to dig deeply into the firm Picardy chalk, constructing underground works that could withstand all but direct hits from the heaviest Allied shells. Thirdly, the defenders had over a year and a half on the Somme before the storm broke with the British bombardment on 24 June 1916 to develop not only their field fortifications and trench systems, but also to rehearse their artillery concentrations and counter attacks (Fig. 8.2). Simply said, thorough German planning and preparation made for the disaster of 1 July 1916 as much as the British Army's own shortcomings.[30]

Jack Sheldon has done for the German Army at the Somme what William Philpott has done for the French. He provides his readers with 'a series of snapshots of an army, which has spent too long in the shadows'. He traces the development of the German defence from late September 1914 through 1 July 1916 to December of that year.

The German defenders in the northern Somme sector (XIV Reserve Corps, commanded by Lieutenant General Hermann von Stein) were subordinated to General Fritz von Below's Second Army. They had benefited from lessons learned in countering a major attack by the Second French Army at Serre on 6–13 June 1915. Lieutenant General Franz Ludwig, *Freiherr* von Soden, the general officer commanding the 26th Reserve Infantry Division, later wrote that this engagement 'was an extremely instructive preparation for the Battle of the Somme, during which the experiences gained at Serre were of the greatest value'.[31] His division held the crucial sector from just south of Serre to Ovillers, just to the north of the Albert-Bapaume road, including the main bastion of the German defence on the Thiepval spur.

Andrew Macdonald devotes considerable attention to the immense effort Below's and Stein's troops spent in preparing to counter the anticipated British offensive during the spring and early summer of 1916. No detail was spared:

> Dugouts, headquarters and observation posts were mined into the ground and camouflaged, as were machine-gun posts. Trench walls were lined with chicken mesh, woven brushwood and planks of timber to reduce the likelihood of their collapsing under shellfire or rain. Duckboards were laid, more trenches were dug with steel loopholes for sentries built into their parapets. Barbed-wire entanglements were thickened, and further back more artillery pits were dug.[32]

As a result of this feverish effort, consuming vast amounts of materiel and requiring months of exhausting labour, by the opening of the British bombardment on 24 June, the German commanders

> ... had spent 18 months converting Second Army's position into a defensive fortress of barbed wire, earthworks and fortified villages. These, along with the infantry and artillery present, had been seamlessly integrated into a defensive system designed to stop any enemy attack with a tremendous weight of co-ordinated artillery and machine-gun firepower.[33]

Significantly, the German defences were at their strongest on the Somme battlefield from Serre to Fricourt. Further south, in the Mametz-Montauban-Curlu sector, they were generally less developed.[34] This deficiency explains why the British XIII and French XX 'Iron' Corps were able to make such relatively good progress here on 1 July 1916. Unfortunately for the British, the main weight of the Fourth Army's attack was applied to German strength in the Serre-Fricourt sector rather than against the comparative weakness further to the south.

There is no doubt that the Germans were extremely skilled and determined at the Somme: 1 July found their defensive system at its most effective. German operations thereafter proved less successful. Never again would the results of one day's fighting so favour the defender. Often their counter attacks proved extremely costly while their trenches and troop concentrations became increasingly subject to devastating British and French artillery fire. Terraine writes about the 'true texture of the Somme', in which Allied assaults were followed by German counter-attacks; and further assaults by counter attacks again.[35] German casualties steadily mounted as their senior commanders insisted that any ground lost had to be retaken immediately. On his first day in post on 3 July, Lossberg recorded:

> Everywhere I went … I issued the order on behalf of the commanding general to fight for every foot of ground and under no circumstances withdraw—even against the strongest fire and superior infantry attacks. Such an order had worked well during the battle in Champagne the previous autumn, and it also served us well in the Somme battle.[36]

Although only a colonel at the time, Lossberg exercised *Vollmacht* – the power of command – as a senior general staff officer on behalf of his commander-in-chief. Thus he was able to direct immediate measures to shore up the German line, whose defenders were exhausted by the Allied onslaught.

Throughout the campaign, the Germans continued to execute local counter attacks, but with one exception in mid September south of Bouchavesnes, they never mustered sufficient resources to mount a major operation.[37] Broadly speaking, the Allies held the initiative throughout on the Somme, able to decide where and when to unleash a fresh blow. With determined troops on both sides, and apparently ample resources available, it is easy to understand how the battle became such a prolonged attritional fight. German losses during the Somme campaign of 1916 accumulated to at least 400,000 and were probably nearer 500,000. While the fighting here might have proved the German Army's 'muddy grave', it continued to fight until 11 November 1918.

The 'Learning Curve' and the Tank

Soldiers adapt and innovate in combat and the technology of war continues to evolve. The degree to which the participants learned on the Somme battlefield has entered military mythology. On 1 July 2016, *The Times* commented that although the battle of the Somme 'was a slaughter', it was 'not in vain', for 'it allowed Allied commanders to learn how to fight a mechanised war on an unprecedented scale'; and that 'it was knowledge that ultimately helped to secure victory.'[38] This description reflects the notion of a 'Learning Curve' – one that posits a steady improvement in the British Army's tactical technique and battlefield technology not only during the course of the Somme campaign in 1916, but also throughout the First World War from 1914 to 1918. This claim has both historical and literary resonance. In his memoir *Soldier From the Wars Returning* (1965), Charles Carrington asserted that 'The British Army learned its lesson the hard way, during the middle part of the Somme battle, and, for the rest of the war, was the best army in the field'.[39] Yet this improving army could not master the enemy defensive system at the battle of Third Ypres between July and November 1917, and was badly handled during the German offensive in the spring of 1918.

There are difficulties with the British 'learning curve' thesis, which is better explained as a process of competitive adaption and development.[40] First, a regular progression in tactical technique did not occur on the Western Front: a series of attacks at the Somme and in subsequent battles demonstrated limited learning since 1 July 1916. Secondly, and this explains in part the preceding issue, the Germans learned at the same time. British historians such as Paddy Griffith cite the adoption of amended tactics and new organisations within the BEF by reference to British General Staff training publications written during the battle of the Somme and in its aftermath.[41] The Germans, however, produced their own reports from the battle and adjusted their tactics. One example stands out: the abandonment of the costly 'ground must be held at all costs' dictum, and the adoption of a more flexible doctrine of 'elastic defence', encapsulated in the *Principles of Command in the Defensive Battle in Position Warfare* (1 December 1916). This new system of defence in depth was designed to force the attacker to expose and expend himself while the defender preserved his strength, counter-attacking when the conditions were favourable.[42]

Sheffield makes much of the 'incomplete victory' resulting from the operation executed by the British XV and XIII Corps on 14 July 1916. Following a five-minute snap bombardment, in a surprise dawn attack five assaulting divisions captured 8 km of the German second position running from Bazentin-le-Petit Wood through Longueval to Trônes Wood. This spectacular initial success, however, could not be exploited. Only a small cavalry force, drawn from the 7th Dragoon Guards and the 2nd Deccan Horse, was on hand by evening to continue the attack. Although the cavalry achieved some local success between High Wood and Longueval, their action proved far too little and far too late to make any substantial impression on the German defence. Sheffield thinks 'a larger body of cavalry ... and an infantry force ... to link up with it' would plausibly have allowed the British to advance almost a mile and a half from Bazentin

Ridge. Moreover, he thinks the capabilities of Kitchener's Armies in general and artillery in particular have been underestimated [43]

It would take much time, experimentation and effort, however, before the British artillery 'system' was perfected in the battles of 1917 and 1918. None the less, German accounts of the Somme attest to the destructive power of the British artillery throughout the campaign.

The next big British offensive on the Somme took place on 15 September 1916. Once again accurate, concentrated artillery played a very big part in the opening successes scored. Yet the debut of the tank in land warfare on that day has prompted considerable attention in the history of the battle. Terraine points out the 'adamantine myth' that resulted. Of the forty-nine Mk I tanks were available on that first day of the tank, only thirty-two were brought into action. Far from being war-winning wonder weapons, the first tanks were slow, crude and clumsy machines. Although spectacular in innovation terms, and representing a welcome boost for British propaganda, the tactical impact of the tank at the Somme on 15 September 1916 was minimal.

A tank may have been 'walking up the High Street of Flers with the British Army cheering behind', as one airman reported, but no decisive operational level breakthrough of the German lines took place here, or anywhere else, for that matter, on the Somme.[44] Churchill, however, believed that the great potential of the tank had been thrown away in its premature employment in insufficient numbers. As Minister of Munitions in 1918 he called for a 'scheme of attack by 10,000 fighting tanks, backed by 10,000 tracked support vehicles'. Any procurement on this scale represented pure fantasy: the greatest number of tanks fielded by the British Army that year was 342 heavy Mk Vs and 72 Medium A 'Whippet' tanks at the Battle of Amiens on 8 August 1918. Their attrition in battle due to either enemy fire or mechanical breakdown was enormous: only six tanks were in action on 12 August on the fifth day of battle.[45]

Conclusion: a Battle Lost or Won?

Apart from the disputed numbers of casualties, the outcome of the battle of the Somme in 1916 remains mired in controversy. Expert historical opinion remains divided. Robert Foley, for example, considers the battle 'a German victory' because 'the Entente forces were unable to break through the German defence and were unable to achieve the victory for which they hoped in July'.[46] William Philpott, however, regards it as an Allied 'Bloody

Victory'. Dependent on how one defines success, such judgements are neither right nor wrong. In eighteenth or nineteenth century warfare, when battles lasted a day or two, victory was usually ascribed to the side that remained on the field of battle and which had forced its opponent to quit fighting. In the protracted trench warfare of the First World War, when attritional battles typically lasted weeks or months, victory or defeat proved less easy to measure. Crude comparisons of casualties provide little reliable guide to the outcome. A much more useful method is to consider the *strategic* result in terms of what happened *after* the battle as opposed to concentrating on the first day. As the Germans conceded the field with their withdrawal over the winter 1916/1917 to the *Siegfried Stellung* (known to the Allies as the Hindenburg Line), the Somme campaign of 1916 can be regarded as an Allied strategic victory, but one won at an inordinate price.

The enduring power of a national mythos, particularly when reinforced by a strong sense of pathos, is reflected in the British government's programme of centenary commemorations of the First World War. When announced by David Cameron on 11 October 2012, it featured the battles on the Western Front particularly associated with blood and mud.[47] Hence the perceived failures of the Somme on 1 July 1916 and of Third Ypres on 31 July 1917 were selected rather than the successes of Messines (7 June 1917), Cambrai (20 November 1917) and Amiens (8 August 1918). Since it does not conform to the overwhelming perception of futility and failure, the counter-narrative of a necessary yet costly victory has little place in the First World War mythology.

In contrast, defeat is suppressed in the folk memory of the Second World War – perceived as a 'good' war (fighting Nazism) as opposed to a 'bad', wasteful and senseless one. While the evacuation at Dunkirk (27 May – 4 June 1940) is remembered as a brilliant operation, the preceding lost battle in France and Flanders is largely forgotten. Unsurprisingly, the successful Normandy landings on D-Day (6 June 1944) will surely always be commemorated more prominently than the monumental disaster at Singapore, which fell on 15 February 1942. This date marked, rather than the first day of the Somme, the greatest catastrophe in the British Army's history, in which the supposedly inferior Japanese 25th Army took no fewer than 80,000 British, Australian, Indian and Malay troops into captivity, adding to the 50,000 already lost during the fighting in Malaya. Defeat can only be accepted as a sacred story if the fight, however forlorn, is bravely and skilfully conducted over a considerable period of time.[48] Hence the Soviet Union was able to convert the gallant defence of Sevastopol during a

250-day siege by German and Romanian forces into a propaganda success when the city finally fell on 4 July 1942.[49] So some physical defeats can become virtual victories in national mythologies.

Whether or not the Somme campaign of 1916 proved a turning point in the First World War, its impact on all three armies involved remained significant. All armies learnt considerably from the battle, albeit at very great loss of both men and materiel. Their respective 'learning curves' were irregular and inconsistent. Moreover, no army of the Somme perfected a way in which to generate an operational level decision despite the steady incorporation of new technologies and tactics. While air power became increasingly important, artillery continued to be the principal destructive arm. The first British tanks proved little more than a novelty; German guns destroyed many which had not already broken down through mechanical failure. Yet the seeds of armoured warfare planted at the Somme were to sprout in the Second World War when the Somme battlefield was fought over once again in much faster and shorter battles of fire and movement.

It is incumbent on military historians to ponder not only on events past, but also to consider their implications for the present and future, and to challenge the popular folklore of a particular nation's story. Perhaps one of the biggest lessons from the Somme campaign of 1916, and of the First World War as a whole, is the enduring importance of multinational cooperation and cohesion. Hence the results of 23 June 2016 cannot be completely ignored alongside those of 1 July 1916.

Yet there is probably another equally fundamental conclusion to be drawn. There remains a vast gap between political rhetoric and reality today over the requirement for strong defences in order to deter war being waged in the first place. The costs of intense and prolonged conflict – as both the world wars of the Twentieth Century amply demonstrate – can be many times more than the required outlays in the years of peace. Speaking of the upcoming First World War centenaries, in 2012 David Cameron promised: 'to honour those who served, to remember those who died, and to ensure that the lessons learnt live with us forever.'[50] He might have reflected on whether, had Britain's armed forces (and particular the Army) been stronger in 1914, there might have been no need for a Somme campaign in 1916.

The grand strategic lesson is that peacetime economies in defence spending may prove short-sighted. Yet if the money remains tight, international alliances and systems of collective deterrence and defence become all the more important.

All armed forces have a duty to learn from previous conflicts, and to make balanced judgements as to the character of future war and to the technologies and tactics required to fight it. There are hard choices to be made and some fundamental truths to accept. Achieving advantage over a well-organised and equipped 'peer' enemy may prove extremely challenging. Hence seldom there are easy shortcuts to battlefield success, let alone to strategic victory. Thus it remains important to expose the myths of the Somme in 1916; and to study wars, campaigns and battles in their wider political, economic and social context.

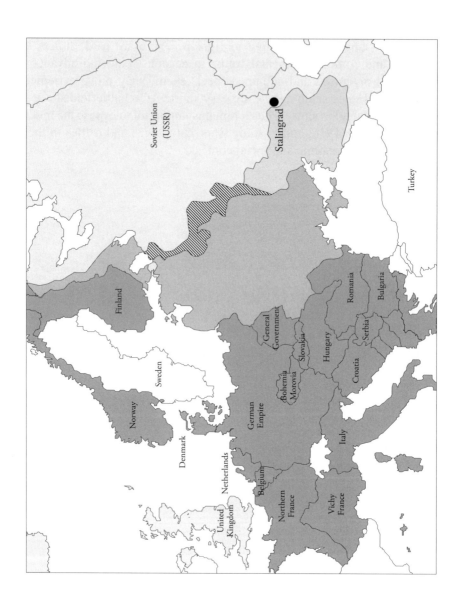

Chapter 9

Stalingrad 1942/43: The Anti-Myth of German National Identity

Andreas Behnke

National myths are meaningful narratives that structure the past, present and future of the imagined communities that nations are. They explain what brought us together, and what the 'strong reasons for staying together' are.[1] They are constitutive of our 'national identities', drawing lines between collective self and other by defining proper spaces and cultural symbols. As such, any political order, however rationally constructed, relies on a 'pre-rational' and 'pre-historical' (in the sense that history can only be written based on it) narrative. To 'disprove' the narrative and the myth it articulates means to 'disprove' a nation's existence.

War in general, and battles in particular, often play significant roles in national mythologies. The mythologization of battles seems to echo the medieval understanding of battle as a judgement of God, as an otherworldly act that founds the being of a nation as a political and historical community, or marks its demise. That battles are still assigned this metaphysical power is itself based on the Clausewitzean mythology of the Decisive Battle, derived from the experiences of the Napoleonic Wars, yet essentialised into a trans-historical truth or law by the Prussian Major-General.[2] To become part of a myth, to remain powerful enough to stir imaginations in a constant 'present' and to elide its confinement to the dusty pages of history books, a battle needs to present its 'other-worldly' nature by producing an unexpected, fascinating outcome, or by determining a dramatic beginning or end.[3] As any critical study of myths reveals, their relevance is always defined in a 'respective present' in terms of their ideological or political instrumentalisation and mobilisation. 'The 'then' (*Einst*) is only experienced in the 'now' (*Jetzt*).[4]

This necessity of contemporary relevance, however, can also negate or undermine the role of war and battle in national mythology. In 1882, in one of the classic texts on national identity, Ernest Renan could still assert that:

> The nation, like the individual, is the outcome of a long past of efforts, sacrifices, and devotions. Of all cults, that of the ancestors is the most legitimate: our ancestors have made us what we are. A heroic past with great men and glory (I mean true glory) is the social capital upon which the national idea rests. These are the essential conditions of being a people: having common glories in the past and a will to continue them in the present; having made great things together and wishing to make them again.[5]

Yet in present times, at least in some countries the role of sacrifice and glory seem to be much diminished when it comes to providing those reasons why we should be together. Be it because we are living in a 'post-heroic age', which no longer knows 'wars fought for great national purposes that can evoke public fervour by armed forces that represent the aroused nation',[6] or be it because of the more recent experience of spectacular failures of the wars in Afghanistan, Iraq and Libya that devalue the metaphysical attributes of historical wars, fighting battles no longer seem to hold our imagination to quite the same extent as before. As Georges Duby wrote, 'Our age chases battles out of its memory and justly so'.[7] Some national myths even build on the explicit rejection of warfare, thus problematizing the role of violence in the constitution of political order and national identity. Prime among these cultures is Germany, or more precisely, the Federal Republic of Germany (FRG), the successor state of the Nazi Third Reich, the regime behind the criminal and genocidal military campaigns of the Second World War. Given that the Nazi regime was (and remains) the constitutive other of the second democratic German republic,[8] the former regime and its mythology of warfare as a continuous 'struggle for survival' had to be rendered as aberration from German history. Hence the battles of the Second World War can never become a straight-forward part of the national mythology of post-1945 and post-1990 Germany. In fact, so strong was the official condemnation of the Nazis' military campaigns that it also erased any reference to the wars Germany fought prior to 1933. The frequently circulated argument that there was a direct line 'from Bismarck to Hitler', from the militarism of Prussia to the wars of expansion and genocide of the Nazis, made the military history of Germany unavailable for the construction of a modern political mythology. A Zero Hour (*Stunde Null*) rather than a particular battle was the 'founding moment' of what was to become the FRG.[9]

One battle of the Second World War still stands out and resonates, if ever more faintly, within the German collective memory of that war, at least for the generation that still experienced it, albeit as children. To the extent that there is still a cross-generational German collective memory, the battle is still imagined as the greatest and costliest defeat of the Germany armies in the Soviet Union, marking the turning point of the war in popular perception.[10] The destruction of the 6th Army, of some 200,000 German soldiers and their allied forces under Lieutenant-General Paulus demonstrated the clear possibility, perhaps even likelihood, of a German defeat in the war.[11]

So the centrality of 'Stalingrad' in the German understanding of the Second World War cannot be doubted. However, this does not mean that the battle served as a mythical event in post-war Germany alone. In fact, the Nazis themselves already struggled to mythologize the military disaster. The Nazi's propaganda minister, Joseph Goebbels, pursued three goals in this regard: to maintain the credibility of the Nazi propaganda machine, which meant that the defeat had to be acknowledged; to turn the military defeat into a moral victory;[12] and thereby to re-arrange conditions within the Third Reich in support of 'total war'. 'The dead should commit the living to an ultimate effort, their sacrifice was supposed to become the standard for what could be expected from people to achieve the *Endsieg* (the ultimate victory)'.[13] The resulting mythologizing emphasised this ultimate commitment: The Nazi's second-in-command Hermann Göring's speech on 31 January 1943, just days before the final surrender of the 6th Army, riffed on Simonides' famous epitaph for the Spartans:

> Stranger, announce to the Spartans that we
> Lie here obedient to their laws.[14]

Göring corrupted this into

> Come you to Germany, report that you have seen us lying in Stalingrad, just as the law, that is, the law of the security of our people, did command.[15]

Further underlining the appeal to blind faith and obedience expressed here was the *Reichsluftmarschall's* previous reference to the Nibelungen's demise in the halls of King Etzel (Attila the Hun), which in effect condemns the soldiers at Stalingrad to death:

> We know of a mighty and heroic tale of a battle without compare, it is called The Battle of the Nibelungs. They too stood in a hall ablaze with fire, slaked their thirst with their own blood, but they fought to the end. Such a battle is raging there today, and in a thousand years every German, with a holy shiver, will still speak of this struggle with awe and remember that despite it all, Germany's victory was decided there.[16]

But at this moment, any attempt to create a foundational myth out of the 'sacrifice' of some 200,000 soldiers could only fail, as the battle became the harbinger of defeat and disaster. The reference to the *Nibelungenlied* and its final mass slaughter perhaps betrays more about the situation than Göring intended. After all, the end of the *Nibelungenlied* does not provide a myth for the 'rebirth of a nation' but rather its demise, with the depiction of gruesome and ultimately meaningless violence.

For the post-war German national identity, 'Stalingrad' is too mobile a signifier and produces too many contradictions to serve as a national myth. The problem here is exposed by Roland Barthes' analysis of myths as semiological systems. Crucially, a myth is a 'second-order semiological system'.[17] As such, it draws on a semiological chain that exists before it. Hence, 'Stalingrad' as a mythological signifier already carries a large number of meanings and associations within it, a 'formless, unstable, nebulous condensation, whose unity and coherence are above all due to its function'.[18] Military-historical narratives usually refer to 'Stalingrad' in the context of the strategic errors committed by Hitler and his generals in over-extending German armed forces in the 1942 operation *Fall Blau*, ordering them to simultaneously attack Stalingrad and the Caucasus and dividing Army Group South into Army Groups A and B.[19] Photographic and cinematic images of the battle provide a signified or reference for the battle that suggests utter devastation and human suffering, chaos, and ultimately military surrender and defeat. The latter, as indicated above, is refracted by the knowledge that these are troops of the Nazi regime, and that this defeat was 'the beginning of the end'. Yet this consolation itself remains refracted by the testimony of unimaginable suffering and death.

The inherently complex structure of 'Stalingrad' as a semiotic system did not prevent its appropriation in the creation of private myths. For many of the German soldiers who fought in, and survived, Stalingrad, their suffering became a value in its own right, extracting them from the criminal nature of the war and the Nazi regime. 'The soldier's ability to endure suffering (*Leidensfähigkeit*) legitimises itself and downright becomes evidence of soldiers' performance, poise and decency'.[20]

Yet any reference to the 'sacrifice' of Germans soldiers is rendered problematic by the battle's historical context of a genocidal military campaign. With more recent historical research demonstrating the involvement of the *Wehrmacht* in the atrocities committed against Soviet and other civilians on the Eastern Front, the traditional assertion of the basic decency of 'the German Soldier' can no longer be maintained. While, as historian Bernd Wegner observes, 'Stalingrad' remains the only battle of the Second World War that is recognised in public memory and in commemorations beyond the private sphere,[21] its public presence is in fact quite limited, with the only Stalingrad memorial standing in the Limburg Cemetery in Germany. Regarding the battle's more recent political instrumentalisation, on 7 May 2015, German Foreign Minister (later President) Frank-Walter Steinmeier met with his Russian counterpart Sergei Lavrov in Volgograd (the former Stalingrad) to lay down wreaths at the Russian memorial for the battle on Mamayev Kurgan. The meeting gained particular poignancy against the backdrop of the Soviet occupation of the Crimea shortly before the anniversary and the continued efforts of Russian-supported troops to conquer territory in Eastern Ukraine.[22]

How then is the relevance of the historical event maintained and reproduced in public and popular imagination? Wegner points to the extensive body of popular literature that emerged in the 1940s and 1950s, and the relevance of the *Stalingradbünde* of old soldiers that kept the memory of the battle alive.[23] Yet with the passing of these soldiers, membership is quickly diminishing. In 2004, the *Bund ehemaliger Stalingradkämpfer e.V. Deutschland*, the registered association of former Stalingrad fighters in Germany, decided to dissolve.[24]

The present analysis therefore proceeds against the backdrop of a fading collective memory about the Second World War and its battles. It focuses on the visual 'archive' of Stalingrad; more specifically the films that 'preserve' and 're-enact' the battle for a non-specific and 'a-historical' audience. This analysis therefore assumes the particular relevance of visual, and in particular cinematic representations of warfare in post-heroic and post-modern societies.

As I have argued elsewhere,

> To Western societies today, warfare is primarily a mediated
> phenomenon. Thus, as we as ordinary citizens of Western
> societies no longer have the experience of warfare ... the mediated
> representation of warfare takes on a particular significance. ...
> [T]he articulation of official discourses on warfare and international
> politics cannot be properly understood without analysing their
> representations in popular culture, and the role played by these in
> the construction of the collective memory of these events.[25]

The primary medium for the vicarious experience of war is arguably film
with its ability to transport the spectator visually, if not emotionally, into
the midst of the battlefield.

The role of film becomes even more complicated when it enters the
realm of war and battles and their role in national mythology. Here, the
particular way the medium film structures our 'sense perceptions' creates
particular interferences with the structure of national myths. To understand
these issues, we need to begin with Walter Benjamin's analysis of film
(and photography) as the quintessential and most significant example of
the work of art in the age of mechanical reproduction.[26]

Unlike traditional works of art, of which we can usually identify an
original, even if the latter is copied or reproduced in a number of ways
throughout history, film is a medium for reproduction; to ask for an
'authentic copy' is clearly meaningless.[27] Film disseminates and distributes
its subject matter in the here and now. It is always present and in-the-
presence, thus 'liquidating' what Benjamin calls the 'aura' of the work of
art, its historical authenticity, given to it by its substantive duration through
history.

> One might subsume the eliminated element in the term 'aura'
> and go on to say: that which withers in the age of mechanical
> reproduction is the aura of the work of art. ... [The] technique of
> reproduction detaches the reproduced object from the domain of
> tradition. By making many reproductions it substitutes a plurality
> of copies for a unique existence.[28]

Benjamin very much disagrees with the enthusiastic expectation that film
would bring back to life 'all legends, all mythologies and all myths, all

founders of religion, and the religions themselves'.[29] Film, he reiterates, entails the liquidation, rather than resuscitation, of 'the traditional value of the cultural heritage'.[30] With that, myth becomes contemporary commodity, circulated and disseminated to a paying audience.

Furthermore, the very production modus of film severs the ties that traditional works of art had with ritual and cult. Hence, 'the existence of the work of art with reference to its aura is never entirely separated from its ritual function. In other words, the unique value of the "authentic" work of art has its basis in ritual'.[31] This aura of authenticity is of course what gives the myth its ability to structure and give meaning to the life of a social community. As reproducibility destroys or liquidates the aura of a work of art, so it affects whatever connection the work has with a ritual. Exhibition value displaces cult value.[32] The spectator of a film exhibition approaches the work of art differently from the audience of a traditional one, such as a play or a concert. Watching a film is a mediated experience that does not appreciate its subject as an integrated whole. A film is composed of different shots and scenes, with different camera positions and angles. How these are put together into a work of cinematic art is decided upon in the process in the cutting room, by the work of the editor. 'Hence, the performance of the actor is subjected to a series of optical tests'. And crucially, this 'permits the audience to take the position of a critic, without experiencing any personal contact with the actor. ... Consequently the audience takes the position of the camera; its approach is that of testing'.[33]

Myth, as mediated by film, loses its ritualised role in lived experience, it becomes subject to re-iterative testing and critical evaluation. Its unquestionable nature evaporates under this gaze. Its role moves from the ritualist to the political,[34] from the semiological to the ideological.[35] Film, one might say, inverts the relationship between (national) myth and the political. While traditionally the former structures the latter through its constitutive narrative, the mediation of myth via cinematic reproducibility subjects the myth to the (ideological) uses of the political realm. The question then becomes how myth is appropriated and re-constituted within different historical and political contexts. Instead of providing continuity through its link to tradition and ritual, cinematised myth becomes an indicator of social and political changes, revealed in its distinct appropriations in different political environments.

In the following section, the analysis will investigate two German Stalingrad movies from 1959 and from 1991/2, respectively, in order to answer the following questions:

What myths, clichés and omissions are promulgated in both movies?

What do these elements tell us about the respective myths about Stalingrad in the Germany of the late 1950 and the country shortly after unification?

The chapter ends with a critical evaluation of the role of these films in the (de)construction of Stalingrad as an element in German national mythology.

Stalingrad, Take 1 (1959)

Hunde, Wollt Ihr Ewig Leben[36] is a film based on a novel by Fritz Wöss, who had actually fought at Stalingrad. The book's title refers to an apocryphal line Frederick the Great supposedly shouted at his retreating soldiers at the battle of Kolin: 'dogs, do you want to live forever?'[37] Book and film were published in a time when West Germany had recently re-created its armed forces (*Bundeswehr*) and become the frontline state of the Cold War. Initial negotiations with the *Bundeswehr* regarding material support for the film started off well, but ultimately collapsed. Then Minister of Defence Franz-Josef Strauß explained that

> These kinds of films are not in the interest of the *Bundeswehr*, because they are limited to the superficial presentation of single events, without balancing them with the – existing – moral grounds for preparedness for military defence (*Verteidigungsbereitschaft*). The time is not ripe yet for a compelling recreation of these fateful events. In any case, your endeavour remains risky, not least with regard to politics. It must be safely assumed that it will stir up emotional discussions in the public. Precisely because of this, a participation of the *Bundeswehr* is unacceptable.[38]

To instigate a debate about the ethics and morals of war by releasing a movie about the most evocative of German defeats only 16 years after the battle and some three to four years after the last of its survivors returned from Soviet PoW camps was too much for a political-military elite that was mostly concerned with re-installing a *Wehrwille* (willingness to defend oneself) within German society. Perhaps Strauß was most concerned about the ending of *Hunde*, when thousands of German soldiers stumble off into a snow-covered distance, wondering if the lesson of Stalingrad would ever be learned. Perhaps he feared that the reconstitution of German military forces could too easily be interpreted as the inability to learn such lessons. Whether the film warranted such concerns seems to be doubtful; contemporary critics called it 'honest' and 'factual'.[39]

The path the movie traces begins with a 'cold start'. A military parade marches in front of Adolf Hitler, and an off narrator tells us

> Parades are splendid to behold. … The eyes are shining, marching forward in unison step. And it ends only when snow and wind weave the palls, to cover what began so brilliantly and confident of victory.

The hubris of Hitler's military plans is here immediately tied to an inescapable fate of death in a cold, remote, snow-covered landscape. Both parade and the images of dead soldiers are drawn from archival material; the whole movie clearly attempts to recreate a documentary atmosphere and verisimilitude.

The following narration from the off sets the historical context:

> In the year 1942, when large parts of the German people still believed in the final victory, in the East more and more signs suggested that things would take a turn for the worse for the German armies, that the Russians were preparing to strike back.

This is the historical background against which the film's narration unfolds. We first encounter its main protagonist, idealistic and Nazi *Ordensburg*-educated Lieutenant Wisse in Kharkov as he prepares for his transfer to the front at Stalingrad. The day before the deployment, he meets and quickly falls in love with Katja, a fair Russian maid who speaks German fluently, because her father loved the language and she taught it in school. His gallant attempt to save her from deportation to Germany wins her heart, and his departure to Stalingrad is turned into a heartfelt, if stilted (or poorly acted) exchange of vows and kisses. The train ride towards Stalingrad is interrupted by a partisan attack; Wisse, together with two new acquaintances, military chaplain Busch and Lieutenant Colonel Kesselbach, takes refuge with a Russian peasant family, with whom the German soldiers share some of their food. The family, which has lost its father in the war, demonstrates it religious beliefs, confirming their basically decent character.

The film then accelerates its narrative development after Wisse arrives at the Romanian unit where he is to serve as an intelligence and liaison officer. Conversations with Romanian and German officers and *Landser* (regular soldiers) quickly establish their respective trustworthiness and bravery. Major Linkmann (perhaps the name alludes to his *linke*, i.e., cheating, character) stands out as a cowardly, opportunistic and egotistical protagonist. The remainder of the film traces the increasingly deteriorating situation for the German soldiers in Stalingrad, contrasting the experiences of the *Landser* with the decision-making of the Generals and Hitler himself. The film is remarkable in this attempt to relate the fate of the ordinary soldiers to the decisions made – and not made – by their military and political leadership. It frequently shows Hitler refusing to take the crisis seriously, rejecting any plan to allow the 6th Army to break out of the Russian encirclement, suggesting the suicide of Paulus (by promoting him to Field Marshal) and finally callously commenting on the news of its demise: 'It was just an army. Raise another one'. Concomitantly, Paulus' stubborn obedience to the orders given by Hitler is rendered as the main factor in the ultimate demise of the Army. A historical myth is invoked when one of his staff officers reminds him of the role that Ludwig Yorck von Wartenburg played in the Napoleonic Wars, when he, against (or without) orders of his king signed the Convention of Tauroggen (30 December 1812) which realigned the Prussian Army, until then a part of the Grande Armeé, in an alliance with Russia. Such bravery to stand up against the monarch or in this case the *Führer*, *Hunde* suggests, is sorely missing in Paulus.

The deteriorating situation is dramatized in the conduct of the respective protagonists. The idealistic Lieutenant becomes increasingly disenchanted with his ideological convictions, as he witnesses and experiences the failure of his superiors to avoid the looming catastrophe. The military chaplain, initially willing to provide solace for the increasingly despondent soldiers, finally gives in to the disappointment with his religion. Major Linkmann reveals himself as the coward we expect him to be; in an attempt to desert and surrender to Soviet forces, he is shot in the back by German *Landser*.

The ultimate surrender, some days after Göring's infamous Thermopylae and Nibelungen speeches quoted above, sees the few remaining soldiers, including some of the main protagonists, gather to march into Soviet captivity. Responsibility for this catastrophe, one soldier exclaims, lies with any officer who could have prevented this [expletive] from happening, all those who insisted on blind obedience – an implied criticism of Paulus' inactivity and docile obedience. The march of the soldiers echoes and links back to the film's initial scenes of the military parade in front of Hitler;

alas, death in PoW camps instead of glory now awaits most of the soldiers. The film closes with the lines 'Perhaps we shall learn from all of this'. 'Or maybe not'. (Fig. 9.1)

Stalingrad, Take 2 (1991/2)

Shot immediately after German unification and ahead of the 60th anniversary of the battle, *Stalingrad*[40] is produced and released within a very different historical context than *Hunde*. And yet, there are striking similarities in narrative elements and protagonists. The movie starts with a black and white screen, introducing the viewer to the historical context of 1942, when :

> German forces have occupied almost all of Europe and parts of North Africa. In Russia [sic!], the second great summer offensive is underway. Its destination: the Caspian Sea and the oilfields of the Caucasus. 6th Army under the command of Lieutenant General Paulus is quickly advancing on the city on the Volga where the cruellest battle of the century will take place: Stalingrad.

For dramatic effect, the screen is displayed without any sound, an eerie silence raises the expectation for the first images. Black and white credits follow, with music dominated by kettledrums, establishing the dramatic nature of the film, and anticipating its doomed finish. The following images of Cervo, an Italian town on the Riviera, underlined by 'typical' Italian mandolin music, offer a jarring contrast. We are witnessing the R&R of *Pionier-Battalion 336*, fresh from the fight at El Alamein, and about to be sent to the Eastern Front at Stalingrad. We encounter the relevant protagonists: there is, again, the idealistic young and inexperienced junior officer, Lieutenant Hans von Witzland and his unit, made up of experienced *Landser* from all over Germany, as their accents reveal. We encounter the Nazi officer, corrupt, selfish and opportunistic and with no regard for the lives of his subordinates. Again we find a military chaplain, who in this version however preaches the Nazi gospel of the German soldier's duty to protect the Western Christian values against Bolshevism. The Lieutenant and his unit travel from their R&R in Italy to the front in Stalingrad by train, with a dramatic cinematic transition when the train drives into the darkness of a tunnel in order to emerge in a dark and cold Russia. The blue and green palette of the Italian Riviera is replaced with grey, dirty green and muted colours. While in *Hunde* a similar transport included meeting a decent and religious Russian peasant family, here the initiating experience is the murderous mistreatment of Russian PoWs by German soldiers. When von Witzland complains to a staff officer, he is sent off with the recommendation not to bother him with such things.

The movie then traces the deteriorating military situation for the German forces after the Soviet Forces' encirclement of Stalingrad; at some point it is noted that the battalion has been reduced from 400 to 62 soldiers. Von Witzmann encounters a female Russian soldier during a search for a comrade; she, much like Katja, speaks German fluently. In this case, it is her mother who was German and made her 'love the language'. And although she betrays his trust when she throws him into the canalisation to let him drown, a later encounter will (re-)establish their personal affection for one another. A stint in a *Strafkompanie* (punitive unit) after forcing the medical treatment of a comrade at gunpoint in a hospital is ended when the protagonists 'volunteer' to defend German positions at the Marinovka airfield against a Russian tank attack. After taking heavy losses, the rag-tag unit withdraws.

A moral breaking point is reached when the remains of the unit, including von Witzland, are commandeered to form a firing squad for the execution of Russian 'saboteurs' (who simply stole some bread) which include a young boy the unit had taken prisoner weeks before. Faced with the expectations of his men to prevent this from happening, and ultimately failing, von Witzland begins to contemplate desertion, no longer feeling bound by his oath. His attempt to reach the last airfield from which the *Luftwaffe* still evacuates wounded soldiers ends in self-inflicted failure, amending his moral failures of desertion and taking tags from dead soldiers on the way to the airfield. The corrupt and at this time delusional Nazi officer meets his destiny, much like Linkmann did in *Hunde*, when challenging von Witzland and his troop to surrender the content of a supply pod (containing *Fliegerschokolade* [methamphetamine-infused aviator chocolate] and medals).

The final moral decisions are made in the 'den' of the Nazi officers, stocked with cognac, food, and other necessities that were kept from the starving *Landser*. Irina, the female Soviet soldier the main protagonist encountered before, is found shackled to a bed, an easy target for collective rape. Instead, a rather vacuous dialogue about moral guilt and redemption ensues, leading to the promise of Irina to lead the remainder of the group towards the German lines (exactly how she plans to cover the approximately

200 miles that the Red Army had driven back German forces by this time remains somewhat unclear). The last scenes see Irina, von Witzland and Private First Class Reiser walk, or rather stumble, across an icy, snow-blown emptiness. Irina is killed when they encounter Soviet forces; her shouting that she is a Soviet soldier has no effect. The final shot of the film witnesses the two remaining soldiers slowly freezing to death, memories of Africa on Reiser's mind: 'The desert is shit, except for the stars', echoing the iconography of 'stars' in Nazi Germany popular culture of the period, which connected the soldiers in far-away theatres of war with their *Heimat* in Germany: '*Heimat, deine Sterne*' (1941), '*Flieger, grüß mir die Sonne*' (1932).[41] (Fig. 9.2)

The Myths of 'Stalingrad' in Changing Times

What then are the myths about 'Stalingrad in these films? If we approach them the way Roland Barthes approaches the myths of everyday artifacts and personae in terms of their basic, un-reflected narratives, their ideological 'what-goes-without-saying' messages,[42] we can discern a set of myths that appear in both films and that structure them in a very similar fashion. At the centre of both film plots is a basically decent German junior officer, loyal to the Nazi regime and its leadership, undergoing a violent rite of passage towards the disillusioned realisation that he has been led astray and that his life has been sacrificed, fighting for a lost cause. He is the victim, rather than the instrument, of Nazi ideology and crimes. At the heart of the battle is the suffering and dying of the German soldiers. The inhumane suffering by the Soviet civilian population is reduced to the decontextualized burning of a village and the shooting of 'saboteurs' in *Stalingrad*. Such conduct, moreover, constitutes the ground for moral qualms for 'decent' German soldiers, reaffirming the basic myth about their character as propagated in these films. As such, they stand on the same moral ground as the Soviet soldier or Soviet civilians. What in the late 1950s resonated with a social narrative that maintained the basic decency of the German *Wehrmacht* soldier and put the blame for the war and its genocidal strategy squarely on Hitler and his satraps is harder to accept in the 1991/2 film. Presenting the main protagonist and the German *Landser* as the reference points for the empathetic German audience creates a deeply problematic moral perspective that the film tries unsuccessfully to supplement with narrative elements about Russian families surviving in the sewer system of Stalingrad, or begging peasants and singing Red Army soldiers. Overall, the film never escapes the seduction of battle action and effects.[43]

In both films, Russian civilians and soldiers are basically decent people, but inferior to the German people. This is mostly effected through a gendering of the characters; the only non-violent encounters are between German heroes and Russian women, with the latter speaking the language of the master. The subaltern can speak, if she speaks the language of the occupier. A variation on the topic appears in *Stalingrad*, where gender in one case is replaced with youth; the young boy captured by the Germans symbolises the relative powerlessness of the Russian protagonists.

Responsibility for 'Stalingrad' is vested in Hitler and his generals, a personalised account of morality that erases the structural conditions Nazi ideology created. Moreover, Nazi officers are compromised not by their affiliation with a genocidal ideology, but via their personal character deficiencies. In both films, the moral depravity of superior officers serves as the foil against which the humanity and decency of the 'ordinary' soldier is produced. The respective historicizing introductions by off-screen narrator and black and white screen not-withstanding, the events narrated in both films centre predominantly on the battle of Stalingrad as such. This temporal and spatial framing has the perverted effect of depicting the German soldiers as defenders, rather than as participants in a war of conquest and annihilation. The fact that they died some 1,400 miles away from home in a genocidal military campaign is silenced in both films, thereby preventing any adulteration of the morality of the German soldiers' suffering.

Ultimately then, both films conjure up the myth that Germans (or German soldiers) were just as much victims of Nazism as the Russians, both soldiers and civilians. This, of course, is the ultimate obscenity of this mythology. It puts the nation that perpetrated the crime on the same level as its victims, denying the latter the triumph of their victory over an inhuman foe. This might have placated a German society still obsessed with extricating itself from its responsibility for the atrocities committed during the Nazi regime and insisting on the 'general decency of the German soldier' in the 1950s. For a Germany that explicitly defines the Nazi regime as its constitutive other, this is but an unfortunate and inappropriate gesture.

Rather than structuring and stabilising the narrative about German national identity across history, the 'Stalingrad' myths in these two German films are subjected to critical reviews within particular historical contexts. In this process, both films erase the events of the battle of Stalingrad and re-place them within contemporary contexts. In this regard the 1959 film is of particular interest. Ostensibly in order to boost its veracity, the director integrates newsreel clips into the narrative of the film. Given that the film itself is shot in black and white, it is sometimes difficult to tell documentary from fictional material. This is of course the intention. Yet this attempt at authenticity has ultimately a very different effect. As it absorbs the first-hand images of the battle into a fictitious plot, it creates a simulation of 'Stalingrad' that overwrites, and thus erases, the historical events. The 'Stalingrad' that viewers claimed to know after watching the film 'was only its aestheticized hyperrealization and so the real event was even more effectively eclipsed and forgotten'.[44] The 1991 film, attempting to produce authenticity via the orchestration and dramatization of extensive battle scenes, ends up with a similar result: 'Stalingrad' as yet another de-historicising action movie with the added bonus that it claims to be 'based on true events'. Yet neither historicity nor authenticity are the result. 'What we are ... experiencing is something else entirely. What is actually occurring – collectively, confusedly, via all the trial and debates – is a transition from the historical stage to a mythical stage: the mythic – and media-led – reconstruction of all these events'.[45] And as such, it absolves us from the guilt, the ambiguity, the violence and the ultimate defeat of Stalingrad, its mythologization depriving it of any mythical power.

Appendix I: Historians' views of most important European Battles

We asked 35 respondents from Canada to Russia and from Norway to Australia what they considered to be the 10 most important European battles. The table below shows the 328 relevant answers, although they are not listed in any order of particular importance. We have included answers relating to battles in the Middle East, which we consider to be of great consequence for Europe. However, we have discounted battles that were neither in Europe nor adjacent areas, e.g. The Battle of Medway, The Siege/Battle of Quebec etc.

29	Waterloo 1815
27	Stalingrad 1942/43
24	Verdun/Somme 1916
19	Lepanto 1571
16	Salamis/Thermopylae 480 BCE
14	Poitiers/Tours 732
13	100 Years' War Orléans 1429 or Castillon 1453 or Crécy 1346 or Azincourt 1415
13	Vienna 1683
12	Trafalgar 1805
9	Cannae 216 BCE
9	Constantinople 1453
9	Marathon 490 BCE
9	Normandy 1944
9	Armada 1588
9	Kursk 1943
7	Austerlitz 1805
7	Hastings 1066
7	Leipzig 1813
6	Borodino 1812

FAMOUS BATTLES

6	Zama 202 BCE
6	Battle of Britain 1940
5	Actium 31 BCE
5	Catalaunian Plains (Châlons sur Marne) 451
5	Moscow 1941
5	Rocroi 1643
5	Sedan 1870
5	White Mountain 1620
5	Marne 1914
5	Sadowa/Königgrätz 1866
4	Bouvines 1214
4	Mohács 1526
4	Gaugamela 331 BCE
4	Manzikert 1071
4	Teutoburg Forest 9
3	Constantinople Conquest of 1204
3	Jutland/Skagerrak 1916
3	Las Navas de Tolosa 1212
3	Lützen 1632
3	Milvian Bridge 312
3	Poltava 1709
3	Plataea 476 BCE
3	Abukir/the Nile 1799
3	Pavía 1525
2	Bannockburn 1314
2	Carthage 146 BCE
2	Constantinople Siege of 717
2	Grunwald 1410 & Tannenberg 1914
2	Hattin 1187
2	Issus 333 BCE
2	Lechfeld 956
2	Leuthen 1757
2	Philippi 42 BCE

APPENDIX I

2	Sevastopol Siege of 1853-56
2	Vienna Siege of 1529
2	Adrianople 379
2	Almansa 1707
2	Blenheim 1704
2	El Alamein 1942
2	Granada 1482-92
2	Kosovo Polje 1389
1	Bir Hakeim 1942
1	Carrhae 53 BCE
1	Cerignola 1503
1	Chaeronea 338
1	Chrysopolis 324
1	Crimea 1920
1	Culloden 1746
1	Dürnkrut 1278
1	Flodden 1513
1	Fontenoy 1745
1	Gallipoli 1916
1	Jena 1806
1	Jerusalem Conquest of 1099
1	Kortrijk Golden Spurs 1302
1	Le Mans 1793
1	Lusitanian War 147
1	Madrid 1808 Dos de Mayo
1	Magenta & Solferino 1859
1	Marignano 1515
1	Mogersdorf 1664
1	Murten 1476
1	Naval Battle of Malta 1283
1	Naval Battle of Terceras 1582
1	Navarino 1827
1	Shipka (Bulgaria) 1877

1	Vouillé 507
1	Wittstock
1	Marston Moor 1644
1	Pharsalos 48 BCE
1	Syracuse 413 BCE
1	Valmy 1792
1	Salado 1340
1	Amiens 1918
1	St Quentin 1557
1	Tudela 1808
1	Moscow 1813
1	Malplaquet 1709
1	Dürnkrut/Marchfield 1278
1	Alesia 52BCE
1	Clavijo (844 ? mythical?)

Appendix II: A comparative Schools' Questionnaire of A-Level (& equivalent) Pupils taking History, 2017

Question: Have you heard of the following? If it is a battle, do you know who won?

	Q2A der Herderschule, Rendsburg, Schleswig-Holstein	The Downs School, Oxon, History A-level Group, 6th form
TOTAL RESPONDENTS	24	32
Roman Empire	Question not asked	26
Holy Roman Empire	Question not asked	27
Trojan War	23	32
Marathon	2	11
Greek Victory	1	9
Persian Victory		1
Thermopylae	3	24
300 Spartans Victory	1	3
Persian Victory	1	9
Cannae	8	13
Carthaginian Victory	6	9
Roman Victory		2
Milvian Bridge	1	7
Victory of Constantine I		6
Victory of Maxentius		1
Poitiers/Tours	2	10
Frankish Victory	2	9
Arab Victory		1
Agincourt	1	12
English Victory		12
French Victory		
Castillon	Question not asked	10
English Victory		4
French Victory		5
Fall of Constantinople	17	21

(Continued)

FAMOUS BATTLES

	Q2A der Herderschule, Rendsburg, Schleswig-Holstein	The Downs School, Oxon, History A-level Group, 6th form
Lepanto	3	10
Christian Victory		2
Turkish Victory		5
Armada	Question not asked	20
English Victory		10
Spanish Victory		4
Vienna 1683	8	13
Christian Victory	1	10
Turkish Victory		
Culloden	Question not asked	3
Catholic Victory		1
Protestant Victory		3
Hanoverian Victory		1
Jacobite Victory		2
Austerlitz 1805	Question not asked	15
British Victory		1
French Victory		2
Austro-Russian Victory		4
Waterloo 1815	23	31
British-Dutch-Prussian Victory	8	21
French Victory		1
Gettysburg 1863	4	16
Northern Victory	1	10
Southern Victory		2
Verdun	13	13
Stalingrad	24	23
German Victory		1
Soviet Victory	15	19
White Mountain 1620	2	Question not asked
Trafalgar 1805	8	Question not askd
British Victory	3	
French Victory		
Leipzig 1813	13	Question not asked
French Victory	2	
Coalition Victory	5	
German-Danish War 1864	23	Question not asked
German Victory	11	
Danish Victory		
Sedan 1870	5	Question not asked

Endnotes

Chapter 1   Introduction to the Second Volume

1. For the arguments, see Yuval Noah Harari: "The Concept of 'Decisive Battles' in World History", *Journal of World History* Vol. 18 No. 3 (2007), pp. 251-66.
2. Indeed, the European Union has financed the construction of museums of commemoration on battlefields from Portugal to Poland.
3. Herder quoted in Isaiah Berlin *Vico and Herder (London: The Hogarth Press, 1992 [1976])*, p. 169.
4. Winston Churchill: 'We shall fight on the beaches', https://www.winston-churchill.org/resources/speeches/1940-the-finest-hour/we-shall-fight-on-the-beaches. Accessed 28 July 2017.
5. Paul Hay du Chastelet: *Traite de la Guerre, ou Politique militaire* (1668), excerpts trs,. by Beatrice Heuser in id. (ed.): *The Strategy Makers: Thoughts on War and Society from Machiavelli to Clausewitz* (Santa Barbara, CA: ABC Clio, 2010), p. 112.
6. George Mosse: *The Nationalization of the Masses: Political Symbolism and Mass Movements in Germany from the Napoleonic Wars Through the Third Reich* (New York: H. Fertig, 1975).
7. For a full typology, see Beatrice Heuser: "Famous Battles: A Typology", in *Famous Battles and How They Shaped the Modern World,* Vol. 1.
8. See the chapter by Mungo Melvin in this volume.
9. Beatrice Heuser: 'Defeats as moral victories', in Andrew Hom & Cian O'Driscoll (eds): *Moral Victories: The Ethics of Winning Wars* (Oxford: Oxford University Press, expected 2017).
10. François-Xavier Nérard: 'Les cimetières mémoriaux de Leningrad: l'impossible deuil?', in David El Kenz and François-Xavier Nérard (eds.): *Commémorer les victimes en Europe (XVI-XXI siècles)* (Champ Vallon: Seyssel, 2011), pp. 197-214.
11. Masada: http://www.jewishvirtuallibrary.org/masada-desert-fortress. Accessed 30 July 2017.

12. http://www.historial.fr for Péronne, accessed on 21 V 2017; http://www.memorial-caen.fr/ accessed on 21 V 2017. Both Péronne and Caen also include virtual online exhibitions.
13. A.V. Seaton: "War and Thanatourism: Waterloo 1815-1914", in *Annals of Tourism Research*, Vol. 26, No. 1 (1999), pp. 130-58.
14. Plutarch: *Life of Alexander*, XV, here in the translation by Ian Scott-Kilvert, Plutarch: *The Age of Alexander* (Harmondsworth: Penguin Books, 1973), p. 267.
15. Polly Low: "Remembering war in fifth-century Greece: ideologies, societies, and commemoration beyond democratic Athens", *World Archaeology* Vol. 35 No. 1 (2003), pp. 98-111.
16. Valerie Hope: "Trophies and Tombstones: Commemorating the Roman soldier", *World Archaeology* Vol. 35 No. 1 (2003), pp. 79-97.
17. G.A.H. [sic!] Guibert: *Journal d'un Voyage en Allemagne fait en 1773* ouvrage posthumé, publié par sa veuve (Paris: Treuttel et Würtz, 1803), Vol. 1 pp. 124-26, trs. by BH.
18. See also A.V.Seaton: "War and thanatourism:Waterloo 1815-1914", *Annals of Tourism Research*, Vol. 26, No. 1 ((999), pp. 130-58.
19. John B. Gatewood, Catherine M. Cameron: "Battlefield Pilgrims at Gettysburg National Military Park", *Ethnology*, Vol. 43, No. 3 (Summer, 2004), pp. 193-216.
20. David W. Lloyd: *Battlefield Tourism: Pilgrimage and the Commemoration of the Great War in Britain, Australia and Canada, 1919-1939* (Oxford: Berg, 1998).
21. Antoine Fleury : « Introduction », in Antoine Fleury and Robert Frank (eds): *Le rôle des guerres dans la mémoire des Européens: leur effet sur la conscience d'être européen* (Paris: P. Lang, 1997), pp. 1-18. See also, Jay Winter : *Sites of Memory, Sites of Mourning : The Great War in European Cultural History* (Cambridge : Cambridge University Press, 2014).

Chapter 2   The Defeat of the Spanish Armada 1588: 'Prose epic of the modern English nation'

1. P. Horden and N. Purcell: *The Corrupting Sea: A Study of Mediterranean History (*Oxford Basil Blackwell 2000) for a discussion of ancient and medieval attitudes to the sea and identity. For Athenian responses to Salamis and sea-power see: R. Osborne (ed. & transl.): *The Old Oligarch: Pseudo-Xenophon's Constitution of the Athenians* (Cambridge: Lactor ,2004) p.17 1.2. Plato *Laws, iv,* 35-42, 705, 949, 952.

ENDNOTES

2. Modern meteorological research has deepened out understanding of the contemporary weather. See: Lamb, H. *Historic Storms of the North Sea, British Isles and NW Europe*. Cambridge UP, 1991.

3. Douglas Knerr: "Through the 'Golden Mist': a Brief Overview of Armada Historiography." *American Neptune* Vol. 49 No. 1 (1989), pp. 5–13.

4. Knerr: "Through the 'Golden Mist'", pp. 5-6.

5. C. Martin and Geoffrey Parker: *The Spanish Armada* (London, Hamish Hamilton 1988), p. 261.

6. The triumph at Cadiz was deliberately under-represented in English literature because any overt celebration of Essex's triumph would have damaged the standing of Lord Robert Cecil, his political rival at Court. A. Payne: 'Richard Hakluyt and his Books.' Hakluyt Society Annual Lecture (1996).

7. Adams had been drawing charts for the defence of the Thames before the battle, see F. Fernandez-Armesto: *The Spanish Armada: The Experience of War in 1588* (Oxford: Oxford University Press, 1988), pp. 112-3.

8. Knerr: "Through the 'Golden Mist'", p. 5-6.

9. Richard Hakluyt: *Principal Voyages*. (reprinted Glasgow: James MacLehose & Sons, 1903) Vol. I, p. xxiv.

10. G.B. Parks: *Richard Hakluyt and the English Voyages* (2nd edn. New York: Frederick Ungar, 1961), p. 176.

11. Parks: 'Richard Hakluyt', p. 179; Hakluyt: *Principal Voyages* (1903), Vol. I p. xxxiii.

12. Payne: 'Richard Hakluyt', p.10.

13. Payne: 'Richard Hakluyt', p.12; J.A. Williamson:. *The Ocean in English History* (Oxford: Oxford University Press, 1941), pp. 79-80.

14. Andrew Lambert.: *Admirals* (London, Faber, 2007), chapter one.

15. Henry VIII fell back on oil painting in 1539 because there is no time to produce a suitable tapestry of 'The Embarkation for the Field of the Cloth of Gold'. See F. Yates: *The Valois Tapestries* London 1959 for a pioneering study of contemporary Tapestry as the art of power, and T. Campbell: *Threads of Splendour: Tapestry of the Baroque* (New Haven: Yale University Press, 2007) for the broader context.

16. Franses, Simon: *Dutch Tapestry in the Golden Age, 1590-1650: Baroque Masterpieces from the Northern Netherlands.* (NY: 2007), pp. 8-19.

17. The Tunis Tapestry cycle is now in the Kunsthistorisches Museum in Vienna.

18. M. Russell: *Visions of the Sea: Hendrick C. Vroom and the origin of Dutch Marine Painting.* (Leiden: Brill, 1983), pp. 149-51. The picture, painted in 1600, currently hangs is a gallery in Innsbruck.

19. Russell: *Visions of the Sea,* pp. 111-3.
20. Justin Dee quoted in Sarah Gristwood "A Tapestry of England's Past" *History Today* Vol. 60 No.9 2010 http://www.historytoday.com/sarah-gristwood/tapestry-england%E2%80%99s-past#sthash.fl4ziuXb.dpuf.
21. Campbell: *Threads of Splendour,* p. 111. This passage is based on a German text of 1613.
22. Justin Dee quoted in Sarah Gristwood 'A Tapestry of England's Past' *History Today,* Vol. 60 No.9 2010 http://www.historytoday.com/sarah-gristwood/tapestry-england%E2%80%99s-past#sthash.fl4ziuXb.dpuf.
23. Simon Turner: "Van Dyck and Tapestry in England", *Tate Papers,* No.17 (Spring 2012), http://www.tate.org.uk/research/publications/tate-papers/17/van-dyck-and-tapestry-in-england, accessed 20 June 2016.
24. S. Farrell: "The Armada Tapestries in the Old Palace of Westminster", *Parliamentary History* Vol. 29 No.3 (2010), pp. 416-40.
25. The tapestry hangings of the House of Lords: representing the several engagements between the English and Spanish fleets, in the ever memorable year MDLXXXVIII (1588), with the portraits of the Lord High-Admiral, and the other noble commanders, taken from the life. Drawn by Clement Lempriere, engraved and published by John Pine in 1739.
26. A theme addressed in the conclusion of this essay.
27. William Pitt, *The Speeches of the Right Honourable the Earl of Chatham in the Houses of Lords and Commons: With a Biographical Memoir and Introductions and Explanatory Notes to the Speeches* (London: Aylott & Jones, 1848), pp. xv-xvi.
28. Emily Ballew Neff: *John Singleton Copley in England* (London: Merrell Holberton, 1995), p. 36
29. S. Gristwood: 'A Tapestry of England's Past', *History Today* Vol. 60 no.9 (2010).
30. Justin Dee quoted in Gristwood "A Tapestry of England's Past".
31. Ernest Hobsbawm, Terence Ranger (eds.): *The Invention of Tradition.* (Cambridge: Cambridge University Press, 1983).
32. J.A. Froude: 'England's Forgotten Worthies' *Westminster Review* (July 1852).
33. Andrew Lambert:*'The Foundations of Naval History': Sir John Laughton, the Royal Navy and the Historical Profession* (London, Chatham 1997); Julian Corbett: *Drake and the Tudor Navy* (London: Longmans, 1898) vol. II p. 284.

Chapter 3   Chatham 1667: A Forgotten Invasion and the Myth of a Moth

1. The account of the Medway attack that follows is based chiefly on P. G. Rogers: *The Dutch in the Medway* (Oxford: Oxford University Press, 1970), 83-115; C. J. W. Van Waning and A. Van Der Moer: *Dese aengemaene tocht*

Chatham 1667 (Zutphen: De Walburg Pers, 1981), especially pp. 39-66, 94-7; J D Davies: 'Chatham to Erith via Dover: Charles II's secret foreign policy and the Project for new Royal Dockyards', *Pepys and Chips: Dockyards, Naval Administration & Warfare in the Seventeenth Century*, Transactions of the Naval Dockyards Society, 8, ed. R Riley (Portsmouth: Naval Dockyards Society, 2012).

2. On 14 December 1941, the Dutch warship *Jan van Brakel* was serving as a convoy escort on the east coast of England when she accidentally struck the anchor buoy of a boom vessel guarding the Medway. The captain signalled the port authorities, '*Van Brakel* damaged boom defence Medway'. The immediate response was: 'What, again?' P M Bosscher: *De Koninklijke Marine in de Tweede Wereldoorlog,* I (Franeker: Wever, 1984), p. 587 n142.

3. F. Fox: *A Distant Storm: The Four Days' Battle of 1666* (Rotherfield: Jean Boudriot, 1994), pp. 346-7.

4. *The Diary of Samuel Pepys*, ed. R. Latham and W. Matthews (London: Bell and Hyman, 1970-83), 21 June 1667. Cf. T. Harris, *Restoration: Charles II and His Kingdoms, 1660-85* (London: Penguin, 2005), p. 74.

5. Marvel: *The Loyal Scot* (1667). For a critical analysis, see D. Baker: *Between Nations: Spenser, Marvell, and the Question of Britain* (Stanford, CA: Stanford University Press, 1997), pp. 128-9, 156.

6. K. Eustace: 'Britannia: Some High Points in the History of the Iconography on British coinage', *British Numistatic Journal* Vol. 76 (2006), pp. 325-7; V. Hewitt: 'Britannia (*fl.* 1st–21st cent.), allegory of a nation, emblem of empire, and patriotic icon', *Oxford Dictionary of National Biography.*

7. For the implications of this, see J. D. Davies: '"Great Neptunes of the Main": Myths, Mangled Histories, and 'Maritime Monarchy' in the Navy of the Stuarts', in A. James Davies and G. Rommelse (eds.): *Ideologies of Western Naval Power 1500-1815* (forthcoming, Abingdon: Routledge, 2018).

8. National Maritime Museum, Greenwich, MS CLI/130.

9. R. Prud'homme van Reine: 'Michiel Adriaenszoon de Ruyter and his Biographer Gerard Brandt', in Prud'homme van Reine, J. R. Bruijn and Rolof van Hovell tot Westerflier (eds): *De Ruyter: Dutch Admiral,* (Rotterdam: Karwansaray, 2011), p. 42. De Ruyter refused the knighthood, but it was given instead to his son Engel.

10. *Pepys Diary,* 14 June 1667.

11. Letter, 'Balls and the Distress in Middlesbrough', *The Daily Gazette* (Middlesbrough), 31 Jan. 1879.

12. Letter, 'Insecurity of the Country in the Case of War', *London Evening Standard,* 3 Dec. 1850.

13. St James's Gazette, 10 June 1887.

14. A. T. Mahan: *The Influence of Sea Power Upon History* (London: Methuen, 1965), p. 132; A. J. Tedder: *The Navy of the Restoration* (Cambrige: Cambridge University Press, 1916), p. 191.

15. *Daily Mail*, 9 July 1917.

16. Western Morning News, 2 Nov. 1935.

17. *Hansard* HC Deb 27 Feb 1961, c.1275.

18. *Hansard* HL Deb 12 June 1991, c.1090.

19. R. Mitchell: 'Macfarlane, Charles (1799-1858), historian and traveller', *Oxford Dictionary of National Biography*.

20. C. L. W. Westergaard: *The First Triple Alliance: The Letters of Christopher Lindenov, Danish Envoy to London 1668-1672* (New Haven: Yale University Press, 1947), 123, 334; C D Van Strien (ed.): *British Travellers in Holland During the Stuart Period* (Leiden: Brill, 1993), 260; C D Van Strien (ed.): *Touring the Low Countries: Accounts of British Travellers, 1660-1720* (Amsterdam: Amsterdam University Press, 1998), p. 14.

21. It was loaned to the National Maritime Museum, Greenwich, for an exhibition in 2012 – the first time it had left the Netherlands since 1667.

22. J. D. Davies: 'Butler, Thomas, sixth earl of Ossory (1634–1680), politician and naval officer', *Oxford Dictionary of National Biography*.

23. A. B. Gardiner: 'The Medal that Provoked a War: Charles II's Lasting Indignation over Adolfzoon's Breda Medal', *The Medal*, Vol. 17 (1990), pp. 11-15, and rejoinder by M Scharloo: 'A Peace Medal that Caused a War?', *The Medal*, Vol. 18 (1991), pp. 11-22 (quotation from p. 21 of latter).

24. The painting had been commissioned within a month of the Medway raid. Its history is examined in detail by J. A. Loughman: 'Paintings in the Public and Private Domain: Collecting and Patronage at Dordrecht, 1620-1749', MS PhD, Courtauld Institute of Art, University of London (1993), pp. 99-105. I am grateful to John Loughman for supplying me with the relevant section of his thesis.

25. British Library, Sloane MS 1786, fo. 177v, fragment of MS pamphlet. Cf. J. Stubbe: *Justification of the present war against the United Netherlands: Wherein the declaration of his majesty is vindicated, and the war proved to be just, honourable, and necessary; the dominion of the sea explained, and his majesties rights thereunto asserted; the obligations of the Dutch to England, and their continual ingratitude. Illustrated with sculptures. In answer to a Dutch treatise entituled Considerations upon the present state of the United Netherlands.* (London: Henry Hills & John Starkey, 1672), pp. 2, 39, 40. The circulation of a particularly offensive Dutch medal was reported in May 1669

in A. B. Hinds (ed.): *Calendar of State Papers, Venetian, 1669-70* (London: His Majesty's Stationary Office, 1937), p. 58.

26. J. Stubbe: *Justification*, pp. 11-28; and id.: *A Further Justification of the Present War Against the United Netherlands* (London: Henry Hills & John Starkey, 1673), 1-3; W. de Britaine: *The Dutch usurpation; or, A brief view of the behaviour of the States-General of the United Provinces towards the kings of Great Britain : with some of their cruelties and injustices exercised upon the subjects of the English nation : as also, a discovery of what arts they have used to arrive at their late grandeur, & c.* (London: Jonathan Edwin, 1672), pp. 1-9; T. W. Fulton: *The Sovereignty of the Seas* (London: William Blackwood, 1911), p. 476. Charles demanded reparation for Van Brakel's insult, and the colours in question were subsequently returned to him.

27. W. de Britaine: *The Interest of England in the Present War with Holland* (London: Jonathan Edwin, 1672), pp. 9-10.

28. Longleat House, Coventry MS 65, fo. 155, Arlington to Henry Coventry, 29 Mar. 1672.

29. Loughman, 'Paintings', pp. 104-105. One copy survives at the Rijksmuseum, Amsterdam.

30. R. Hutton: 'The Making of the Secret Treaty of Dover, 1668-70', *The Historical Journal*, Vol. 29 (1986), pp. 297-318; J D Davies: 'Chatham to Dover via Erith'.

31. R. Prud'homme van Reine, *Rechterhand van Nederland: Biografie van Michiel Adriaenszoon De Ruyter* (Amsterdam: Arbeiderspers, 1996), pp. 342-59.

32. http://www.npogeschiedenis.nl/speler.WO_NOS_771921.html, accessed 1 June 2016.

33. Rogers: *Dutch in the Medway*, p. 174.

34. See the review by Gijs Rommelse, https://jddavies.com/2015/05/11/the-film-and-the-facts-about-the-movie-michiel-de-ruyter/ [accessed on 9 Feb 2017].

35. Dr Gijs Rommelse, head of History at the Haarlemmermeer Lyceum, Hoofdorp: personal communication to the author, 13 June 2016.

36. Frits de Ruyter de Wildt: personal communication to the author, 13 June 2016.

37. See *inter alia* http://londonist.com/2016/06/farage-and-geldof-in-bizarre-thames-flotilla-face-off, accessed 21 September 2016; Tweets referencing 'Medway' and '1667' dated 15 June 2016.

38. Nevertheless, at least three commemorative conferences took place concerning the events in June 1667, one in Chatham and the other two in Amsterdam.

39. A. Scheffer: *Roemruchte jaren van onze vloot* (Baarn: Wereldvenster, 1966), p. 161.

40. A. Doedens and J. Houter: *1666: de ramp van Vlieland en Terschelling* (Franeker: van Wijnen, 2013), pp. 233-73.
41. Figures from R. Winfield: *British Warships in the Age of Sail, 1603-1714* (Barnsley: Seaforth, 2009).
42. In 1938, Clyde Grose observed, dispassionately and correctly, that 'Pepys is our only authority for the statement that on the night of the Medway disaster Charles and the Duchess *(sic)* of Castlemaine were playing at hunting a poor moth in Monmouth's lodgings', before adding the loaded barb, 'but at least he did things like that'. C L Grose: 'Charles the Second of England', *The American Historical Review*, Vol. 43 (1938), p. 539.
43. *Pepys Diary*, 13 June 1667.
44. Even one of Charles II's sternest modern critics is full of praise for his decisive response to the Dutch attack: R. Hutton: *The Restoration* (Oxford: Oxford University Press, 1985), pp. 269-70.
45. *Pepys Diary*, 13 June 1667.

Chapter 4   Vienna 1683 and the Defence of Europe

1. This research was made possible by the hospitality of the Austrian Landesverteidigungsakademie and a small research travel grant of the University of Reading. Special thanks are due to Hofrat Dr Erwin Schmidl.
2. Constantinople was referred to by the (East) Romans simply as 'the City' (*polis*), whence the Turkish deformation of Greek στην πόλη, 'to the city', which became 'Istanbul'.
3. The Turkish *kızıl* can mean both 'bright red' (as opposed to *kırmızı* = crimson) and 'golden'.
4. László Nagy: 'Ungarn im Jahre 1683', in Austrian Commission for Military History (ed.): papers of the *International Congress of Military History* (Vienna: Federal Ministry for the Defence of the Country, 1983), pp. 187-98.
5. Richard Kreutel & Karl Teply: *Kara Mustafa vor Wien: 1683 aus Sicht türkischer Quellen* (Graz: Styria, 1982), p. 61f.
6. Andrew Wheatcroft: *The Enemy at the Gate: Habsburgs, Ottomans and the Battle for Europe* (London: Pimlico, 2009), p. 13f.
7. Fahri Çeliker: 'Zweite Türkenbelagerung Wiens und Ursachen der Misserfolge' in *International Congress of Military History* (1983), p. 172.
8. Jan Wimmer: 'Der Entsatz von Wien 1683: Planung und Realisierung', in *International Congress of Military History* (1983), p. 199.
9. Text in Isabella Ackerl: *Von Türken belagert – von Christen entsetzt: das belagerte Wien 1683* (Vienna: Österreichischer Bundesverlag, 1983), p. 30f.
10. Wimmer: 'Der Entsatz von Wien 1683', pp. 199-219.

ENDNOTES

11. Johannes Sachslehner: *Wien Anno 1683: Ein europäisches Schicksalsjahr* (Vienna: Pichler Verlag, 2004), pp. 157, 164-66. The abduction of locals as slaves finds its echo also in local records where spouses asked for special permission to re-marry, as the fate of the abducted individuals was uncertain. Problems of bigamy arose on a few occasions when the missing spouses managed to escape and make their way home years later; again, parish records are reliable sources here.

12. After 1683, volunteers from other parts of the Habsburg empire would be moved to some of the depopulated villages. See Ackerl: *Von Türken belagert,* pp. 176-80

13. Sachslehner: *Wien Anno 1683,* p. 164f.

14. Ackerl: *Von Türken belagert,* pp. 134-8; Sachslehner: *Wien Anno 1683,* p. 308.

15. The Kahlenberg or naked mountain, later renamed Leopoldsberg or Leopold's mountain, and the Sauberg or sow mountain, later confusingly renamed Kahlenberg.

16. Sachslehner: *Wien Anno 1683,* pp. 308, 310.

17. 'Wie die Arbeit, so der Lohn' (Feb. 1684), etching on display in the Wienmuseum, Vienna.

18. Richard Kreutel & Karl Teply: *Kara Mustafa vor Wien: 1683 aus Sicht türkischer Quellen* (Graz: Styria, 1982).

19. Thomas Barker: *Double Eagle and Crescent: Vienna's Second Turkish Siege and its Historical Background* (Albany: State University of New York Press, 1967).

20. See Athena Leoussi: "Introduction", in Athena Leoussi (ed): *Famous Battles and How They Shaped the Modern World* (Pen & Sword, 2018), Vol. 1.

21. *1. April 2000* (Wolfgang Liebeneier – Regie; Ernst Marboe & Rudolf Brunngraber – Script, 1952 for the Austrian Government).

22. Janusz Tazbir: 'Die Legende vom Wiener Entsatz', in *International Congress of Military History* (1983), pp. 221-32; Patrice Dabrowski: *Commemorations and the Shaping of Modern Poland* (Bloomington, IN: Indiana University Press, 2004), pp. 49-74.

23. José Alvarez Nunco: 'The Formation of Spanish Identity and Its Adaptation to the Age of Nations', in *History & Memory,* Vol. 14, No. 1/2 (Fall 2002), pp. 13-36.

24. Anne Cornelia Kenneweg: 'Antemurale Christianitatis', in Pim de Boer, Heinz Duchhardt, Georg Kreis (eds): *Europäische Erinnerungsorte* Vol. 2 *Haus Europa* (Munich: Oldenbourg, 2012), p. 73.

25. Paul Knoll: 'Poland as "Antemurale Christianitatis" in the Late Middle Ages', *The Catholic Historical Review,* Vol. 60, No. 3 (Oct., 1974), p. 393.

26. Knoll: 'Poland as "Antemurale Christianitatis"', p. 381; Alan Davies: *The Crucified Nation: A Motif in Modern Nationalism* (Brighton: Sussex Academic Press, 2010), p. 13.

27. Ibid., pp. 381-401; Kenneweg: 'Antemurale Christianitatis', p. 77.

28. Text in http://emperors-clothes.com/milo/milosaid.html accessed on 3 X 2015.
29. Péter Ötvös: review of *Das Ungarnbild der deutschen Historiographie*. Ed. By Márta Fata (Stuttgart: Franz Steiner 2004), in Zsolt K. Lengyel (ed.): *Ungarnjahrbuch* No. 28 (Munich: Ungarisches Institut, 2007), p. 511f.
30. Andrew Wheatcroft: *The Enemy at the Gates: Habsburgs, Ottomans and the Battle for Europe* (London: Pimlico, 2009), pp. 245-65.
31. https://www.youtube.com/watch?v=edFQTZpf8yM accessed on 4 October 2015
32. Wheatcroft: *The Enemy*, p. 268.
33. For example, in a local election campaign of 2010, a right-wing political party in Austria explicitly drew on the imagery of the Turkish Wars in a comic strip pitting a superman against [Kara] Mustafa who was planning to put an extra-large minaret on the St Stephen's cathedral in the centre of Vienna. See Ernst Petritsch: "Die Schlacht am Kahlenberg", de Boer, Duchhardt, & Kreis (eds): *Europäische Erinnerungsorte* Vol. 2 *Haus Europa*, p. 413.
34. Thomas Petersen: "Sorgen und Hilfsbereitschaft: Die Einstellungen der Deutschen zur Flüchtlingskrise", *Forschung und Lehre* 23rd Year (January 2016), pp.18-21, using data from opinion polls of the Allenbach Institute.

Chapter 5   Culloden 1746: Six Myths and their Politics

1. Thanks particularly to Doreen Mackie Fergusson, for all her invaluable help with my field work and research, and to Ulrike Seeberger, who knows more about Scottish culture than many a Scot.
2. Lindsey Bowditch, Hilary Horrocks et al: *Cùil Lodair – Culloden* (Edinburgh: The National Trust for Scotland, 2014), p. 5.
3. Christopher Duffy: *The '45* (London: Cassell, 2003); Jeremy Black: *Culloden and the '45* (Stroud, Glos: Sutton, 1990); Peter Harrington: *Culloden 1756: The Highland Clans' Last Charge* (London: Osprey, 1991).
4. Dauvit Horsbroch: "'Tae see oursels as ithers see us'": Scottish military identity from the Covenant to Victoria, 1637-1837', in Steve Murdoch & A. Mackillop (eds.): *Fighting for Identity: Scottish Military Experience c. 1550-1900* (Leiden: Brill, 2002), p. 105.
5. Steve Murdoch "Introduction", in Steve Murdoch (ed.): *Scotland in the Thirty Years' War 1618-1648* (Leiden: Brill, 2001), p. 19f.
6. John L. Roberts: *Clan, King and Covenant: History of the Highland Clans from the Civil War to the Glencoe Massacre* (Edinburgh: Edinburgh University Press, 2000), p. 235.
7. Jeremy Black: *Culloden and the '45* (Stroud, Glos: Sutton, 1990, ppb 2000), pp. 107, 132, 177.

ENDNOTES

8. Christopher Duffy has impressively reconstructed the evolving weather conditions in different parts of the United Kingdom during the campaign, see *The '45*, pp. 312, 380-91.

9. Black: *Culloden and the '45*, p. 190.

10. Ibid., p. 183.

11. Bowditch, Horrocks et al: *Cùil Lodair – Culloden*, p. 64.

12. John Prebble: *Culloden* (London: Pimlico, 2002), p. 132.

13. Black: *Culloden and the '45*, p. 203.

14. Quoted in Sabine Volk-Birke: "Einigkeit für Recht und Freiheit? Grossbritannien am Rande des (Bürger-)Krieges 1745/46", in Stefanie Stockhorst (ed.): *Krieg und Frieden im 18. Jahrhundert: Kulturgeschichtliche Studien* (Hanover: Wehrhahn Verlag, 2015), pp. 260-2.

15. Quoted in Volk-Birke: "Einigkeit für Recht und Freiheit?", p. 260f.

16. On the socio-political history of kilt and tartan, see Matthew Dziennik: "Whig Tartan: Material Culture and its Use in the Scottish Highlands, 1746-1815", *Past and Present* No. 217 (Nov. 2012), pp. 117-47.

17. J.E. Cookson: "The Napoleonic Wars, Military Scotland and Tory Highlandism in the Early Nineteenth Century", in *The Scottish Historical Review* Vol. 76 No. 1 (April 1999), pp. 60-75.

18. Robert Clyde: *From Rebel to Hero: the Image of the Highlander, 1745-1830* (East Linton, East Lothian: Tuckwell Press, 1995), pp. 150-3.

19. Linda Colley: *Britons: Forging the Nation* (New Haven: Yale University Press, 1992).

20. Colin Kidd: *Subverting Scotlands Past: Scottish Whig historians and the creation of an Anglo-British Identity, 1689- ca. 1830* (Cambridge: CUP, 1993)

21. The link is made, for example, in Phil Sked: *Culloden* (The National Trust for Scotland, 1997), p. 27; Terry Deary: *Bloody Scotland* in the Series *Horrible Histories* (London: Scholastic, 1998), p. 138.

22. Colin Kidd: *Subverting Scotlands Past: Scottish Whig historians and the creation of an Anglo-British Identity, 1689- ca. 1830* (Cambridge: CUP, 1993); Andrew Mackillop: "The political culture of the Scottish Highlands from Culloden to Waterloo", *The Historical Journal* Vol. 46 No. 3 (2003), pp. 511-32, esp. p. 513.

23. Black: *Culloden and the '45*, p 80.

24. J. Barke (ed): *Poems and Songs of Robert Burns* (Fontana: 1983), p. 552, quoted in Horsbroch: "'Tae see oursels as ithers see us", p. 106.

25. "A Short History of Scotland", in Miles Kington (ed): *Punch History of Scotland* (London: Robson Books, 1977), p. 39.

26. Sir Walter Scott: *Waverley, or 'tis sixty years since* (1814; Harmondsworth: Penguin, 1972), p. 492.

27. Sir Walter Scott: *Redgauntlet. A Tale of the Eighteenth Century.* In Three Volumes. (Edinburgh: Printed for Archibald Constable and Co. Edinburgh; And Hurst, Robinson and Co., London, 1824).

28. Volk-Birke: "Einigkeit für Recht und Freiheit?", p. 271f.

29. William Ewart Lockhart: *The White Cockade* (1899), Kelvingrove Museum and Art Gallery, Glasgow.

30. "My bonnie Moorhen", in Peter Kay: *A Jacobite Legacy from Bonnie Dundee to Bonnie Prince Charlie* (Loughborough: Soar Valley Music Publications, 1995), p. 46.

31. Ibid., pp. 35 and 41.

32. Ibid., p. 40.

33. Ibid., p. 44.

34. "The Highland Widow's Lament", Kay: *A Jacobite Legacy,* p. 47.

35. "Will ye no come back again?", Kay: *A Jacobite Legacy,* p. 34.

36. http://movingimage.nls.uk/film/2256 accessed on 4 VI 2017.

37. John Buchan: *Midwinter* (London: Hodder & Stoughton, 1923).

38. Bram Stoker: *The Lady of the Shroud* (1909; Ware, Hereforshire: Wordsworth, 2010), p. 198.

39. Richard Cook: "The Home-Ly Kailyard Nation: Nineteenth-Century Narratives of the Highland and the Myth of Merrie Auld Scotland", *English Literary History* Vol. 66 No. 4 (Winter 1999), pp. 1053-73.

40. Directed by C. C. Calvert, http://www.silentera.com/PSFL/data/B/BonniePrince Charlie1923.html accessed on 5 XII 2015.

41. For an excellent survey of the films, but also other interpretations of Culloden, see John R. Gold, Margaret M. Gold: "'The Graves of the Gallant Highlanders': Memory, Interpretation and Narratives of Culloden", *History and Memory*, Vol. 19, No. 1 (Spring/Summer 2007), pp. 5-38.

42. Gold & Gold: 'The Graves of the Gallant Highlanders', pp. 16-21.

43. Peter Womack: *Improvement and Romance: Constructing the Myth of the Highlands* (Basingstoke: Macmillan, 1989), p. 1.

44. For a more detailed history of the Culloden site, see Gold & Gold: "'The Graves of the Gallant Highlanders'", pp. 21-31.

45. UK Tourism statistics 2012, http://www.tourismalliance.com/downloads/ TA_327_353.pdf accessed on 10 III 2013.

46. Visit Scotland statistics, http://www.visitscotland.org/research_and_statistics/ tourismstatistics/national_statistics/international_statistics.aspx, accessed on 10 III2013.

ENDNOTES

47. http://clan-donald-usa.org/CDCMS/, accessed on 5 XII 2015.

48. http://www.gla.ac.uk/media/media_122689_en.pdf, accessed on 30 IV 2017.

49. http://www.blair-castle.co.uk/castle_history_evolution.cfm, accessed on 21 XI 2015.

50. Dziennik: "Whig Tartan", p. 120.

51. Source: Peter Lynch: *The History of the Scottish National Party* (Cardiff: Welsh Academic Press, 2002), p. 16; for later results, BBC News.

52. Malcolm Chapman: *The Gaelic Vision of Scottish Culture* (London: Croom Helm, 1978), p. 20.

53. Ian Donnachie & Christopher Whatley (eds.): *The Manufacture of Scottisch History* (Edinburgh: Polygon, 1992), see especially Charles Withers: "The Historical Creation of the Scottisch Highlands", pp. 143-56.

54. NTS: *Culloden* (Edinburgh, 1990), cited in Gold & Gold: "Graves of the Gallant Highlanders", p. 32.

55. Anon.: *The Story of the Gael - A reproduction of the Murals in the National Trust for Scotland Visitor Centre at Culloden* (s.l., s.e., pamphlet, ca. 1976).

56. In 2016 Gabaldon told the broadcaster Cathy MacDonald for the BBC's Gaelic Alba channel, the author says: 'I've walked a lot of battlefields. Most are not haunted - that one is.' "'I feel the ghosts of Culloden' says Diana Gabaldon who is moved to tears", *The Daily Record* (30 Sept. 2016).

57. Gold & Gold: "'The Graves of the Gallant Highlanders'", pp. 26-32.

58. Black: *Culloden and the '45;* Prebble: *Culloden* to name but two.

59. James Mitchell, Lynn Bennie, & Rob Johns: *The Scottish National Party: Transition to Power* (Oxford: OUP, 2012), pp. 110F, 157.

60. For categorisations of different types of nationalism, see Hans Kohn: *The Idea of Nationalism* (New York: Macmillan, 1944).

61. Founder of the 7:84 Theatre Company – named after the much-cited 1970s statistics that 7% of the population of the UK own 84% of its assets.

62. *The Cheviot, the Stag and the Black, Black Oil* (1973), see http://www.you-tube.com/watch?v=sb3qbFcLYZc accessed on 10 June 2014.

63. Mircea Eliade: *Myth and Reality.* Willard Trask tans. (New York: Harper & Row, 1963, repr. 1968), pp. 11, 14.

64. Quoted in Fred Freeman (ed.): *To be the nation again: songs that have reflected and informed opinion in Scotland* (Ceol Mor Productions, 1999).

65. Blind Harry called him 'of whole lineage and true line of Scotland', P. Hume Brown: *History of Scotland* Vol. 1 (Cambridge: Cambridge University Press, 1911), p. 41, D.J. Gray: *William Wallace: the King's Enemy* (London: Robert Hale, 1991), p. 27f.

66. Kington (ed.): *Punch History of Scotland*, p. 38f.

FAMOUS BATTLES

Chapter 6 Waterloo 1815 - the Battle for History

1. The story of Waterloo has been told and retold on many occasions. Among recent histories are Jacques Logie: *Waterloo: The 1815 Campaign* (Stroud: Spellmount, 2006); Andrew Roberts: *Waterloo: Napoleon's Last Gamble* (Leicester : W. F. Howes, 2005); and Gordon Corrigan: *Waterloo: A New History of the Battle and its Armies* (London: Atlantic Books, 2015).

2. Jeremy Black: *Waterloo: the Battle that Brought Down Napoleon* (London: Icon, 2011) p. xiii.

3. Andrew Field: *Waterloo: The French Perspective* (Barnsley: Pen & Sword Military, 2012), p. 238.

4. For a fuller discussion of the different national narratives of the battle, see Alan Forrest: *Great Battles: Waterloo* (Oxford: 2015).

5. Bernard Coppens: *Waterloo: les mensonges. Les manipulations de l'histoire enfin révélées* (Brussels: 2009).

6. Oskar Cox Jensen: *Napoleon and British Song, 1797-1822* (Basingstoke: Palgrave Macmillan, 2015), pp. 116-24.

7. *The Daily Telegraph* (20 June 2015).

8. Pierre Nora (ed.): *Les lieux de mémoire* 7 vols., (Paris: Gallimard, 1984-92).

9. *Le Monde* (6 December 2005).

10. Etienne François and Uwe Puschner (eds): *Erinnerungstage: Wendepunkte der Geschichte von der Antike bis zur Gegenwart* (Munich: Beck, 2010).

11. Bruno Colson: *Leipzig: La Bataille des Nations, 16-19 octobre 1813* (Paris: Perrin, 2013).

12. Karen Hagemann: 'Celebration, Contestation and Commemoration: The Battle of Leipzig In German Memories of the Anti-Napoleonic Wars', in Alan Forrest, Karen Hagemann and Michael Rowe (eds): *War, Demobilization and Memory: The Legacy of War in the Era of Atlantic Revolutions* (Basingstoke: Palgrave Macmillan, 2016), pp. 335-52.

13. Kirstin Schäfer: 'Die Völkerschlacht', in Etienne François and Hagen Schulze (eds): *Deutsche Erinnerungsorte* (3 vols, Munich: 2001), Beck, 2001), Vol. pp. 187-201.

14. Jens Mastnak: *Die King's German Legion, 1803-1816. Lebenswirklichkeit in einer militärischen Formation des Koalitionskriege* (Celle: 2015).

15. Jasper Heinzen: 'A Negotiated Truce: The Battle of Waterloo in European Memory since the Second World War', *History and Memory* 26 (1974), p. 50.

16. Nick Foulkes: *Dancing into Battle: A Social History of the Battle of Waterloo* (London: Weidenfeld & Nicolson, 2006), p. 21.

17. Philippe Raxhon: 'Le Lion de Waterloo, un monument controversé', in Marcel Watelet and Pierre Couvreur (eds): *Waterloo, lieu de mémoire européen* (Louvain-la-Neuve: Bruylant, 2000), pp. 151-60.

18. Lotte Jensen: 'The Dutch against Napoleon: Resistance Literature and National Identity, 1806-13', *Journal of Dutch Literature* 2/2 (2012), pp. 5-26.

19. Peter Hofschröer: *The Waterloo Campaign: The German Victory* (London: Greenhill Books, 1999).

20. Richard Mayne, Douglas Johnson and Robert Tombs (eds): *Cross Channel Currents: 100 years of the Entente Cordiale* (London: Routledge, 2004), p. xiv.

21. *The Sunday Times Magazine*, 12 June 2016, p. 17.

22. Holger Hoock: *The King's Artists: The Royal Academy of Arts and the Politics of British Culture, 1760-1840* (Oxford: Clarendon Press, 2003), p. 254.

23. Peter Hofschröer: *Wellington's Smallest Victory: The Duke, the Model Maker and the Secret of Waterloo* (London: Faber, 2004).

24. Stuart Semmel: 'Reading the Tangible Past: British Tourism, Collecting and Memory after Waterloo', *Representations* No. 69 (2000), p. 12.

25. Christopher Woolgar: 'Writing the Despatch: Wellington and Official Communication', in Woolgar (ed.): *Wellington Studies* Vol. 2 (Southampton: 1999).

26. Hansard: *The Parliamentary Debates from the Year 1803 to the Present Time* (London: 1803-20), 23 June 1815.

27. Stuart Semmel: 'British Uses for Napoleon', *Modern Language Notes* 120 (2005), p. 745.

28. Robert Southey: *The Poet's Pilgrimage to Waterloo* (London: Longman & Co., 1816); Walter Scott: *The Field of Waterloo: A Poem* (Edinburgh: 1815).

29. Philip Shaw: *Waterloo and the Romantic Imagination* (Basingstoke: Palgrave Macmillan, 2002), p. 195.

30. Rory Muir: *Wellington: Waterloo and the Fortunes of Peace, 1814-52* (New Haven, CT: Yale University Press, 2015), p. 41.

31. Claude-Michel Cluny: *Waterloo, mythologie des lieux* (Paris: Ed. de la Différence, 2012), p. 138.

32. Emmanuel de Las Cases: *Le Mémorial de Sainte-Hélène*, ed. Marcel Dunan (2 vols., Paris: Gallimard, 1955), Vol. 2, p. 255.

33. Huw Davies: *Wellington's Wars: The Making of a Military Genius* (New Haven: CT: Yale University Press, 2012), p. 247.

34. R. E. Foster: *Wellington and Waterloo: The Duke, the Battle and Posterity* (Stroud: Spellmount, 2014), p. 153.

35. James Mulvihill: *Notorious facts: Publicity in Romantic England, 1780-1830* (Newark, DW: University of Delaware Press, 2011), p. 32f.; Andrew Franta: *Romanticism and the Rise of the Mass Public* (Cambridge: CUP, 2007), pp. 1-3.

36. On memories of Peterloo: see Robert Poole (ed.): *Return to Peterloo* (Manchester: 2014).

37. See, for example, Melvyn Thompson: *St George's (Kidderminster): a Waterloo Church* (Kidderminster: 2009).

38. On the adulation of Nelson, see Colin White: '"His dirge our groans – his monument our praise": Official and Popular Commemoration of Nelson in 1805-06', in Holger Hoock (ed.): *History, Commemoration and National Preoccupation: Trafalgar, 1805-2005* (Oxford: OUP, 2007), pp. 23-48. On the sadness that engulfed the nation on hearing of his death, see also John Sugden: *Nelson, The Sword of Albion* (London: Vintage Digital, 2012), p. 836f.

39. John Cookson: *The British Armed Nation, 1793-1815* (Oxford: Clarendon Press, 1997), p.126f.

40. Linda Colley: *Britons: Forging the Nation, 1707-1837* (New Haven, CT: Yale University Press, 1992), pp. 11-18.

41. Christine Haynes: 'Making Peace: The Allied Occupation of France, 1815-18', in Alan Forrest, Karen Hagemann and Michael Rowe (eds): *War, Demobilization and Memory: The Legacy of War in the Era of Atlantic Revolutions* (Basingstoke: Palgrave Macmillan, 2016), pp. 51-67.

42. Jean-Marc Largeaud: *Napoléon et Waterloo: la défaite glorieuse de 1815 à nos jours* (Paris: 2006), p. 354.

43. Stephen Clarke: *How the French Won Waterloo (or think they did)* London: Cornerstone Digital, 2016), p.117.

44. *Loc. cit.*

45. Jacques Garnier: 'Pierre-Jacques-Etienne Cambronne, vicomte', in Jean Tulard: *Dictionnaire Napoléon* (2 vols, Paris: Fayard, 1999), Vol. 1, p. 355.

46. Gérard Gengembre: *A vos plumes, citoyens! Ecrivains, journalistes, orateurs et poètes, de la Bastille à Waterloo* (Paris: Gallimard, 1988), p. 127.

47. Michael Broers: *Napoleon: Soldier of Destiny* (London: Faber and Faber, 2014), pp. 416-17.

48. Jarosław Czubaty: *The Duchy of Warsaw: 1807-15: A Napoleonic Outpost in Central Europe* (London: Bloomsbury Academic, 2016), pp. 195-216.

49. Shaw: *Waterloo and the Romantic Imagination*, p. 1.

50. Hervé Dumont: *Napoléon: L'épopée en 1000 films. Cinéma et télévision de 1897 à 2015* (Lausanne: Ides & Calendes, 2015), pp. 618-25.

51. France, Assemblée nationale, Communiqué de Presse de Jacques MYARD, Député, Maire de Maisons-Laffitte, 15 June 2015.

ENDNOTES

Chapter 7   Gettysburg, 1863, and American National Identity

1. Lincoln: 'Inaugural Address', 4 March 1861, *Collected Works of Abraham Lincoln (CWAL)*, ed. by Roy P. Basler (New Brunswick: Rutgers University Press, 1953), Vol. 4, p. 264.

2. Scott Bowden and Bill Ward: *Last Chance for Victory: Robert E. Lee and the Gettysburg Campaign* (New York: Da Capo, 2001), p. 34; Alan T. Nolan, *Lee Considered: General Robert E. Lee and Civil War History* (Chapel Hill: University of North Carolina Press, 1991), p. 79.

3. Carl Schurz: *The Reminiscences of Carl Schurz*, 3 vols. (New York: McClure, 1907/08), Vol. 3, pp. 10-11.

4. Schurz: *Reminiscences*, Vol. 3, p. 12.

5. James Longstreet: 'Lee in Pennsylvania', in: *Annals of the Civil War*, ed. by Alexander Kelley McClure (Dayton: Morningside, 1988), p. 421. Longstreet concluded his discussion of their conversation with a reference to Lee's official after battle report in which he stated that he, Lee, had not intended to fight a general battle. It seems obvious that Longstreet added that reference to cast doubt on all of Lee's official statements.

6. Arthur James Freemantle: *Three Months in the Southern States* (New York: Bradburn, 1864), p. 256.

7. *New York World*, reprinted in *Annals of the Civil War*, p. 427.

8. Longstreet to A.B. Longstreet, 24 July 1863, *Annals of the Civil War*, p. 414.

9. Longstreet: *Annals of the Civil War*, p. 393.

10. Ibid., p. 404.

11. Margaret Mitchell: *Gone With the Wind* (New York: Macmillan, 1936), p. 380.

12. Address of Edward Everett, 19 November 1863 (Boston: Little, Brown and Co. 1864), p. 33.

13. Lincoln, Address of 19 November 1863, *CWAL*, Vol. 7, p. 23.

14. Gary W. Gallagher (ed.): *The Myth of the Lost Cause and Civil War History* (Bloomington: Indiana University Press, 2000), p. 1; Wolfgang Schivelbusch, *Die Kultur der Niederlage* (Berlin: Alexander Fest, 2001), p. 75.

15. Jefferson Davis: *The Rise and Fall of the Confederate Government*, 2 vols. (New York: Appleton, 1881), Vol. 1, p. 80. Prior to the war and during the conflict, leading Confederate politicians such as Vice President Alexander H. Stephens were less reluctant to call slavery the real reason for secession. Even if one wants to give Davis the benefit of the doubt and declare states rights to be at the heart of the problem, slavery still figures prominently as the only federal vs. states rights issue under debate.

16. Report of the History Committee of the U.C.V., Made at the Reunion of Confederate Veterans, held at Richmond, Va, May 30th-June 3d, 1907, by George L. Christian, in: *The Confederate Cause and Conduct in the War Between the States*, ed. by Hunter McGuire and George L. Christian (Richmond: L.H. Jenkins, 1907), pp. 178-80.

17. Edward A. Pollard: *The Lost Cause: A New Southern History of the War of the Confederates* (New York : E.B. Treat, 1866), p. 409.

18. Edward A. Pollard: *The Third Year of the War* (New York: Charles B. Richardson, 1865), p. 35.

19. As quoted in Carol Reardon: *Pickett's Charge in History and Memory* (Chapel Hill: University of North Carolina, 1997), pp. 68-9.

20. Reardon: *Pickett's Charge*, p. 3.

21. LaSalle Corbell Pickett: *The Bugles of Gettysburg* (Chicago: F.G. Browne and Co., 1913), p. 120. Mrs. Corbell Pickett appears to imply that her husband led the charge from the front. There is no indication that he was near the scene of the battle. What is clear is that he survived the attack physically completely unharmed.

22. William Faulkner: *Intruder in the Dust* (New York: Random House, 1948), pp. 194-5.

23. Woodrow Wilson: 'Address in Gettysburg', 4 July 1913, in *Selected Addresses and Public Papers of Woodrow Wilson*, ed. by Albert B. Hart (New York: Boni and Liveright, 1918), pp. 10-13.

24. Roosevelt, as quoted in M. Keith Harris: *Across the Bloody Chasm: The Culture of Commemoration Among Civil War Veterans* (Baton Rouge: Louisiana State University, 2014), p. 9.

25. MacKinlay Kantor: *Long Remember* (New York: Tom Doherty, 1934), pp. 342-3.

26. Jeffrey M. Parrotte: *History and Memory in Gettysburg*, Syracuse University Media Studies, no. 6 (2012), p. 36.

27. Newt Gingrich und William R. Forstchen: *Gettysburg: A Novel About the Civil War* (New York: St. Martin's Press, 2003), pp. 5, pp. 492-3.

28. Ralph Peters: *Cain at Gettysburg* (New York: Tom Doherty, 2012), pp. 368, 522.

29. Alice Fahs and Joan Waugh (eds.): *The Memory of the Civil War in American Culture* (Chapel Hill: University of North Carolina Press, 2004), p. 4.

Chapter 8   Busting the Myths of the Somme 1916

1. I am indebted not only to William Philpott's scholarship on the battle of the Somme of 1916, but also for his informative and helpful comments made on a draft of this chapter.

2. As reported by Martin Tooth, BBC News, at http://www.bbc.co.uk/news/blogs-the-papers-36679970, accessed on 26 February 2017.
3. A. J. P. Taylor: *The First World War. An Illustrated History* (London: Hamish Hamilton, 1963), p. 140. Page reference is to the Penguin Books edition of 1966.
4. Arthur Bryant: *English Saga 1840–1940* (London: Collins, 1940) p. 288.
5. http://www.britishlegion.org.uk/remembrance/ww1-centenary/somme-100/somme-100-toolkit/ accessed on 11 February 2017.
6. Taylor: *First World War*, p. 140.
7. Bronislaw Malinowski: *Magic, Science, and Religion and Other Essays 1948* (New York: Doubleday, 1948), p. 96. I am grateful to Dr Abby Day for bringing Malinowski's work to my attention.
8. Ibid., p. 117.
9. The British Official History describes a series of battles at the Somme in 1916, the first of which is termed the 'Battle of Albert'.
10. Charles Messenger: *Call-To-Arms, The British Army 1914–18* (London: Weidenfeld & Nicolson, 2005), p. 134.
11. Jack Sheldon: *The British Army on the Somme 1914 – 1916* (Barnsley: Pen & Sword, 2007); Andrew Macdonald: *The First Day of the Somme* (Auckland: HarperCollins, 2016).
12. John Terraine: *The Smoke and the Fire: Myth and Anti-Myths of War 1861–1945* (London: Sidgwick & Jackson, 1980); Paddy Griffith: *Battle Tactics of the Western Front. The British Army's Art of Attack 1916–18* (New Haven & London: Yale University Press, 1994); Gary Sheffield: *The Somme* (London: Cassell, 2003). Sheffield's earlier work, *Forgotten Victory. The First World War: Myths and Realities* (London: Headline, 2001), Chapter 7, 'The Year of the Somme', is particularly useful in debunking a number of myths of the battle.
13. Strictly speaking, there were five Kitchener 'new armies', labeled K1 – K5, each consisting of six divisions. In total, thirty New Army divisions were raised.
14. Many of the divisions, however, included a mixture of regular and new army battalions owing to the swapping of brigades as the New Army divisions joined the BEF.
15. Martin Middlebrook: *The First Day of the Somme, 1 July 1916* (London: Allen Lane, 1971). References are to the Penguin edition of 1984.
16. Ibid., Appendix 5, p. 330.
17. Sheffield: *The Somme*, p. 47. References are to the paperback edition of 2004.

18. Although ascribed as a New Army division, three of the 30th's thirteen battalions were regular: the 2nd Wilts and 2nd Green Howards in the 21st Brigade and the 2nd Bedfords in the 89th Brigade.
19. Accessed from http://www.yorkshireeveningpost.co.uk/news/offbeat/the-young-leeds-pals-who-died-in-a-moment-1-6234556, originally published on 11 November 2013, on 12 February 2017. I am grateful to Tim Lynch for drawing my attention to this story. Incidentally, the ground was bone dry on 1 July 1916; the attack started at 0730, and its unlikely that the men were weary at the beginning of the operation.
20. Similar points surrounding the 'futility and failure' are made by Andrew Robertshaw: *Somme. 1 July 1916. Tragedy and Triumph* (Oxford: Osprey, 2006), p. 1. He provides a very balanced and readable account of the opening of the Somme offensive from the British and German perspectives.
21. Statistics and commentary are drawn from Terraine: *Smoke and Fire*, Table C, Casualties in Five Major British Battles 1916–18, p. 46. The comparisons also need to take into account the scale of the actions involved.
22. Ibid, Table B, Some Occasions of Heavy Loss, 1914–18, p. 45.
23. Peter Simkins: *Chronicles of the Great War. The Western Front 1914* (Godalming: Bramley Books, 1997), p. 114.
24. Captain Wilfrid Miles: *History of the Great War* based on official documents by direction of the Historical Section of the Committee of Imperial Defence: *Military Operations. France and Belgium, 1916*: [Vol. II] *2 July 1916 until the end of the Battle of the Somme* (London: Macmillan, 1938), pp. 558-9.
25. North of the Somme: 39th and 11th Divisions of XX Corps; south of the Somme: the 2nd and 3rd Colonial Divisions of I Colonial Corps and the 61st Division of XXXV Corps.
26. William Philpott: *Bloody Victory. The Sacrifice on the Somme* (London: Little, Brown, 2009), p. 438.
27. For example, A. H. Farrar-Hockley, *The Somme* (London: B. T. Batsford, 1964), p. 153 and pp. 155–7 describes the attack of the French Sixth Army on 1 July 1916 north of the Somme (XX Corps) in less than a page, and that to the south (I Colonial and XXXV Corps) in just over two.
28. Philpott: *Bloody Victory,* p. 349.
29. Ibid., p. 399.
30. Farrar-Hockley: *The Somme*, p. 133, however, reminded his readers: 'The British are apt to exult in their own military mistakes and to extol in the successes of their enemies'. There is some truth in this observation, as evidenced by the public reaction to the fateful charge of the Light Brigade at the battle of Balaklava on 25 October 1854.

31. Sheldon: *The British Army on the Somme 1914 – 1916*, p. 70.

32. Andrew Macdonald: *The First Day of the Somme*, p. 83.

33. Ibid., p. 106.

34. There were important exceptions: Bois Y opposite XX Corps north of the Somme, for example, was a formidably constructed defensive position akin to the Leipzig redoubt at Thiepval.

35. Terraine: *Smoke and Fire*, pp. 121-3.

36. David T. Zabecki and Dieter J. Biedekarken (eds.): *Lossberg's War: The World War I Memoirs of a German Chief of Staff* (Kentucky: University Press of Kentucky, 2017) p. 212.

37. Philpott: *Bloody Victory*, p. 377. Several newly raised German divisions were cut to pieces by French firepower.

38. As reported in BBC News, http://www.bbc.co.uk/ncws/blogs the-papers-36679970, accessed on 26 February 2017.

39. Charles Carrington: *Soldier from the Wars Returning* (London: Hutchinson, 1965), p. 120.

40. See William Philpott: 'Beyond the 'Learning Curve': The British Army's Military Transformation in the First World War', 10 November 2009, https://rusi.org/commentary/beyond-learning-curve-british-armys-military-transformation-first-world-war accessed on 26 March 2017.

41. Griffith: *Battle Tactics*, pp. 76–9. The publications he mentions include: SS 119, Preliminary Notes on the Tactical Lessons of Recent Operations (July 1916); SS 135, Instructions for the Training of Divisions for Offensive Action (December 1916); and SS 143, Instructions for the Training of Platoons for Offensive Action (14 February 1917).

42. See Timothy T. Dupfer: 'The Dynamics of Doctrine: The Changes in German Tactical Doctrine during the First World War, *Leavenworth Papers*, no. 4, U.S. Army Command and Staff College, July 1981, pp. 11–21.

43. Sheffield: *The Somme*, p. 85. The cavalry achieved considerably more than the myth of being mowed down by machine-gun fire.

44. At Courcelette, however, a tactical break-through was achieved according to one German eye-witness – the future chancellor Franz von Papen. The British high command, being unaware of the promising situation, failed to exploit it. See Philpott: *Bloody Victory*, p. 367. Additionally, Sheffield: *Forgotten Victory* (p. 148), makes a valid point about the contemporary utility of the new armoured vehicles: [The] 'penny-packeting' of tanks to allow them to give maximum support to the infantry was a sensible way to use the small number of technically unreliable tanks available. The simple truth [however] was that

Haig expected too much of the new machine[s] on 15 September [1916]. At that time the tank was not a war-winning weapon.'

45. Based on Terraine: *Smoke and Fire*, pp. 148-54.

46. Robert T. Foley: 'The Somme: The German Perspective', 14 June 2006, http://www.open.edu/openlearn/history-the-arts/history/the-german-perspective# accessed on 26 February 2017.

47. The transcript of the speech is at https://www.gov.uk/government/speeches/speech-at-imperial-war-museum-on-first-world-war-centenary-plans, accessed on 11 February 2017.

48. Beatrice Heuser: 'Defeats as moral victories', in Andrew R. Hom, Cian O'Driscoll and Kurt Mills (eds): *Moral Victories: The Ethics of Winning Wars* (Oxford: Oxford University Press, 2017), pp. 52-68.

49. A matter explored by Mungo Melvin: *Sevastopol's Wars. Crimea from Potemkin to Putin* (Oxford: Osprey, 2017), pp. 536–7.

50. David Cameron's text is at https://www.gov.uk/government/speeches/speech-at-imperial-war-museum-on-first-world-war-centenary-plans, accessed on 11 February 2017.

Chapter 9   Stalingrad 1942/43: The Anti-Myth of German National Identity

1. Peter Sloterdijk: 'Der starke Grund, zusammen zu sein. Erinnerungen an die Erfindung des Volkes', *Die Zeit*, (2 January 1998), http://www.zeit.de/1998/02/Der_starke_Grund_zusammen_zu_sein.

2. Gerd Krumeich: 'Einleitung: Schlachtenmythen in der Geschichte', in: Gerd Krumeich and Susanne Brandt (eds.): *Schlachtenmythen. Ereignis – Erzählung - Erinnerung* (Köln: Böhlau Verlag 2003), p. 5.

3. Krumeich: 'Einleitung', pp. 3-4.

4. Krumeich: 'Einleitung', p. 5.

5. Ernest Renan: '"What is a Nation?", text of a conference delivered at the Sorbonne on March 11th, http://ucparis.fr/files/9313/6549/9943/What_is_a_Nation.pdf.

6. Edward N. Luttwak: 'Towards Post-Heroic Warfare', *Foreign Affairs* (May/June 1995).

7. Georges Duby: *The Legend of Bouvines. War, Religion and Culture in the Middle Ages.* (Cambridge: Polity Press 1990), p. 178).

8. Andreas Behnke: 'The Theme that Dare Not Speak its Name: *Geopolitik*,Geopolitics and German Foreign Policy Since Unification', in: Stefano Guzzini (ed.) *The Return of Geopolitics in Europe? Social Mechanisms and Foreign Policy Identity Crises* (Cambridge: Cambridge University Press 2012), pp. 101-26.

ENDNOTES

9. The Battle of Berlin in the last days of the Third Reich is only a part of the overall catastrophic defeat of Nazi forces throughout Germany.

10. Arguably, the Soviet 'Operation Bagration' from June to August 1944, which caused the collapse of the German Army Group Centre with more than half a million German soldiers dead or wounded, is the more dramatic and costly event in the war. Yet although it sealed the defeat of Nazi Germany, it lacks the character of a dramatic 'turning point' to be as effective as 'Stalingrad' is.

11. Whether Stalingrad actually was the 'turning point' is contested. As research into memoirs and letters of German soldiers and officers of Operation Barbarossa indicates, there was a growing awareness among them already in late 1941 and early 1942 that the German strategy had failed and that the war could not be won any more.

12. Editors' note: see also Beatrice Heuser: 'Defeats as moral victories', in Andrew Hom & Cian O'Driscoll (eds): *Moral Victories: The Ethics of Winning Wars* (Oxford: Oxford University Press, 2017), pp. 52-68.

13. Bernd Wegner: 'Der Mythos "Stalingrad" (19 November 1942 – 2 Februar 1943)' in: Krumeich and Brandt (eds.) *Schlachtenmythen,* pp. 183-97.

14. Here in Emma Aston's translation, see chapter 4 of Volume 1.

15. Quoted in Berthold Seewald: 'Die Spartaner waren gar nicht so nett', *Die Welt* (3 April 2007), http://www.welt.de/kultur/kino/article792092/Die-Spartaner-waren-gar-nicht-so-nett.html, author's translation.

16. Quoted in Sven Felix Kellerhoff: 'Wie die Deutschen vom Ende in Stalingrad erfuhren', *Die Welt* (31 January 2013), http://www.welt.de/geschichte/zweit-er-weltkrieg/article113266162/Wie-die-Deutschen-vom-Ende-in-Stalingrad-erfuhren.html, author's translation. See also 'Stalingrad – der größte Heroenkampf unserer Geschichte', *Völkischer Beobachter* (2 February 1943), Bundesarchiv, BArch, RW 4/264b fol. 424, https://www.bundesarchiv.de/oef-fentlichkeitsarbeit/bilder_dokumente/03385/index-48.html.de.

17. Roland Barthes: *Mythologies* (London: Vintage Books 2009), p. 137.

18. Barthes: *Mythologies*, p. 143.

19. See for instance Raymond Cartier: *Der Zweite Weltkrieg. Band 2: 1942-1944* (Munich and Zurich: R. Piper & Co. Verlag 1982), pp. 658-85.

20. Wegner 'Der Mythos "Stalingrad"', p. 190.

21. Wegner 'Der Mythos "Stalingrad"', p. 185.

22. In light of these developments, German Chancellor Angela Merkel had refused to attend the next day's victory parade on Moscow, see: 'German and Russian diplomats pay tribute to Stalingrad victims', *Deutsche Welle* (7 May 2015), http://www.dw.com/en/german-and-russian-diplomats-pay-tribute-to-stalin-grad-victims/a-18437830, 22 June 2016 (2015).

23. For a review of these meetings see Michael Kumpfmüller: 'Ob Recht oder Unrecht. Stalingrad erinnern oder: Warum sich Vergangenheit nicht bewältigen läßt', *Die Zeit*, (12 October 1990), http://www.zeit.de/1990/42/ob-recht-oder-unrecht.

24. See limburg.de: 'Stalingrad-Denkmal am Hauptfriedhof', http://www.limburg.de/index.phtml?La=1&sNavID=1680.202&mNavID=1680.4&object=tx%7C1680.797.1&sub=0; research on the Internet suggests that there are still some associations active in Austria.

25. Andreas Behnke and Benjamin de Carvalho: 'Shooting Wars: International Relations and the CinematicRepresentation of Warfare', *Millennium: Journal of International Studies*, Vol. 34 No. 3 (2006), p. 935.

26. Walter Benjamin: 'The Work of Art in the Age of Mechanical Reproduction' in: Walter Benjamin *Illuminations*. Edited and with an Introduction by Hannah Arendt (London 2015: The Bodley Head).

27. Benjamin, 'The Work of Art', p. 215.

28. Ibid.

29. Abel Gance: 'Le Temps de l'Image est Venu!', *L'Art Cinematographique*, Volume 2 (1927), p. 96, http://www.film.uzh.ch/dam/jcr:d78a8e82-12d7-4ee8-8862-2475ecdbab40/Gance_1927_le%20temps%20des%20images.pdf, author's translation.

30. Benjamin, 'The Work of Art', p. 215.

31. Ibid., p. 217.

32. Ibid., p. 219.

33. Ibid., p. 222.

34. Ibid., p. 218.

35. Barthes, *Mythologies*, pp. 109ff; see also Andrew N. Leak: *Barthes: Mythologies* (London: Grant and Cutler 1994), p. 9.

36. Dir. Frank Wisbar, Deutsche Film Hansa GmbH (1959); re-issued by Kinowelt GmbH (2009).

37. 'Dogs' here is a literal translation which does not quite capture the by now archaic meaning of 'Hunde' in German. An Internet search produces 'rascals', 'bastards', 'rogues' and 'scoundrels' as possible translations.

38. Quoted in: 'Frei nach Schiller', *Der Spiegel*, (15 April 1959), p. 67, http://magazin.spiegel.de/EpubDelivery/spiegel/pdf/42625075.

39. See 'Frei nach Schiller', p. 67.

40. Dir. Joseph Vilsmaier, Bavaria Film GmbH (1993).

41. The latter tune has undergone a rather effective deconstruction to tease out the Rock'n'Roll in it by the German group Extrabreit, cf. https://www.youtube.com/watch?v=u9yrdQW8NVA

ENDNOTES

42. Neil Badmington: 'Introduction to the 2009 Edition' in Roland Barthes, *Mythologies*, p. xi.
43. For a critical review, see Andreas Kilb: 'Neue Kameraden', *Die Zeit*, (22 January 1993), http://www.zeit.de/1993/04/neue-kameraden.
44. William Merrin: *Baudrillard and the Media. A Critical Introduction* (Cambridge: Polity Press 2005), p. 66.
45. Jean Baudrillard: *The Transparency of Evil. Essays on Extreme Phenomena* (London & New York, NY: Verso 1993), p. 92.

Index

INDEX

INDEX

FAMOUS BATTLES

INDEX